THE ATLANTIS SYNDROME

To the memory of my Father

THE ATLANTIS SYNDROME

PAUL JORDAN

SUTTON PUBLISHING

This book was first published in 2001 by
Sutton Publishing Limited · Phoenix Mill
Thrupp · Stroud · Gloucestershire · GL5 2BU

This paperback edition first published in 2003

British Library Cataloguing in Publication Data
A catalogue record for this book is available from the British
Library

ISBN 0 7509 3518 9

Typeset in 10/12pt Photina.
Typesetiing and origination by
Sutton Publishing Limited.
Printed and bound in Great Britain by
J.H. Haynes & Co. Ltd, Sparkford.

CONTENTS

Acknowledgements

I should like to thank Drs Ruth Whitehouse, John Wilkins, Jane Renfrew and Ken Feder for the very helpful vetting of my manuscript and Professors Colin Renfrew and Garrett Fagan for their generous comments.

INTRODUCTION

Having passed through many incredible adventures from the Pacific Ocean into the Mediterranean via the Indian Ocean and Red Sea, and then out through the Strait of Gibraltar, cruising a while to pick up treasure from Spanish wrecks in Vigo Bay, Captain Nemo's *Nautilus* submarine headed south-west into the Atlantic, some time in the early 1860s.

Professor Arronax, the captain's uninvited guest, noted one morning that *Nautilus* had come to rest in a shallow sea at a longitude of about 16° and latitude around 32°, 'one hundred and fifty leagues from land' as he puts it in his story: in other words, about 450 nautical miles off the coast of Morocco, north of the Canaries and just south-east of Madeira. Then the captain invited the professor on an underwater stroll that he was certain would interest him greatly. That stroll involved a submarine climb up a small mountain beneath the sea. The professor tells the story.

The mountain rose no more than 200 or 250 metres above the level of the sea bottom, but on the other side, from twice that height, it commanded the depths of this part of the ocean floor. My eyes ranged widely over a large area lit by violent flashes of light. In fact, this mountain was a volcano.

Fifteen metres from the peak, in a rain of stones and cinders, a large crater was pouring forth torrents of lava which fell in a cascade of fire into the midst of the liquid mass. In this way, the volcano lit the ocean floor like an immense torch, even to the extreme limits of the horizon. I said that the submarine crater threw out lava, but there were no flames. Flames need the oxygen of the air to feed on, and cannot develop under water; but streams of lava, having in themselves the means of their incandescence, can attain a white heat, fight vigorously against the surrounding water and turn it into vapour by contact.

Captain Nemo taking the altitude of the Sun.

INTRODUCTION

There under my eyes, ruined, destroyed, lay a town – its roofs open to the sky, its temples fallen, its arches dislocated, its columns lying on the ground, from all of which one could still recognize the massive character of Tuscan architecture. Further on, some remains of a gigantic aqueduct; here the high base of an Acropolis, with the floating outline of a Parthenon; there traces of a quay, as if an ancient port had formerly abutted the ocean with its merchant ships and war-galleys. Further on again, long lines of sunken walls and broad deserted streets – a perfect Pompeii beneath the waters; such was the sight that Captain Nemo had brought me to see.

Where was I? Where? I must know at any cost. I tried to speak, but Captain Nemo stopped me with a gesture and, picking up a piece of chalk stone, went up to a black basalt rock and traced the single word –

ATLANTIS

What a light came into my mind! Plato's Atlantis, the Meropis of Theopompus, that continent denied by Origen, Porphyry, Iamblichus, D'Anville, Malte-Brun and Humboldt who placed the story of its disappearance in the realm of legend, though its existence was entertained by Posidonius, Pliny, Ammianus Marcellinus, Tertullian, Engel, Buffon and D'Averzac. I had it now before my eyes, its ruins bearing undeniable witness to the catastrophe that overtook it. The scene of its destruction lay beyond Europe, Asia and North Africa, beyond the columns of Hercules, where these powerful sons of Atlantis had lived, against whom the first wars of ancient Greece were waged. It was Plato himself who wrote the history of mighty deeds in those distant, heroic days. Through the strangest of destinies, I was now standing on a mountain of the lost continent.

Whilst I was trying to fix every detail of this grand landscape in my mind, Captain Nemo remained motionless, as if turned to mute stone, leaning on a mossy rock. Was he dreaming of those generations long since disappeared? Was he asking them the secret of human destiny? And then the

Nemo and Arronax at Atlantis.

moon appeared through the waters, throwing her pale rays on the buried continent. It was but a gleam, but what an indescribable effect! The Captain rose, cast one last look on the immense plain and bade me follow him. We came down the mountain rapidly and I saw the lantern of the *Nautilus* shining like a star. The Captain walked straight to it, and we got on board as the first rays of light whitened the surface of the ocean.

Writing in the late 1860s, Jules Verne – with only a little artistic licence – based his visit to the ruins of Atlantis in *Twenty Thousand Leagues under the Sea* on the accounts of

Atlantis that were available to educated Europeans in the nineteenth century. All of this available material went back, as it still does, to Plato, in whose writings the name and idea of Atlantis first appear; there is no prior mention in Greek or any other writings before the time of Plato, who died in 347 BC. The other classical writers, and later European ones, whom Verne puts into his Professor Arronax's account were simply retailing and commenting upon Plato's remarks about Atlantis – either for or against its existence as the worthy professor notes. Theopompus wrote just a few years after Plato's time but in Verne's day and still in ours his writings are known only at second-hand in the works of later classical authors. His distant continent, inhabited by Meropians among others, has been identified with Atlantis by some subsequent writers but seems not to have been the same place in his view. He appears to write of it as still in existence and never destroyed in some cataclysm as is central to Plato's account, and no other details of the two stories concur beyond a suggestion by Theopompus that the inhabitants of his distant continent once contemplated an invasion of Europe. Some people have thought that the Meropians' continent represents a dim acquaintance in classical times with the Americas, long before the Vikings or Irish monks or Columbus got there, but the details of the account are too fanciful to inspire confidence. And some people since Renaissance times have wanted to associate Plato's Atlantis, too, with the Americas in some way – perhaps as the vanished source of the ancient American civilizations (as well as of the Old World's first civilizations) or as having been, before its destruction, close to the Americas, perhaps somewhere among the West Indies.

Verne sees his Atlantis as a classical sort of city, evidently much like Plato's Athens albeit with 'Tuscan architecture', and he duly puts it out in the Atlantic but not too far from the Pillars of Hercules, which was the name used in classical times for the Gibraltar point-of-exit out of the Mediterranean. He follows Plato further in crediting the long-vanished Atlanteans with waging war against the Greeks. Though he does not directly attribute the destruction of Atlantis to volcanic mayhem (Plato mentioned only an earthquake), the still-active

The end of Atlantis, from a French book of 1872.

crater of his underwater volcano dominates the entire scene he conjures up for us of an overthrown ancient civilization – indeed it provides the light we see it by. Something like a volcano appeals to the modern mind as a natural means by which a great ancient civilization might have been brought down, and practically erased from the archaeological record, as happened with Pompeii until archaeology brought it to light. Verne's volcano is a part of the developing constellation of details that often run together in the full realization of the Atlantis story, as is his location among Atlantic islands like the Canaries and Madeiras. Of course, such details vary with different theories about Atlantis: comets sometimes instead of volcanoes, Caribbean islands instead of islands closer to Africa. In this book we shall be assembling the full complement of features that have accrued to the Atlantis story since Plato's time, and taking a particular interest in the underlying ideas and attitudes that sustain the enduring image of Atlantis – the 'Atlantis Syndrome', the concurrence of 'symptoms', if you like, that make up the Atlantis vision. Everyone responds to this vision, especially in our science fiction-conscious times. Indeed the idea seems to speak to some predisposition in the human psyche to believe in the Golden Age, forgotten cataclysms, superior beings remote in time or space, help or warning from powers outside ourselves. The vision doesn't have to be called 'Atlantis' and there have been many locations for it in this world, or even on other worlds. A whole set of related ideas comes together in 'Atlantis' – a syndrome for us to explore in detail, asking whether there's any truth in it and, if there isn't, why such a set of ideas has proved so enduring.

Volcano apart, Jules Verne (whose story of Captain 'Nobody' and his amazing submarine was published in 1870) scarcely embroiders Plato's account of Atlantis at all. The other writers he mentions are standard classical authorities or (mainly French) writers of the eighteenth and nineteenth centuries. Some of these latter authors had begun to speculate about a possible location of Atlantis in or near the New World but had not gone very far with it: it was to be an American writer who would give Atlantis a whole new lease of life a dozen years after Verne's pioneering science fiction novel was published. Ignatius Donnelly would go well beyond Plato and initiate a school of archaeological speculation that found favour with some academics for a while but is now repudiated in all orthodox academic circles – and enthusiastically maintained in the world of 'alternative archaeology' at the same time. Donnelly's successors have gone as far beyond him as he went beyond Plato.

But before getting deep into Donnelly and what has come after him, we need to know what the first writer about Atlantis had to say in detail, and to ponder what he meant by it. What sort of man was it who launched Atlantis?

1

PLATO'S UNFINISHED BUSINESS

It was said of Oscar Wilde that if you thought his plays were funny, well you should just have heard him talk! Something of the sort seems to have been the case with the Athenian philosopher Plato, too, though not in the humorous line. Philosophers have not always been known for their literary powers but Plato stands second only perhaps to Nietzsche for his stylish and imaginative handling of philosophical ideas. His achievement was all the more remarkable at a time when the idea of writing and publishing literature of any kind was a relatively new one. It is thought that, unusually among classical authors, we still possess all the works of Plato, who lived and wrote in Athens more than 2,300 years ago. Such was his standing in classical, later medieval and Renaissance times that all his written works have come down to us. (Oddly enough, the only work of Plato's that remained in currency in the Dark Ages was the first two-thirds of his *Timaeus* – in which Atlantis first appears – in the form of 'a crabbed Latin version', valued for its cosmological speculations.)

And yet Plato himself seems to have considered his writing as a lesser thing than his work with his students in the Academy he founded in his native Athens in about 387 BC. In one of his books (the *Phaedrus*) he has Socrates deliver a none too favourable verdict on the worth of written works, and in his seventh epistle (if a genuine piece of his) he contrasts the lower value of the written word with that of the precious intercourse between living minds engaged in philosophical enquiry. His own philosophical writings are cast in the form of conversations between thinking men, exploring social, moral, scientific and generally philosophical issues. He himself never figures in them and a prominent role is usually given to his mentor Socrates, who left behind no written work of his own. Almost always, the other characters of his dialogues are real people whose historical existence is attested. A couple of anonymous participants may have been introduced to speak directly for Plato's own opinions, but he may very well have also wished his own views on others of his characters, especially Socrates. His readers, of course, would never have thought for one moment that they were being treated to verbatim records of conversations that ever actually took place and we, in our turn, must always remember that, with Plato, we are facing philosophy with literary style and imagination. Plato lived, moreover, to the ripe old age of eighty, and his views changed through life as do ours; so no doubt did his morale and his intellectual grip.

What Plato wrote about Atlantis was the fruit of his old age and it is no detraction from his genius to observe that this Atlantis material is awkwardly introduced, inconsistently developed and ultimately aborted in an unfinished trilogy of works that Plato appears to have abandoned, or at least set aside, in order to finish one last major piece. That was the *Laws*, which lacks literary sparkle altogether and espouses a rather bleak and illiberal vision of a practical arrangement of politics and legal measures: the nearest thing Plato at the end of his life could conceive to an ideal state in a far from ideal world.

Plato's philosophy as a whole is a basically rationalistic attempt to arrive at a system of absolute validity not only in scientific terms but also in the realms of politics, law, ethics and theology. An aristocrat by descent, with both conservative and democratic connections, he lived in disillusioning times and the circumstances of his own life were especially unsettling to him. A refuge of universal philosophical validity in a troubled world was his goal. By the time he was thirty, Plato had seen the overthrow by Sparta of the Athenian empire that had grown up after the defeat of the Persians in 479 BC, and then civil strife in the city of his birth. The judicial execution of Socrates in 399 BC had driven him into temporary exile, during which he may have visited Italy, including Sicily for the first time, and also Egypt though he himself never said so. (He would have been able to read about Egypt in the work of Herodotus who did go there just before Plato's time.) Back in Athens, he gave up on any idea of a career in domestic politics and concentrated his attentions on his Academy, the reputation of which shone in the fields of mathematics, science (especially biology) and philosophy. The grove of the Academy must have been a welcome retreat from the disappointing outside world: a place where notions of an ideal society could be elaborated in works like the *Republic* without any uncomfortable consequences as a result of trying to realize them in the actual world.

But Plato was destined to make a foray into practical politics after all – not in Athens but far away in the west, on the island of Sicily, with perhaps predictably lowering outcome. Probably not long after the completion of the *Republic*, with its vision of an austerely communistic and wisely authoritarian society, Plato was invited to the commercially wealthy city of Syracuse, in 367 BC, to take a guiding hand in the education of its future ruler Dionysius. But the young man turned out to be unsuitable material for the role of philosopher-prince and soon dismissed Plato and his Sicilian backers. Plato made unavailing attempts to rescue the situation but finally came away from Sicily in 360 BC with an abiding distaste for the materialistic excesses and gross sensuality of the way of life he had witnessed in Syracuse. Thus by the time he was seventy, Plato had added to the disillusionment of his experiences of Athenian politics the fresh disappointment of an educational experiment gone wrong and the practical failure of his political ideals in the face of commercial interests and wealthy power play.

At home in Athens, Plato returned to his work with his students, wrote up his Sicilian experiences and turned again to more substantial philosophical writing. In perhaps 355 BC he embarked on what was intended to be a trilogy of dialogue pieces that would express his mature, if not indeed senescent, outlook on God, Nature and Man's place in the world and in history. The three works were to be the completed *Timaeus*, the incomplete *Critias* and the never started *Hermocrates*, the whole sequence covering a series of conversations that might have taken place in 421 BC, during an annual Athenian festival that was a bit like Christmas but in mid-August. Plato himself would have been about seven at the time of the conversations he purports to record. The lively readability of much of Plato's work is well expressed in the opening of the *Timaeus*, which features the same cast as the earlier *Republic*.

> Socrates: One, two, three – but where, my dear Timaeus, is the fourth of my guests of yesterday, our hosts of today?
> Timaeus: He's gone sick, Socrates, for he would never have missed our meeting if he could help it.
> Socrates: Then the job of filling in for him goes to you and our friends here, no?
> Timaeus: Sure, and we'll do our best. It wouldn't be right, after the splendid hospitality we had from you yesterday, if we – those who are left of us – failed to entertain you in return.

Socrates, who would have been about fifty, is as usual the anchorman of the discussions, but in what we have of the planned trilogy Timaeus, an astronomer from Locri in Italy, and then the Athenian Critias (who was Plato's great-grandfather) hog the conversation. (Hermocrates, interestingly enough, was a Syracusan general who would go on to fight with Sparta against Athens, nearly fifty years before Plato's own Sicilian involvement.)

The *Timaeus* begins by harking back to the *Republic*, with Socrates again characterizing an ideal sort of self-sufficient state where everyone knows his place and no one engages in trade or piles up unnecessary wealth. He says he would like to know how such a state would get on in practice, in particular how it would face up to war. This is in itself a strange start to a philosophical work that will be principally concerned with scientific matters rather than social or ethical issues. Before Timaeus can get on with those matters, Critias (who would have been about ninety years old) comes in with his first version of the story of Atlantis, claiming without overwhelming plausibility that the ideal polity outlined by Socrates has powerfully reminded him of something he heard about Athens from his own grandfather (also named Critias) during another annual festival (this time in October) when he himself was a young boy. We may recall that the Critias of these conversations is Plato's own great-grandfather, and Plato would himself have been but a boy when these festive conversations are supposed to have taken place. The coincidences of the two sets of circumstances do rather shout 'artist at work'.

Be that as it may, Critias proposes to make a brief contribution about this Athens of old and, in a way that has impressed many modern commentators on the story he tells, he goes on to assure his hearers that what he will unfold is 'though strange, entirely true'. We need not make too much of that declaration at this point since Plato on more than one occasion in his writings introduces plainly mythological material with similar assurances. In the *Gorgias*, for example, a story about the Isles of the Blessed (the Greeks' idea of Heaven) and Tartarus (their version of Purgatory and Hell) begins with a similar assurance, put into the mouth of Socrates this time, who urges his hearers to 'listen then to a very fine story, which I suppose you will regard as fiction, but I consider to be fact, for what I am going to tell you I shall tell as the actual truth'. Again, in connection with another myth about immortality and reincarnation in the *Meno*, Plato has Socrates say that it is 'something true . . . and fine'. In general, Plato, though morally an enemy of lies and falsehood, was prepared to see the value of higher 'truths' in myth – in which he pioneered a philosophical approach to religious assertions that is still very much with us today. On occasions, he was prepared to interpret myth in the same way that many modern writers on 'Atlantological' themes do: as scientific history remembered in mythological terms. At the start of the *Timaeus* the story of Phaethon, who once lost control of the fiery chariot of his sun-god father and scorched the earth until Zeus brought him down with a thunderbolt, is interpreted as an objective astronomical event. 'Now this tale as it is told has the appearance of a myth, but the truth of it lies in the movement of celestial bodies as they circle the world and in the destruction after long periods of time of things on earth in a great conflagration.'

At other times, Plato seems simply to have resorted to casting his material in fictional terms for the sake of his readers: in the *Statesman*, the man from Elea says 'we have to bring in some pleasant stories to relieve the strain, there is a mass of old legend which we must now use for our purpose'. And what he brings in at this point is not in fact real Greek myth at all but a first outing for Plato's idea of cyclical destruction and renewal. In the *Phaedrus*, Plato comes close to admitting to the process of invention we see at work in his Atlantis story, when Phaedrus observes that 'it's easy for you, Socrates, to make up tales from Egypt or anywhere else you care to'. So all in all, although he never calls his Atlantis story a myth, there is no reason to think that Plato handled it in any way different from his approach to the mythical material served up elsewhere in his work. It was, in any case, a literary convention of the classical world to present invented material (like statesmen's speeches for example) as straight report. On a perhaps less elevated level, journalists follow the same course to this day. Plato went so far in his *Parmenides* to have Socrates converse at length with someone he never met and there are stories in later commentators on Plato to the effect that Socrates himself complained before his death about the stuff 'that young Plato' was putting into his mouth.

The Critias of Plato's intended trilogy is, we recall, Plato's own great-grandfather, all of ninety at the time of the tale. He says he got his story as a boy from his own grandfather, another Critias, who was the son of one Dropides – a relative, perhaps even a brother, of the man with whom the story really starts (the genealogy of Plato's family is not really all that clear). This chain of descent has taken us back to some time not so long after 600 BC and to a very important early Athenian named Solon, who thus turns out to be a distant ancestor of Plato. Solon, himself an aristocrat descended from the last kings of Athens, was the man who ended exclusive aristocratic control of the Athenian government in favour of control by the merely rich, with some relief for the worst burdens upon the poor and a more humane law code for all. For his good works he became known as one of the Seven Wise Men of Greece. He was also renowned as the first great poet of Athens, though his poems have not come down to us.

When his reforms were in place, Solon left Athens to travel abroad on business and, so the story goes, to avoid having to be around if and when his reforms were modified. Some time after 600 BC, his travels took him to Egypt: not the Egypt of the glory days of New Kingdom pharaohs like Ramesses II of Thebes, let alone the remote Old Kingdom rulers of Memphis, but an Egypt that had known recent defeat and decline and cultural discontinuity – an Egypt that had had to come to terms with a reduced role in the world, to the point where Greek merchants secured for themselves an independent trading emporium at Naucratis on the Delta coast, rather like the Kontors of the Hanseatic League in late medieval Europe. At the time of Solon's visit, Egypt was embarking on a renewal of state power and cultural pride centred upon a Delta town called Sais by the Greeks, after which this whole late era of Egyptian history is known as the Saite Period. In those days the new Egyptian élite looked back to the great days of Egypt's earlier history with intense enthusiasm, eager to restore as far as they could the religious rites, the pharaonic traditions, the very language of olden times, though all these things had been greatly altered through the vicissitudes of history. Not unnaturally, they frequently overdid it – rather like Victorians 'restoring' churches and building new gothic palaces. Much about their own past they misunderstood and inadvertently distorted – and they were not above downright invention as when, for example, they forged an inscription by the pyramids to look like an ancient record of Khufu's doings at Giza of nearly two thousand years before, full of anachronisms. This was the latter-day Egypt to which Solon came: still recognizably the inheritance of former days but decadent from its former glory and much altered by involvement in the realities of the wide world of the sixth century BC.

In Saite Egypt, according to the younger Critias as he tells his story to Socrates and the others, Solon conversed with Egyptian priests who opened his eyes to the long-forgotten history of his own city of Athens in Greece. For Athens as he now heard had once been the best governed state in the world – not unlike the ideal state proposed by Socrates earlier – before one of a long series of world cataclysms obliterated all memory of it, except in the records of the Egyptians. These records, we are to understand, Solon himself saw carved in hieroglyphs on pillars of stone. It should be noted straightaway that we now possess no Egyptian records that describe an early state of Athens or its destruction in a cataclysmic flood. In general, the Egyptian records pay little or no heed to the goings-on of foreign countries, which held no interest for the self-contained and self-satisfied Egyptians unless they happened for the moment to directly impinge on Egypt. Nor do Egyptian records afford a picture of an ongoing system of world cataclysms, either by fire or flood as Solon's informant sketches in for him. They do not, in fact, with even the maximum extrapolation, go back much beyond 3000 BC, whereas Solon's priestly guide tells him that Egypt's history began eight thousand years before the chat they are having, and the history of Athens began a thousand years before that! In the light of archaeology in both Greece and Egypt, we know that 10,500 years ago there was no Athens, only

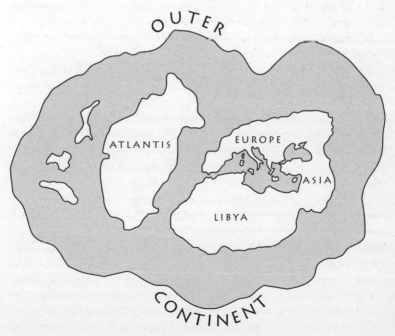

Plato's Atlantean geography, with an outer continent surrounding all.

Late Stone Age hunting bands, and a not dissimilar foraging way of life was being pursued in the Nile Valley, too. Not even farming, let alone civilization, had yet come to either of these places in 8600 BC. Something is wrong with the dates the Saite priests are said, in Plato's account of two hundred years later, to have quoted from their records to Solon. There could be several explanations for this situation, as we shall see. Meanwhile, it is worth quoting at length the words Plato puts into the mouth of Critias as a report of what the priests told Solon some time soon after about 600 BC.

> The records tell how great a power your city stopped once when that power assaulted all Europe and Asia, coming in from the Atlantic Ocean. In those days that ocean could be traversed, for there was an island in it in front of the strait you call the Pillars of Hercules. This island was larger than Libya and Asia put together, and from it the voyagers of those times could reach other islands, from which the whole of a continent on the opposite side of that ocean could be reached – a continent truly deserving the name. For all the parts we know within the strait I spoke of seem to be but a bay with a narrow entrance, while that outer sea is the real ocean and the land that wholly surrounds it really deserves the name of continent.

The Egyptian priests, as per the younger Critias as per Plato, seem to have been telling his grandfather's relative Solon that there was a true continent on the other side of the Atlantic, rather as Theopompus is reported to have told of a continent on which the Meropians lived. It may be tempting for us to identify this continent with the Americas but we should note that it was evidently not Atlantis itself – that was an (admittedly enormous) island in the Atlantic Ocean according to Critias, much nearer the gateway to the little Mediterranean world at the Strait of Gibraltar. As for that island of Atlantis:

> Now on this island of Atlantis, there grew up an extraordinary power under kings who ruled not only the island itself but many other islands and parts of the continent; more than that, they were rulers, inside the strait,

of North Africa as far as Egypt, and of Europe to the borders of Italy. This concentrated power tried in one fell swoop to enslave your country and ours and all the region within the strait. That was when, Solon, the power of your city became clear to all people for its courage and strength. Athens was at the forefront in bravery and the arts of war. First as the leader of Greece, then forced to stand alone by the defection of the others, she faced the ultimate danger, defeated the invaders and set up her trophy. Those peoples not yet enslaved she saved from slavery, and all the rest of us within the boundary of the Pillars set up by Hercules she unstintingly freed.

Two important points should be noted here. First, the Saite priest is telling Solon that Atlantis warred against both Athens and Egypt so, since he has already said that Egyptian history goes back eight thousand years at the time of the chat with Solon (a thousand years less than that of Athens), the war must have taken place after 8600 BC. Secondly, we may well notice, as classical scholars have since the eighteenth century, that the account of plucky little Athens' stand against Atlantis, at the head of her allies or sometimes alone, bears a striking resemblance to the role that classical Athens saw herself as having so nobly played against the Persian invaders of Greece a century before Plato's heyday. The wind-up of the story should now be heard in full from the mouth of Critias reporting the Saite priest, since it reminds us that the purported emphasis of his interjection into the *Timaeus* is not really on Atlantis at all but rather on Athens.

Afterwards there came a time of extraordinary earthquakes and floods; there came a terrible day and night when all your warships were swallowed up by the earth and the island of Atlantis also sank beneath the sea and disappeared. So now the ocean beyond the Pillars of Hercules cannot be traversed, the way blocked by mud just below the surface of the sea, left behind when the island settled down.

We may briefly comment that the Greeks of Plato's time cannot have had much familiarity with the Atlantic Ocean beyond the strait if they thought it was unnavigably blocked with mud. It is possible that it suited the wily Phoenician merchants who did sail into the Atlantic to have this story put about – we know they were prepared to go to some lengths to protect their trade monopolies. Herodotus has a similar story of unnavigable shallows in the Indian Ocean encountered by Egyptians sailing out of the Red Sea. It has been suggested that Plato's unnavigable shoals, albeit of mud, reflect some dim acquaintance of the Phoenicians with the Sargasso Sea of weed and marine life reached on the western side of the Azores. More likely the Phoenicians were spinning yarns about their trading post at Tartessus on the estuary of the Guadalquivir north of Cadiz – metals were their chief target there – which was finally shut down by heavy silting sometime after 500 BC.

At all events, Critias has reminded his hearers that this noble Athens of old went down along with Atlantis, some time (he doesn't say how long) after the war that evidently itself occurred at some date after 8600 BC: the simultaneous demise of Athens and Atlantis is in line with Plato's notion of general cyclical catastrophism. He ends with a not altogether convincing effort to reinforce the notion of an ideal state previously floated by Socrates.

So, Socrates, I have given you a brief account of the tale told by old Critias as he heard it from Solon. When you were talking yesterday of your state and its citizens, I remembered this story and was surprised to note at how many points your account exactly agreed, by some miracle, with Solon's.

Of course, Socrates had had absolutely nothing to say about Atlantis, of which he and the other two had plainly never heard. And his ideal state bore no great resemblance to the version of old Athens reported at this stage by the younger Critias, except insofar as in general terms the past heroics of this long-forgotten Athens are of the sort Socrates was looking for from his ideal society. As a preface to a book about the creation of the universe and mankind's place in it, handled by Timaeus in the rest of the text in a scientific sort of spirit, the story of old Athens and its war with Atlantis sits rather awkwardly. The fact that Plato went on in the second work of this trilogy to make so much more of Atlantis suggests that the planting of the story in outline in the *Timaeus* was a planned move, to trail the all-important theme of the *Critias* which we can only conclude was to be a moralistic overview of ancient history (with Hermocrates in the last of the trilogy to take us on into the modern history of the Greek world). But the manner in which the story of Atlantis seems to run away with Plato in the *Critias* into obsessive and irrelevant detail and then comes to an abrupt, unfinished end may equally suggest that the ageing Plato lost his way with his material here and in the end could get no further with it. One story about Plato from much later times pictures him dying at his desk like Karl Marx, in the middle of a piece of writing – but the uncompleted *Critias* may have prompted this idea rather than be evidence of it. (Another story says he died at a wedding feast.) If the *Laws* really was Plato's last work, then he may have turned to this dry and bleak production (which itself is thought to show signs of incomplete revision) as his last best chance to express his final outlook on human affairs, abandoning the trilogy that he could neither develop nor rework around the obstacle of Atlantis. He died in 347 BC at the age of eighty.

The account of Atlantis contained in the *Critias* is much longer and more detailed (to the point of tedium) than the one we have taken from the *Timaeus*; it is also, in the matter of dates, somewhat at odds with the previous work. For it begins, 'Now firstly we must recall that 9000 is the total of years since the war occurred, as is recorded, between the dwellers beyond the Pillars of Hercules and all that dwelt within them, the war we have now to relate in detail.' (Because the *Critias* is unfinished, we never do get to the war.) Note that the war, which was by implication dated to sometime after 8600 BC in the *Timaeus*, is now said to have occurred at about 9420 BC, nine thousand years before the particular festival of 421 BC at which the ongoing conversation is taking place. 'Recorded' or not, this dating looks like sloppiness on Plato's part, and inspires no confidence in any notion that he was anxious to relay historical facts in a scrupulous manner. Rather it looks as though the old man didn't really care about these details, since the point of his story lay somewhere else altogether than with writing history.

After a brief reiteration of the broad outline of the story from the *Timaeus* – Athens in command on one side, kings of Atlantis on the other, from an island greater than Libya and Asia, now sunk by earthquakes, leaving a barrier of mud – Critias promises that his account will go on to cover the history of all the nations of the time (which it never achieves) but must begin with the main protagonists of the war, starting with Athens. Very interestingly, there is no initial claim here that the information comes from records in Egypt: we simply have Plato's mouthpiece of the moment, Critias, telling us all about it. What he says first is that in times of yore the gods allotted themselves various parts of the world and Athena and Hephaestus got Athens – it is extremely unlikely, to say the least, that any ancient Egyptian records could ever have made this claim. Even if they did, allowing for identification of some Egyptian god and goddess with Hephaestus and Athena (such as Khnum and Neith), we are not likely to regard the claim as historical fact.

Critias goes on to revisit the scenario, already announced in the *Timaeus*, of succeeding cataclysms to explain why no one in Athens in his day knows anything of the early years of their city beyond a few names traditionally handed down. The survivors, 'unlettered, mountain people', of each episode of earthquake and flood were having too hard a time surviving at all to bother with history. Critias sagely remarks that enquiry into history is something that comes with city life 'in company with leisure, when people see that they are now furnished with the everyday necessities, and not before'. And so 'the names of the ancients, without their doings, have been preserved'. Then Plato seems to remember the Egyptian records as a corroboration for names that have come down in Athenian tradition and claims that Solon was given some of them by the priests of Sais in the course of describing the war between Athens and Atlantis – but as we never get to the war in this unfinished work, so we never hear any more of them in any context describing their part in it. Critias then continues with an extended account of the constitution of Athens of nine thousand years before, once more with no suggestion that this information comes from Egyptian sources – although Critias has, we recall, previously claimed that it was precisely the miraculous match between the ideal state of Socrates and the old Athens revealed to Solon in Egypt that made him remember the Atlantis story in the first place.

The picture Critias now unfolds of the Athens that fought Atlantis is indeed uncannily like the ideal state proposed in Plato's previous work, the *Republic*, written before 370 BC. He reports that in this old Athens a military élite looked after the state from the heights of the Acropolis, with the support of a skilled class of craftsmen living on the lower slopes and another class of farm workers in the fields beyond. The city was self-sufficient and all goods were held in common, with the warriors receiving enough (but no more than they needed) from the people they guarded. Nothing changed or was meant to change from generation to generation. Life was uncomplicated by greed or ambition. Nobody engaged in trade or empire-building. Needless to say, this state of affairs certainly bore no resemblance to the Athens of Plato's own time and, we are entitled to think, not very much to any earlier version of Athens either. At the same time, memories of the simpler ways of just a couple of centuries earlier, before the expansion of commerce and wealth-based power factions, may well have come down to a man like Plato as a more desirable image of how life ought to be.

At this point Critias throws in some eminently sensible theorizing to show how a previously more abundant agricultural situation of nine thousand years before might have deteriorated to the less favourable conditions of his own day through land erosion, though the claim that the soil of the Acropolis in Athens was eroded away in one single night of extraordinary rain at a time of earthquake and flood is not geologically sound. There is a hint that details of the former extent and condition of the Attic hinterland of Athens were passed on by the Egyptian priests to Solon – and, again, we can only point to the extreme unlikeliness of this claim in the light of our own knowledge of Egyptian records, and to the impossibility of there having been an advanced agricultural settlement of Attica in 9600 BC. There were, however, still some traces surviving of the Mycenaean city of Athens in

Plato's time – old walls on the Acropolis, for example, that were already more than six centuries old. Plato might have got his idea of some former city of immense antiquity from remains like those.

In line with the noble picture of old Athenian society of yore already painted, Critias tells us that the public buildings of the warrior élite and their priestly adjuncts were 'devoid of gold and silver, which they nowhere used; on the contrary, they aspired to a middle ground between luxurious ostentation and meanness and built their houses tastefully, in which they and their children's children grew old and handed them on in unaltered succession to others like themselves'. We shall see that this situation is in marked contrast to the life of the Atlanteans. Critias concludes his word picture of the joys of ancient Athenian life: 'So it was that these people, of the character described and always dealing justly both with their own land and with Greece as a whole, were famous throughout all Europe and Asia both for their physical beauty and for the perfection of their moral virtue, and were of all men then alive the most renowned.' If the Egyptian priests really gave all this to Solon, it might be thought that they were taking flattery of a visiting Athenian businessman a bit far.

Now comes a score of lines from the *Critias* that would be especially hard to swallow if we were still unsceptical about the true historical value of what we are hearing. Critias says he is going to frankly inform us of the character of the people on the other side in the war, 'if we have not lost recollection of what we heard when we were children'. So, he is going to do it from memory, it seems. A few lines later he is claiming that Solon had made notes on what his Egyptian sources told him with a view to using the story in his own poetry and these notes are now in his possession. It isn't entirely clear whether these are comprehensive notes on the whole story or only notes about the names of the people involved in the war – perhaps only the latter, since Critias says he learnt them all by heart as a child. (He is ninety at the supposed time of telling, remember.) People who want to take Plato literally about Atlantis make much of the alleged possession by Critias of these notes, which might account perhaps for the disproportionate detail of what follows about Atlantis, if we could also believe in the extraordinary records of the Egyptian priests on which the notes were based. The business of the names is curious in itself for Plato seems to be trying to take care of an obvious objection to his account if it gives utterly Greek names to people of Atlantis. The explanation offered is that Solon was first given Egyptian names for these Atlantean folk by the priests of Sais but went on to discover that the Egyptians had translated the meaning of the original Atlantean names into their own Egyptian language: when the underlying meaning of these names was explained to him, Solon was able to turn them into Greek. 'Therefore if the names you hear are just like our own names, do not be at all surprised.' That procedure would certainly have had the merit of keeping things simple for Plato's readers.

Quoting now from Solon's account of Atlantis as he heard it as a boy (aided perhaps by the notes in his possession) Plato's Critias continues with his characterization of the Atlanteans, telling us first that the gods' allotments gave Atlantis to Poseidon, who settled the island with children he got by a mortal Atlantean woman named Cleito, after carrying out some large-scale modifications of the local scenery in a way that cannot, of course, be literally true. The god broke down hills, created circular belts of water and caused springs to bubble forth. He begat in biblical style five pairs of half-mortal sons and divided up the island into ten princedoms, giving his first-born named Atlas the best portion as king of all. (All this cannot by any stretch be other than mythological.) The island and the sea in which it lay were named after Atlas. Evidently part of the huge island reached practically to the Atlantic coast of Spain since one of Poseidon's other sons, Gadirus (his Atlantean name, no less, rendered as Eumelus in Greek) seems to have bequeathed a remnant of his name to the area around what we call Cadiz and the Greeks called Gades.

Unlike their austere Athenian contemporaries, these Atlanteans are said to be conspicuously rich 'and the wealth they possessed was so great that the like had never been seen before in any royal house and will likely never be seen again'. Though their island is marvellously abundant in every sort of natural provision – precious metals, animal life (including elephants), trees and fruit and vegetables – these Atlanteans are not content with self-sufficiency and import goods from their empire abroad. And again unlike the Athenian rulers, no king of Atlantis was modest enough to pass on his seat unaltered to his successors for 'as each king received it from his predecessors, he added to its adornment and did all he could to overtake the king before, until in the end they made an abode that was amazing to see for the scale and beauty of the workmanship'.

The main city of Atlantis, where its overlord resides, is an arrangement of rigidly circular design, whose centre stands nearly 10 kilometres from the sea – with allowance for the variability of ancient measures. This central island's outer wall is plated with the mystery metal orichalcum (only a name in Plato's time, probably representing a memory of a zinc-copper alloy occasionally produced in the ancient world), and beyond this circles an annular inner harbour. Beyond that in turn comes a ring island whose wall is plated with tin, then a second circular harbour (linked by a covered canal to the inner one) and another ring island with a bronze-clad wall, itself encircled by a great harbour communicating by canal to the interior and outwards to the sea, with a matching canal leading inland to the irrigated plain behind the city. The whole area of the outer city beyond the great annular harbour is filled with the houses of its people, up to the stone walls that encircle the entire place. Plato's description of the city is sufficiently detailed and precise to make possible a definite plan of the Atlantean capital, whose geometric perfection in the spirit of Pythagoras would be enough to arouse suspicion of invention by itself.

The wealth and lavish appointments of this chief city of Atlantis are elaborately pictured and at length: silver-covered temples (including Poseidon's own) with huge gold statuary inside and out (including statues of both gods and private persons) and roofs of ivory ornamented in gold and silver (and orichalcum), gardens, gymnasia, a racecourse, shipyards full of triremes and their gear. The whole account reads like an obsessive reverie of no-expense-spared luxuriousness (in sharp contrast with the previously described modesty of the Athenians), which it is frankly inconceivable that Solon or

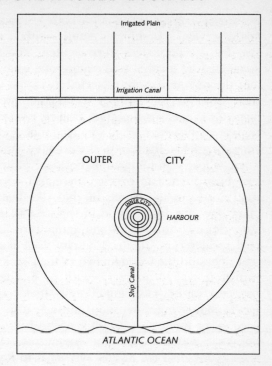

Atlantis City, as
described by Critias.

anybody else could have got from Egyptian records. It is not
difficult, however, to see how Plato's imagination could have put
this picture together from his own experience and from what
the Greeks knew of the barbarian world beyond their own
culture. Babylon, for example, as written up by Herodotus (who
died at about the same time that Plato was born), furnished a
fair example of luxurious living, so far gone in decadence as to
feature hanging gardens, while the Medes' capital at Ecbatana
was encircled by seven ring walls of many different hues with
tunnels through them. The Phoenician ports of Gades (Cadiz)
and Tartessus on the Atlantic coast of Spain (outside the Pillars
of Hercules) may also have contributed to Plato's theme – the
latter's decline before his time appears to have left behind a
scene of muddy dereliction at the mouth of the Guadalquivir
that he may have found suggestive. The aggressively commercial
Phoenician city of Carthage on the North African coast

possessed a great circular harbour surrounded by docks that could service 220 ships at a time, with a central island where the fleet headquarters were located. The round harbour was connected by a canal to a square one and both these harbours and the city itself were protected inside an outer wall; moreover the central keep of Carthage was further enclosed by a wall of its own. Carthage was the great trading rival of Syracuse in Sicily, the very city where Plato's educational and political ideals had come to grief in the face of the ambition and greed of the erring pupil whose moulding into the ideal philosopher-prince Plato had been invited to oversee. Syracuse, too, possessed features that closely match details of the Atlantean capital: it was the chief city of a large island in the west (if not huge and in the Atlantic), rich in mineral and agricultural wealth, with hot and cold springs like Atlantis. The city itself was one of the largest and richest in the world known to the Greeks and was divided up into four walled quarters, with its citadel on a promontory between two harbours full of ships. Its location on the edge of a fertile plain ringed by mountains is also mirrored in Plato's account of the rest of Atlantis, as put into the mouth of Critias. Syracuse was moreover the enemy of Athens and its greedy ruler Dionysius I did invade Tyrrhenia in Italy as the Atlanteans were supposed to have done according to Critias, who continues with his memories of what the Egyptian priest told Solon.

> Firstly, then, according to the account, the whole place rose sheer out of the sea to a great height, but the part around the city was a smooth plain that enclosed it, itself encircled by mountains that stretched to the sea: this plain had a level surface and was rectangular in shape, 3000 stades long and 2000 stades wide in the middle, counting up from the sea.

This would be something like 550 by 370 kilometres, but we are not told how extensive are the mountainous areas beyond the plain (though they are full of villages, streams, lakes, meadows, timber and wildlife). Even if the mountains covered a lot of ground, it is clear that the dimensions now being quoted fall a long way short of an island greater than North Africa and Asia put together, even as they were known in

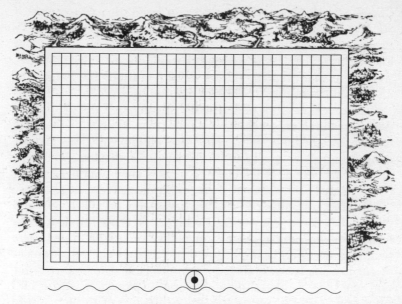

The Plain of Atlantis.

Plato's day, as previously claimed by Critias. The maximum dimensions of the triangular island of Sicily are about half the measurements given for the plain of Atlantis.

Atlantis, incidentally, also bears a passing resemblance to the home of Nausicaa in Homer's *Odyssey* which is worth noting, being described in her own words as:

> surrounded by high battlements, with an excellent harbour on each side and approached by a narrow causeway where the curved ships are drawn up to the road . . . you will see near the path a fine poplar wood . . . where my father has his royal park and garden . . . where trees hang their greenery on high . . . served by two springs . . . there is the meeting place of the people, built up on either side of the fine temple of Poseidon with blocks of quarried stone bedded deeply in the ground . . . walls of bronze topped with blue enamel tiles run round the court . . . golden doors on posts of silver . . . the lintel of silver too and the door handle of gold.

27

Corfu has the best claim to have been the prototype of Nausicaa's homeland of Phaeacia, though report of some Phoenician trading post has been proposed as its inspiration also. Plato distrusted poets (to the point of floating the suggestion that even the *Iliad* and *Odyssey* should be banned in an ideal state) but he would have known his Homer.

Critias follows his account of the general geography of Atlantis with a description of a prodigious system of trenches and irrigation ditches on the plain and an impressive assessment of the manpower available to the rulers of the ten Atlantean princedoms both in peacetime and in war. The powers of each of these princes are described as comprehensively autocratic, 'punishing and putting to death whomsoever he willed', though curtailed between the princes by divine precepts handed down from Poseidon and recorded on pillars of orichalcum in the temple of Poseidon at the centre of the island. The princes meet at regular intervals to review their obligations to one another and seal their compact under the laws of Poseidon with a bull hunt and sacrifice, cutting the bull's throat 'over the top of the pillar, raining down blood over the inscription', after which 'all the princes dressed themselves in the most beautiful sable robes and sat on the ground beside the cinders of the sacrificial victims through the night'. Plato was no friend of unchecked monarchies nor of greedy living but his story of Atlantis allows that the rulers of Atlantis continued for a long while in godly ways despite their wealth and power and only went off the rails when their all-too-human nature got the better of them. We shall quote the *Critias* to the end from this point until it breaks off in mid-sentence:

For many generations, as long as their divinely-inherited nature stayed strong in them, they were responsive to the laws and well disposed to their divine kin. For the intentions of their hearts were true and altogether noble, and they showed gentleness along with wisdom in dealing with the vicissitudes of life and in their relations with one another. So they scorned everything but virtue and made light of their riches, bearing the burden of their huge possession of gold and other goods; in that way their wealth did not intoxicate them with pride so that they should lose self-control and go to the bad; rather in sobriety of mind they realized that all good things are increased by goodwill in harness with virtue, whereas the hot pursuit and worship of such goods not only leads to the loss of the goods themselves but also to the loss of virtue with them. As a result of thinking so and of the continuation of their divine nature, all their wealth had grown to the greatness we previously described. But when the proportion of divinity within them grew faint and weak through continual mingling with a large dose of mortal blood, and the human disposition came to dominate, then in the end they lost their goodness through an inability to bear the burden of their goods and became ugly to anyone with the eyes to see it. For they had lost the fairest of their goods from the most precious of their parts – but in the eyes of those who have no gift of seeing what makes the truly happy life, it was now more than ever that they appeared superlatively fair and blessed, filled as they were with ungoverned ambition and power. And Zeus, the God of gods, who rules by the unalterable law, in that he has the gift of seeing these things, marked how this righteous race was in an evil way and resolved to punish them, so that they might come through chastisement to a better way. He therefore called together all the gods to that place they honour most as it stands in the centre of the Universe and overlooks everything that comes into existence; and when he had assembled them, he spoke thus . . .

So ends Plato's launch of Atlantis on the world, interrupted in the course of a very un-Egyptian but very Platonic expression of a dire warning to his fellow Athenians of the mid-fourth century BC: it may be, a warning to us all. But it is interesting, to say the least, to recall that in the *Timaeus*, both virtuous Athens and vicious Atlantis went down together in the course of a natural catastrophe of overnight floods, one of Plato's ever-recurring cycles of destruction that would be followed by renewal for Athens, but not apparently for Atlantis, gone for good. In a completed *Critias*, the Atlanteans would presumably have been first divinely chastened (by war with Athens?) and perhaps reformed, only to be swept away in a natural catastrophe in the end.

2

PLATO'S PURPOSE

Plato's Athens of the *Timaeus* and *Critias* partly reflects – with ideological exaggeration – a memory of his native city of a century or two before his time and before commercial wealth and factionalism had spoiled it: the rather nobler Athens that had lingered long enough to be at the forefront of the struggle against the despotic, luxury-loving Persian invaders of Greece.

Those Persians played their part in the generation of the Atlantis story: invaders who threatened Greece in the early fifth century BC, having already conquered Egypt among so much more. Something of the Persians' habits and deeds found its way into the story of Atlantis, along with topographical and cultural details picked up from Carthage and Babylon. On the one hand, the Atlanteans are definitely barbarians in the Greek sense: they don't speak Greek (they didn't have Greek names before translation, we recall) and so can only have stuttered out the same sort of bub-bub-bub that was the hallmark of barbarians everywhere and gave them their general name; they live in ostentatious luxury and their form of government is untempered monarchy (albeit under the rule of law at its best), just as you would expect of barbarians.

On the other hand, the Atlanteans have also taken on much of their flavour from the Greek world, especially from Sicily in the very geography of their island and its chief city, along with its naval prowess, its wealth and its greed – so much so that Plato's story of the nemesis of Atlantis could be read in part as a prolonged retrospective gripe about his disillusioning involvement in the island's affairs. But, of course, it was not Syracuse in the end that prompted Plato: it was his own city of Athens in his formative years and his adulthood, an Athens in decline from greatness and virtue as a result, as he saw it, of the corruption of wealth and power and barbarous habits of life. In response to the Persian emergency Athens had built itself a league of alliances that it subsequently went on to turn into an exploitative commercial empire for its own ostentatious benefit, until war with the Spartans – who had remained much closer to Plato's ideals of society – ruined that empire and reduced Athens to political infighting. It was into his picture of Atlantis in decline that Plato put all that he found disagreeable about Athens and the wider Greek world of his day, near the end of a long and disillusioning life.

The wealthy despots of Atlantis, like the demagogues of Athens on the eve of disaster, control not only their own land but many more islands (even parts of the continent beyond them, with inroads into North Africa, Italy and Egypt); their capital city is a masterpiece of artificial construction like the Athenian capital rebuilt after the Persian wars; its central temple complex is a riot of ivory, silver, gold (and even orichalcum) with gigantic statuary – like the Athenian Parthenon with its big barbarous statue of Athena, only more so; the palaces of its rulers are lavishly decorated and appointed, just as wealthy citizens of Plato's own day had turned to private ostentation in their own homes, sometimes rivalling the grandeur of public buildings. The Atlantean capital of the *Timaeus* and the *Critias* is, above all, the Athens of Plato's own day, writ large for effect. And the gods, it seemed to Plato, had already embarked on the destruction of overweening Athens, not yet with Atlantean earthquake and flood but with war and defeat, loss of empire and domestic strife. There is no reason to think Plato expected natural catastrophe to soon ensue on a large scale at Athens (those details in his Atlantis story were products of his artistry) but even for such details there were prototypes close to home. When Plato was less than one year old, severe earthquakes shook much of Greece, with marine effects as related by the historian Thucydides that might well have a direct bearing on Plato's Atlantis story.

At Orobiae in Euboea the sea sank away from its existing shoreline and then swept back up in a huge wave, which submerged part of the city and left some of it underwater when it retreated, so that what was once land is now sea. Those of the local inhabitants who were unable to escape by running up to higher ground were lost in the flood. An inundation of the same sort occurred at Atalante, the island off the coast of Locris; here parts of the Athenian fortifications were swept away and one of two ships drawn up on the beach was broken up.

An Athenian ship destroyed and an island called Atalante part-flooded! This is practically a sketch in miniature for events in the aftermath of the war between Athens and Atlantis, as told by Critias – and never mind any Egyptian records. Nearer in time to the writing of the *Timaeus* and *Critias*, there had been landslip and flooding following an earthquake in the Gulf of Corinth, leading to the submergence of the three localities of Helice, Aegina and Bura in 373 BC. According to Diodorus Siculus in the first century BC, 'entire cities with their inhabitants disappeared'. Helice in particular suffered badly, being lost altogether with its famous temple of Poseidon (no less)! No bodies were ever found and shoals thereafter made navigation hazardous.

It is just possible that, in a very general way, memories of an earlier and greater catastrophe than those mentioned above in the Gulf of Corinth and Euboea may have come down to Plato to stoke his imagination as he set to work on his Atlantis story. It is even possible that Solon (or Plato himself, if he ever got to Egypt) derived some vague idea of this catastrophe from Egyptian records – though, if that was the case, none of those records have come down to us. They would not have been records of a war between Athens and Atlantis in 9000 BC or so or of the destruction of an island in the Atlantic Ocean, but of events of only a thousand years before which took place in the Mediterranean Sea. And they would do nothing to establish any credibility for the precise historical and geographical assertions in Plato's work.

The events in question afflicted a non-Greek civilization that flourished on Crete and other Aegean islands before the Greeks themselves rose to power on the Greek mainland, then on the islands. This is the civilization we know as 'Minoan', which went back in its origins about as far as Egyptian history did, to around 3000 BC. Its heyday ran from about 2100 to 1500 BC, contemporary with the Egyptian Middle Kingdom and early New Kingdom. The Egyptians appear to have traded with Minoan Crete from their New Kingdom city of Avaris in the Delta and their records and tomb paintings feature what may well be Cretans, though as they have come down to us the records have nothing to say about war with Egypt (or Athens), earthquake, flood and collapse. Indeed, they suggest no detailed knowledge at all of Aegean culture on the Egyptians' part. It is modern archaeology that has revealed the destruction by natural disaster of a particular Minoan community on an island we now sometimes call Santorini after St Irene (the Greeks called it Thera) and the final decline of the entire Minoan civilization somewhat later on.

At one time some archaeologists believed that report of the catastrophe on Thera, reflected also in problems for nearby Crete itself, and of the collapse of Cretan culture at much the same time, might have somehow reached Plato (very likely via Egypt) and played its part in the creation of the Atlantis story – either by supplying inspiration to his artistic imagination or in the form of direct information, misunderstood perhaps in matters of chronology and geography. It is possible that Egyptian records, lost since Solon's or Plato's time, might have told something of a natural disaster that struck part at least of the Minoan world and of the subsequent decline of Cretan power, despite what we have said of the lack of details about other civilizations that Egyptian records generally show (as is certainly the case with what we have from them about Crete). It is just possible, too, that Solon or Plato might have got hold of the wrong end of the stick about the size (and location) and antiquity of the vanished civilization of Crete, perhaps by somehow accidentally inflating figures by a factor of ten – so that nine hundred years before Solon became nine thousand and the island's dimensions were similarly enlarged (though Plato's description of Atlantis would still bear no resemblance to Crete).

It would remain odd that Herodotus, who visited Egypt (including the temple at Sais) before Plato – or after Solon, if you prefer – and related many a tale told him by his own sample of Egyptian priests, mentions nothing resembling a Cretan catastrophe and collapse, let alone Atlantis. Some of what his Egyptian informants apparently told Herodotus is so fantastical that we may be tempted to think they were impostors or were having him on, or that he wasn't too concerned with plausibility as long as it all made a good exotic story: perhaps Solon or Plato felt the same way. (Interestingly, though, Herodotus did suggest that the Egyptians possessed records of the Trojan War, which may well have not passed Plato by. And it seems clear that Plato drew on Herodotus to a considerable extent in his presentation of the Atlantis story – the longevity of Egyptian civilization is emphasized in Herodotus, as is its immunity to the effects of meteorological changes during its long course.)

Overlooking the silence of Herodotus (and other Greek writers before Plato) on the topic of anything like Atlantis, some people have argued that Solon mistook the Egyptian numerals himself (it is unlikely that native Egyptian speakers could have done so), or noted them down wrongly or misremembered them, when he was acquainting himself with the supposed Egyptian records; or perhaps Critias or Plato himself made the error, so that Plato had to face the fact that the huge lost island could not possibly be inside the Mediterranean and had to be located outside. This is all speculation, since we have no Egyptian records (nor report of them from anybody else) to show that they ever wrote up even a vague account of the destruction of Thera and disappearance of the Minoan power. The same grave charge of sheer speculation has to be brought against the ingenious suggestion that, to the Egyptians, Crete was indeed a large island to the west with other islands about it and a mainland – Europe – beyond; and that it could be said moreover to lie between Libya and Asia if by Asia we understand, as the Greeks did, modern Anatolia. Plato, so this conjecture runs, might have misunderstood a note by Solon to the effect that Atlantis lay between (*meson*) Libya and Asia as meaning greater (*meidzon*) than Libya and Asia. Sheer speculation!

It was a letter in *The Times* of London which first suggested, anonymously in 1909, that it was the sudden end of Minoan culture in about 1450 BC (as revealed by archaeology) that lay behind the story of Atlantis. Just before the Second World War, observation of the obviously volcanic destruction of Thera was combined with the archaeology of the cultural collapse (which involved fire at several sites) to create a picture of the end of a glittering civilization, then believed to have been a great maritime empire, brought on by a terrible natural disaster. News of the whole thing, probably already somewhat garbled, might have reached Egypt to be recorded well enough to prompt Solon and Plato nine centuries later. The eventual occupation of Crete by Mycenaean Greeks a thousand years before Plato might have supplied the idea of the Athenian defeat of the Atlanteans.

Volcanic activity in the vicinity of Thera was noted by classical authors like Pliny in the first century AD and the ongoing volcanic nature of the island group of Santorini (all that is left of Thera) was well known in the nineteenth century: Captain Nemo visits it in *Twenty Thousand Leagues under the Sea*, without relating it in any way to Atlantis (though the suggestion had been first made in 1855 that Thera was indeed Atlantis, after an initial discovery of archaeological material on the island). But the dates of any major eruptions of the volcano, whose caldera clearly forms the basis of the island ring today, were long unknown. After the Second World War oceanographic research discovered two layers of volcanic ash traceable to Thera in the sediments on the bottom of the eastern end of the Mediterranean, the lower one of some considerable geological age but the upper one radiocarbon dated to later than 3000 BC. Ash from Thera was also found to cover much of Crete and many a Cycladic island. (Thera-Santorini is the southernmost of the Cyclades, only about 110 kilometres north of Crete.) It was further discovered that Thera had blown up in a colossal explosion that possibly exceeded the ferocity of the Krakatau eruption of 1883. Both at Thera and Krakatau, the final cataclysm had come after a series of minor disturbances with earthquakes. The Indonesian volcano furnished a vivid picture of what might have happened with Thera: after months of pumice showers came four explosions so violent they were heard 3,000 kilometres away in Australia and darkness fell over much of Java and Sumatra; hundreds of kilometres away from the volcano's core, shock waves broke windows and cracked walls; by the finish two-thirds of Krakatau had collapsed into the sea, sending out seismic sea waves (tsunamis) up to 30 kilometres high that drowned over 35,000 people. When we note that Santorini's caldera is four times wider than Krakatau's, and a third deeper, we can guess at the vast impact of Thera's eruption, but when exactly did it occur?

From the late 1960s on, excavations at Akrotiri on Thera showed that two thick pumice layers cover archaeological material of about 1550–1500 BC in the form of pottery of a style called Late Minoan IA discovered in the ruins of abandoned houses. The lower and earlier pumice layer is about 5 metres thick and a bit weathered, so evidently the volcano held off for a little while after its first eruption before the big bang which deposited the upper pumice layer to a maximum thickness of 60 metres, after which the spent volcano fell into the sea. The date of *c.* 1500 BC derived from the pottery for the time immediately preceding the start of trouble agreed fairly well with a radiocarbon date of 1559 ± 44 on the carbonized remains of a tree destroyed by the first pumice deposition. So Thera's sequence of eruptions seems to have begun around 1500 BC and the events could be thought to have been on a scale (with associated earthquake phenomena over a wider region) capable of bringing down a whole civilization centred on Crete, just over 100 kilometres from the volcano. Shocks, pumice hails, consequent fires, giant waves and months of darkness might easily have laid low the Cretan empire – and news of all this must have reached Egypt and been worth noting.

Unfortunately the volcanic theory of Cretan collapse started to unravel as soon as it was proposed, since archaeology had already suggested 1450 BC, not 1500, as the date of the sudden decline of Minoan civilization, which coincided on Crete with a subsequent pottery phase called Late Minoan IB. (After that, the archaeological record attests to the presence of the Mycenaean Greeks.) Late Minoan IB never reached Thera (so close to Crete) before the end came, though it did reach islands further away, which strongly suggests that cultural evolution continued on Crete and other Minoan islands for several decades after Thera was abandoned as a result of the volcanic débâcle. Geological research does not allow for more than a year or two to cover the entire sequence of eruptions at Thera – Krakatau went from beginning to end in a few months. On Crete, at Nirou Khani, moreover, lumps of pumice have been found buried in cups of the Late Minoan IA period, with no association of LM IB material, under the threshold of the door to a shrine, as appeasements no doubt to the gods who had unleashed the Theran volcano on the Minoan world – plainly these shrine deposits well pre-date the end of Cretan civilization. Elsewhere on Crete, at Zakros, ash particles have been found in an LM IA level sealed under LM IB remains. There is evidence to suggest that life was disrupted on Crete by the explosion of Thera, but clearly it was not brought to a stop – indeed, cultural vitality was revived for at least another generation with the attractive 'marine style' of LM IB, featuring dolphins, starfish, octopuses and other sea life.

In any case the effects of the eruption were not as severe away from Thera as the Krakatau parallel might suggest, with only moderate ash falls detected on Crete and tsunamis of no more than 8 metres recorded on its northern coast: it is unlikely that agriculture was much impeded by the ash or that Minoan ports and fleets were wiped out by the waves. The selective destruction of some but not all Cretan sites does not look like the result of a single earthquake of volcanic origin, and may well be owed to arson rather than to nature. Modern archaeological opinion, moreover, is less inclined than formerly to regard the Minoan civilization as an aggressive maritime empire, while evidence based on tree-ring growth and ice core analysis has been put forward (and also disputed) to indicate an earlier date for the eruption, before 1600 BC. Radiocarbon dating of grain carbonized by the eruption also suggests too early a date (in the range of 1630–1530 BC) for the end of Minoan civilization.

Further parallels between Plato's Atlantis and Minoan Crete that were once pressed home look less impressive now. Knossos, Minoan Crete's capital, was really nothing like Plato's Atlantis save for the polychrome exuberance of its decoration. The bull-dancing scenes of Minoan wall paintings and bull-capture depictions on a pair of Minoan cups are even less reminiscent of the Atlantean bull sacrifices described by Plato than are the pharaonic rituals of Egypt to do with bulls, or the bull sacrifices of Plato's Greece for that matter. Certainly, the Minoans were as fond of baths as Plato's Atlanteans, but there were definitely no elephants on Crete. We know that Plato was familiar with Crete (he toyed with the idea of founding an experimental society there) and it seems unlikely he would not have recognized something of Crete in any notes of Solon or in any Egyptian records if Crete was really the basis of his tale. In any case, Plato mentions no volcano in connection with Atlantis (though the minerals and hot springs are rather volcanic features), which would be an odd omission if ancient report of Thera and Crete had come down to him. He was perfectly familiar with vulcanism at Mount Etna in his own time on Sicily and, presumably, with the fate of Empedocles in that volcano's crater.

It is clear, then, that no detailed description of Minoan Crete and its decline can have directly inspired Plato through Solon and Critias from any accurate Egyptian documentation. All that can be said is that vague records of a natural catastrophe on a Mediterranean island, some of the after-effects of which may have been witnessed in Egypt, and of a decline in the scope of a former trading partner *might* have reached Plato from Egyptian sources. We may as well say, and it is at least as plausible, that the same Mesopotamian legend of a great flood that inspired the compilers of Genesis also came through, by a different transmission, to Plato. That is not saying much and we may well be more impressed with the memories of earthquakes and floods much closer to home and much closer in time that Plato could draw on from places like Atalante and Helice when he came to cook up Atlantis.

Like his fellow Greeks in general, Plato was almost bound to be in awe of the antiquity of Egypt and the long reach of its historical records which the Egyptians themselves mythically exaggerated: cause enough for him to wish his history of Atlantis on Egyptian priests. We could go on speculating that Egyptian annals, and indeed still surviving reliefs, of their struggles with a coalition of 'Sea Peoples' who harried the Delta region around

1200 BC may also have contributed to the story of Atlantean aggression – but what is the point? Nothing about the real historical doings of these people has any bearing on Plato's purpose in writing of Atlantis and any details of their real history that may have come through, faint and distorted, into Plato's imaginative account are really so paltry and irrelevant to his purposes that they are no better than curiosities by the time we get to them. And uncertain ones at that, after due allowance for necessary changes of dates, dimensions, locations, names, topographical details, etc., etc. The same goes for attempts to link the Atlantis story to the fall of Troy as perhaps derived from an alternative to Homer's telling via Egyptian records, or to Phoenician sailors' tales of the loss of Tartessus to silting, or to folk memories of flooding in the Mediterranean or Black Sea (or North Sea, or off the Atlantic coast of North Africa) as the glaciers melted at the end of the last ice age. And the same goes, as we shall see, for attempts to trace Plato's story back to Crô-Magnon culture of fifteen thousand years ago or to the megalith builders of western Europe after 5000 BC or to early settlements of Cuba trading with Phoenician merchants – or for that matter to any of a multitude of other Atlantis prototypes in the North Sea, the Baltic, the Black Sea, the Arctic Ocean, the Anatolian interior, under the southern ice-cap or in outer space. To one degree or another, all these scenarios involve such a deal of reinterpretation (with violence) of Plato's actual words that the end result is ridiculous.

As the pioneer analyst of ideas of vanished civilizations L. Sprague de Camp (to whom all subsequent writers owe so much) put it in his *Lost Continents* of 1954: 'You cannot change all the details of Plato's story and still claim to have Plato's story. That is like saying the legendary King Arthur is "really" Queen Cleopatra. All you have to do is to change Cleopatra's sex, nationality, period, temperament, moral character, and other details and the resemblance becomes obvious.' James Guy Bramwell, in his *Lost Atlantis* of 1938, put it very succinctly: 'either Atlantis is an island in the Atlantic Ocean, or it is not Atlantis at all'. And we may add that nor is it Atlantis if what was lost bears no resemblance whatever to Plato's elaborate description of the place and turns out instead to involve the flooding of a few hunter-gatherers or primitive farmers of the late Stone Age.

In doing violence to Plato's story of Atlantis so as to make it fit some theory of ancient disasters or lost lands or previously unrecognized ancient ocean crossings, Plato's purpose in writing of Atlantis in the *Timaeus* and *Critias* is completely overlooked. Indeed, the character of Plato's entire life's work is disregarded. Plato wanted, through philosophical dialogue, to arrive at a scheme of life that was at the same time rational and scientific and yet still capable of encompassing the moral and religious aspects of human nature. The trilogy of the *Timaeus*, the unfinished *Critias* and the unwritten *Hermocrates* was intended to develop the theme of mankind's place in the whole universe of being from first principles: from the origins and nature of the world through history to an understanding of how life might best be lived by human beings. Evidently to link the *Timaeus* back to the *Republic*, with its social concerns, and to herald the purpose of the entire trilogy, Plato planted the first sketch of Atlantis by Critias (in response to Socrates' musings on an ideal state) before Timaeus got on to the main business of this first part of the whole, which was cosmology and physics and biology. The *Critias* returns to Atlantis at the start of what was to be an account of human history from the earliest days, incorporating the not so unreasonable idea at the time of a great cyclical process of successive human communities on the up and on the slide as natural (or divinely ordered) catastrophes repeatedly saw off the old and brought on the new.

This cyclical view of history was probably owed to the Babylonians and was further developed only a little after Plato's time by Bcrossus of Cos, himself of Babylonian extraction. We are so used to the Judaeo-Christian, Marxist, evolutionary perspective on human affairs – with beginning, direction, steps along the way and ends in view – that we can easily forget that cultures lacking these prejudices are very likely to see the world in terms of great cycles, endlessly repeating, of catastrophe and renewal and catastrophe again: the Aztecs of Mexico, for example, shared this vision with the Babylonians and Greeks. The last book of Plato's trilogy, the *Hermocrates*, featuring a Syracusan general who had fought against Athens in Plato's own younger years (and thus after the time in which the trilogy is set), would have gone on to deal with modern history and, presumably, to reinforce the moral and social ideas Plato wished to promote. (Plato's last work, the *Laws*, in effect covers this ground.)

The story of Atlantis in the *Critias* is certainly building to a climax of divine wrath against the unjust when it breaks off, and it is made very clear that the turpitude of the Atlanteans lies in their greedy pursuit of wealth and power for its own sake and to the loss of their own virtue. By contrast with the austere, self-sufficient simplicity and moderation of their Athenian contemporaries, the Atlanteans live in barbarian splendour at the centre of an empire, with obscenely rich and self-aggrandizing kings who think nothing of battering nature with huge irrigation schemes and city engineering works or of plundering the mineral wealth of their island to decorate their palaces in extravagant style. The ordinary people of Atlantis, too, live in showy houses, enjoy warm baths without regard to season and prefer going to the races than to the gym. All this smacks of the barbarian world of the Persians, Babylonians and Egyptians of Plato's time; sadly for him, it also smacks of the excesses of some rich Greek cities, too, including his own. In showing that the Atlanteans have finally gone wrong not so much because they are barbarians as because they cannot, in the end, stand up to the pressures of wealth and power that are typical of barbarian states, Plato is arguing that it is certain sorts of political and economic organization that spoil human life and bring peoples down. With the instincts of an artist as well as the clarity of mind of a great thinker, Plato could see the way his world was going and created a minatory vision of the undoing of an ancient wealthy empire to warn his fellow Greeks in all the city-states of what was in store for them in an ever more commercial and materialistic age, with the semi-barbarian kingdom of the Macedonians waiting in the wings.

Alexander of Macedon, carrying warfare to the Persians on their own ground at the head of a Greek army, went on to create a vast new empire embracing most of the ancient world. And so he brought into being something even more like Plato's Atlantis than anything Plato saw around him in his own day, making the Greek world itself more barbarian and oriental in the process. Plato would have deplored the Hellenistic way of life ushered in by Alexander's conquests even more than he distrusted the tendencies of his own time, regarding all such materialistic and flashy forms of existence as death to the pilgrim spirit of enquiry into truth that he valued above all else. This is what the Atlantis story is all about: an analysis of what has gone wrong with Plato's world, an uncannily prophetic vision of what is about to go even more wrong with it and a warning – not just to his own city or his own country or his own times – of what will always go wrong when wealth and materialistic pride become the be-all and end-all of human life. Plato's Atlantis is thus a warning to us all – and not a piece of history writing in any way.

That judgement seems to have been shared by Plato's most illustrious pupil, the philosopher Aristotle, who was interestingly enough the son of the court physician of the Macedonian kings and for a while served as tutor to the young Alexander of Macedon. With Aristotle we are in the maddening position of knowing most of his works only in the form of lecture notes or quotes in later writers' books. It is from a quote in Strabo's *Geography*, of the early first century AD, that we know what Aristotle thought about the Atlantis story. Aristotle, too, talked of shallow mud beyond the Pillars of Hercules but he ranked Plato's account of Atlantis with fictional devices in Homer and declared that 'he who created it also destroyed it', showing that he regarded it as a literary creation for philosophical ends. Coming from someone who was a prominent pupil of Plato's, this remark strongly suggests that Plato made no informal claims among his students for the historical authenticity of his story and that there was no acquaintance with Atlantis as a piece of common knowledge of the day (even in the sketchiest form) among the educated people of the Greek world.

This conclusion is buttressed by the complete absence of references to the island of Atlantis by any writer before Plato, even one like Herodotus who had visited Egypt before Plato was born (paying a call to that same temple at Sais at which Solon was supposed to have learned of Atlantis). It was Herodotus who first referred to the waters beyond the Pillars of Hercules as the 'Atlantic Ocean', a natural enough extension of the name of the Atlas Mountains of north-west Africa to the great sea beyond them. It is a fair surmise that Plato, first inspired by report of the flooding of Atalante (some 100 kilometres from Athens) which happened when he was about one year old, was tickled by the similarity of that little island's name to the root (Atlant– in Greek) of the name of Homer's mythical Atlas and the mountain range named after him. (Atlas was supposed to have been turned to stone to hold up the heavens or the whole globe of the earth – hence the modern usage of 'atlas'.) When Plato assigned dimensions and grandeur to his Atlantis that the Mediterranean could not contain, he put his island out into the Atlantic Ocean, so-named since the time of Herodotus who as we recall never mentions any Atlantis. We know of a work, written just before Plato's time, by one Hellanicus of Lesbos, that was actually called *Atlantis*, but it had nothing to do with Plato's story and was a mythological treatise on the daughters of Atlas – 'Atlantis' means daughter of Atlas!

Aristotle stands at the head of a long line of disbelievers in Atlantis, in the ancient world and in later times. There were some classical believers in Atlantis, however. Another pupil of Plato's called Crantor is said, in a work written more than 700 years later at the very end of the classical tradition of philosophy, to have accepted Atlantis as history and to have believed the claim of Critias that the full story was recorded on pillars to be seen in Egypt. What Proclus said in the 430s AD about a since lost work of Crantor's of about 300 BC cannot count for much. A range of ancient authors including Theophrastus (a pupil of Aristotle who was over twenty when Plato died), Posidonius (writing about 70 BC), Strabo and Philo of Alexandria (a few years AD), Tertullian (about AD 200) and Ammianus Marcellinus (fourth century AD) regarded Atlantis as history. On the other hand, Longinus (first century AD), Origen (around AD 230), Iamblichus (AD 300) and Porphyry (died AD 305) were among those who regarded Atlantis as myth and allegory. Pliny, who died in the eruption of Vesuvius in AD 79, was open-minded but sceptical about it, while Plutarch (who died in AD 120) was evasive but contributed a name (about 450 years after Plato) for the priest who told Solon all about Atlantis: Senchis, which might derive from the same Egyptian name that we know as Shoshenk or Sheshonk (a pharaoh of about 925 BC).

That same Proclus of about AD 430 who credits Crantor with believing in Atlantis is himself ambivalent about the historical validity of the story, witnessing to inconclusive debate about the matter in Alexandria, where the great library evidently held no documentation to corroborate the story. But to him we owe the sole hint we have (and it is not a very persuasive one) that anyone in classical times ever knew anything about Atlantis that was not directly traceable to Plato's writings. Proclus refers to a work by a now obscure historian and geographer of perhaps the first century BC (up to 500 years before his time) named Marcellus. None of his writings have come down to us but they included, according to Proclus, a book called *Ethiopic History* that he thought might corroborate Plato up to a point. In it, it seems, Marcellus reported that various explorers of the Atlantic Ocean beyond the Pillars of Hercules had brought back stories of islands in the sea and that a lively controversy had gone on among the scholars of Alexandria as to the Atlantean significance of these islands. Nothing very surprising about that – many ships of several nations had ventured into the Atlantic and found some of the closer islands off the African and European coasts by 100 BC. Alexandrian scholars would inevitably have remembered Plato when they considered these islands.

But Marcellus, says Proclus, mentions three other islands 'of immense extent, one of them sacred to Pluto, another to Ammon and the middle one to Neptune, the size of which was a thousand stades'. We recall that the plain, without its mountainous fringe, of Plato's Atlantis was 3000 by 2000 stades in extent, but even these figures suggested a whole island much smaller than 'Libya and Asia put together' which is how Plato elsewhere characterizes Atlantis. This island of Marcellus is at least much bigger (at going on for 200 kilometres long) than any island we know among the Canaries, Madeiras, Cape Verdes or Azores which explorers of his time might have reached in the Atlantic. However, ancient measurements were always flexible and ancient reports were often exaggerated. But Marcellus is not done, for his explorers 'also add that its inhabitants preserved from their ancestors the memory of the Atlantic island that existed there, and was really wonderfully great, which for a long while ruled all the islands in the Atlantic Sea and was itself also sacred to Neptune'.

Neptune was the Roman equivalent of Poseidon, the founder god of Atlantis according to Plato. But then this sea-god was the founder and patron of many a maritime community. (Pluto was the Hades of the Greeks and Ammon the great god of latter-day Egypt.) At face value, Marcellus (according to Proclus) is reporting an island group, known by about 100 BC, whose inhabitants recalled a greater island in their midst, with an empire rather like the one Plato gives to Atlantis. The simplest explanation for this claim (and the simplest are always to be preferred) is that Marcellus and his informants were, not surprisingly, influenced by Plato's renowned writings about Atlantis, and so Marcellus via Proclus is not reliable independent corroboration at all. The same can be said for remarks once attributed to Aristotle about an island found by the Carthaginians a few days' sail into the Atlantic, with woods, fruit trees and navigable rivers: this was, in fact, the work of one of several later 'pseudo-Aristotles' posing as the master. There really is, then, no source of the Atlantis story other than Plato and no later ancient author ever reported seeing the old Egyptian records again or ever hearing another word out of an Egyptian – even in Alexandria – about Atlantis or anything remotely resembling it.

Clearly, sailors' tales circulated of islands in the Atlantic, sometimes based on fact, for the geographers of the day to mull over, and it was reasonable to speculate (as our Pseudo-Aristotle and Theopompus evidently did) that there might be other continents as well as islands across oceans remote from the Mediterranean world, rather as we speculate today about other solar systems. ('It is probable that there are many other continents separated from ours by a sea that we must cross to reach them, some larger and others smaller but all, save our own, invisible to us . . . As our islands are in relation to our seas, so is the inhabited world in relation to the Atlantic, and so are many other continents in relation to the whole sea; for they are as it were immense islands surrounded by immense seas.' *Pseudo-Aristotle*) But nothing in the classical geographers' writings offers independent corroboration of Atlantis. And nothing in modern geology allows for the former existence of a now vanished island-continent whose surviving remnants might be the Azores or Canaries or Madeiras, as we shall see when we come to the theories of Ignatius Donnelly.

For the moment, at this early stage of our diagnostic work on the Atlantis Syndrome, when we still have only Plato to go on, we need to establish what key features of the idea of Atlantis we have garnered so far. Let us set aside what we now know of Plato's purpose in writing of Atlantis (crucial though it is to understanding how the whole idea of Atlantis was generated), acknowledging that later writers about the vanished island have lost all track of the claims made by him for Athens vs. Atlantis and usually all track of his moral outrage against the vices of the Atlanteans, too. (Like many another moral artist, Plato has succeeded in making his villains more compelling than his saints.) Let us concentrate instead on the bits of the tale that have come through as standard components of Atlantis speculation – in other words, on what of Plato's account is still around in the thoughts of Atlantologists, the basic material that Plato laid down on which others have built.

The key idea is, of course, of a vanished civilization, a whole sophisticated way of life lost without trace, save in some very select ancient records known to a precious few. This is not an Egyptian idea. The Egyptians thought their way of life was very old, with king lists that seemed to take them back at least four thousand years by Saite times. There were, admittedly, some confusing gaps and overlaps in their records (as a result of periods of social disturbance when records failed or several rival rulers ruled at once) that made the true span hard to calculate – but that only left the way open to thinking it might be longer than it was. They thought, moreover, that predynastic times (before the first kings with recorded names reigned) had seen successions of semi-divine rulers going back for thousands upon thousands of years to very remote days when the gods themselves walked the earth. Despite the periods of disturbance (and there were three major ones in Egyptian history), the Egyptians did not believe – whatever the Saite priests are supposed to have told Solon – in long-separated episodes of cosmic cataclysm when fire and flood wiped out most of humanity and its historical memory. But we know that Plato did believe in such a scheme of human history. And this was a not unreasonable idea for the enquiring minds of the Greeks to have hit upon when they faced the fact of human existence without the benighted reliance on religious traditions of most peoples of the ancient world, but also without the benefits of archaeology, geology and evolutionary biology to guide them. Plato selected the Egyptians as the transmitters of knowledge about the remote past because of the general Greek regard for the venerable longevity of Egyptian civilization. If anyone was going to know about previous states of the world, it was the Egyptians. There may even be a gentle joke on his contemporary detractors in Plato's scene-setting in Sais for his Atlantis narrative. Rival philosophers had, according to a later tradition at least, accused Plato of pinching his social ideals as detailed in the *Republic* from the Egyptians – so in the *Timaeus* and *Critias* he openly attributed knowledge of Atlantis to them. In his next and last work, the *Laws*, he returns to the antiquity of Egypt, making his anonymous Athenian speaker declare that Egyptian art of ten thousand years ago was just as good as it is today 'and I'm not talking loosely, I mean literally ten thousand'.

Inadvertently, with his insistence on the age and accuracy of the Egyptian annals (as a literary device, really), Plato generated an important feature of the Atlantis idea that would never leave the scene: that, despite the general ignorance of humanity, including its scholars, about the true history of the world, there is rich and rare ancient information to be gleaned in exotic places by the enlightened few in the know. This information isn't always in the form of ancient texts (it can be 'encoded' in star maps and temple layouts and hoary mythologies) but texts are never very far away – or the promise of them at any rate, as is the case with the Atlantean Hall of Records under the Sphinx that recently failed to show up by the millennium as advertised.

Plato's depiction of the Atlanteans' style of life as opulent and artificial, beyond the stern dreams of their Athenian rivals, started something too. Never mind that he really meant to highlight the moral dangers of luxury and power: what he hereby contributed to the grand Atlantis vision of later times is a picture of wealth, technological prowess and mastery of nature. If anyone wants to see riches, materialistic sophistication and bold dealings with the physical world as the hallmarks of civilization, then Plato has for them conjured up a supercivilization on Atlantis and rather inadvertently boosted the idea of a long-lost Golden Age. What he has signally not done, however, on any reading, is to credit his Atlantis with the oodles of 'ancient wisdom' that are now *de rigueur* for vanished supercivilizations. Plato's Atlanteans are engineers but not scientists and certainly not sages. They have not built their civilization with a high technology otherwise unknown in the ancient world, they are not master-astronomers and they are not wise enough to avoid the pitfalls of their wealth and power.

The civilization of Atlantis is not, as Plato tells it, the first in the world (Athens, at least, is as old and no doubt there have been others before them in the long cycle of human existence) nor is it the fount of civilization from which all other cultures have borrowed their inspiration. It isn't a patch on Athens: it's just richer, greedier and more artificial. It has an empire but there is no suggestion of nineteenth-century missionary humbug about that – Plato's Atlantean empire isn't bringing enlightenment to lesser breeds. It would be left to Plato's successors, in the days of much later empires, to correct his errors and omissions in matters of ancient wisdom and enlightenment.

The location of Atlantis and the nature of its end are parts of the Atlantis Syndrome that Plato established in only a general way – many of his successors have moved Atlantis about a good deal, sometimes out of the Atlantic altogether, and, instead of earthquake and flood, emphasis has shifted on to volcanoes and even cometary collisions to account for the island's destruction. Not many Atlantologists think Zeus did it any more, or Ammon-Ra or any sort of god or God.

From Plato, then, western thought received the notion of a spectacular ancient civilization destroyed practically without trace in a remote region no longer easy to investigate, out beyond the Mediterranean and European world, tantalizingly remembered in the lost records of another ancient civilization almost as mysterious as Atlantis itself. The story was just a matter of curiosity for the geographers, historians and philosophers of the classical world, nothing more. When the pagan culture of the West was overrun by Christianity, with its reliance on the traditions of one small Levantine nation as its sole guide to history, interest in Atlantis disappeared – the Bible had nothing to say about it. (The sixth-century monk Cosmas did, however, make the suggestion that the 'Timaeus' had really picked up on the Flood story familiar in the Bible via a 'Chaldean' – latter-day Babylonian – tradition.) It would take the discovery of a new world across the Atlantic to revive interest in Atlantis, and in the process the Atlantis notion would itself be turned into something new.

3

NEW WORLD,
NEW ATLANTIS

Numerous islands of the eastern Atlantic are nearer to Carthage than was the original homeland of the Carthaginians in the Levant at the eastern end of the Mediterranean. The Madeiras are the nearest of all, but well out in the Atlantic, and there is no archaeological evidence to show that the Phoenicians went there from Carthage, though they might have visited them. Genoese sailors reached them before the middle of the fourteenth century and they are clearly shown on the Laurentian portolano of 1351. Thereafter the Portuguese settled the Madeiras, finding no human beings there nor indeed any land mammals at all.

Further south, the Canary Islands (which are closer than the Madeiras to the Atlantic coast of Africa) were known to the classical world after report of an expedition there of about 40 BC reached Rome from the client king, Juba II, whom the Romans had set up in Mauretania: Plutarch and Pliny both wrote of the Canaries. The Moors were there in AD 999 and later on the sailors of several European powers visited the islands, until they passed to Spain in 1479. Close as they are to the North African coast, the Canaries were inhabited by a Berber-speaking people (now extinct as a separate group) living a Late Stone Age sort of life. Very likely Phoenician sailors had encountered them long before the expedition related by Juba. The Cape Verde islands are still further south and not as near to the coast as the Canaries but, again, there is every chance that Phoenician (and Moorish) explorers reached them on occasion: the Portuguese were there from 1460, after a possible Venetian visit in 1456. No previous inhabitants are recorded. The British Isles, too, were within Phoenician reach and a Greek contemporary of Plato's got as far as Britain and the mouth of the Rhine. All or any of these island groups relatively near the Atlantic coast of Africa and Europe may have contributed to a Mediterranean sailors' folklore of fabulous islands in the Atlantic Ocean in classical times (when the Canaries in particular were identified with the mythical Isles of the Blessed where the most fortunate of the dead went to their reward). Echoes of that classical lore (some of it perhaps transmitted by Moorish sailors from North Africa and Spain), as well as the mentions by writers like Pliny, encouraged explorers of the European Renaissance to search these islands out again.

The Azores, much further away from land in the midst of the Atlantic, were not discovered until 1427, by the Portuguese who found no traces of human habitation or visitation on them, though the Moors have been credited with reaching them on the basis of the writings of an Arab geographer of the first half of the twelfth century. (Report of stray finds of a bracelet, interlocking rings and stone discs from the sea off the Azores might relate these items, if they ever existed at all, to some recent historical origin.) Renaissance scholars were bound to remember Plato as more and more of these island groups in the Atlantic came into the orbit of European knowledge in the fifteenth century, with the Azores in particular looking like a possible remnant of the vanished island-continent of Atlantis. But it was not until the discovery of new, previously unsuspected and quite alien cultures in the New World, on the other side of the Atlantic, that speculation about Atlantis was vigorously renewed. Forty years after Columbus came to the Bahamas in 1492 and opened the way for the exploration of the Central American mainland after 1498, the Italian scientist and poet Girolamo Fracastoro suggested that the Indian cultures encountered in the Americas were latter-day remnants of the civilization of Atlantis. (He also theorized that diseases are spread by minute organisms, that fossils are the remains of ancient life-forms and that the planets all circle a fixed point.) In relating the

Indians of America to Plato's Atlantis, Fracastoro was following the tradition of his day of trying to make new discoveries conform with what the respected authorities of the classical world had had to say on any given topic (with the Bible as the ultimate authority, of course). It was a reasonable idea at the time in the current state of knowledge of history and geography; and we all try to fit new things into our existing schemes as a first resort. But with his suggestion about the Americas, Fracastoro gave a new direction to the story of Atlantis which others soon followed. In 1553 Francisco Lopez de Gomara took up that suggestion in his *General History of the Indies*, and the proposal was made to call north or south America 'Atlantis' – the Elizabethan mathematician and astrologer John Dee put the name on a map (he also claimed to summon up spirits from Atlantis). Sir Francis Bacon built on the idea in his unfinished utopian work *The New Atlantis*, published after his death in 1627, a fictionalized vehicle – complete with what sound like aeroplanes and submarines – for his philosophical and political views, rather like Plato's work. (Bacon even anticipated something like the cinema with his New Atlanteans' 'houses of deceits of the senses, where we represent all manner of juggling, false apparitions, impostures and illusions, and their fallacies'.) John Swan's *Speculum Mundi* of 1644 concluded that America was indeed close by if not part of the western end of Plato's 'Atlantick Island'. A few years later, a work by the Jesuit scholar Athanasius Kircher contained a map of such beguiling plausibility (if upside-down to our eyes) that we can see just how Atlantis ought to have looked, riding in the mid-Atlantic. Under Kircher's influence the idea that the biblical Flood and the end of Atlantis were one and the same was revived.

At this stage, Plato's Atlantis functioned only as a convenient explanation for the existence of the Indian cultures of the Americas, which were tacitly assumed to have been incapable of generating themselves yet evidently were not to be easily traced back to any known Old World civilization. The idea of Atlantis had thus advanced a pace beyond Plato: it had not been totally destroyed, not sunk wholly without trace; its island home might be gone (or almost gone, if the Azores were a tiny relic of it) but

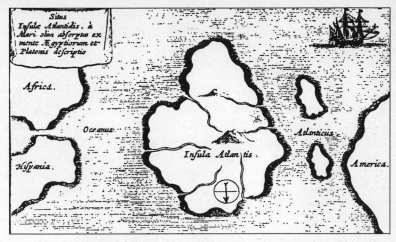

Atlantis according to Athanasius Kircher in 1664.

its heritage lived on in however debased a form in the peoples of America. What was more, Atlantis now appeared as a fount of civilization, a source and origin for later cultures. Perhaps it was the source for cultural developments other than just those of the Americas: in due course, it would not be too great a step to see it as the source of some Old World civilizations, too. After all, Plato said the Atlanteans had conquered parts of North Africa and Italy and now it was known that there were pyramids in Mexico as well as in Egypt. While the Bible's version of the ancient history of the world, and especially of the Jews' part in it, remained unquestioned, Atlantis could hardly be posed as the fount of all civilization all over the world, but in the end that step too was bound to be taken.

The idea of American Indian origins in Atlantis, even of a possible location of Atlantis close to or in the Americas, was supported by such scholars of the late eighteenth and early nineteenth centuries as Georges Buffon, the French naturalist (who ran into trouble with the theologians of the Sorbonne over his views on the longevity of earth history), and the Prussian explorer and scientist Alexander von Humboldt, who pioneered the idea of continental drift between Africa and South America. While Buffon thought that Atlantis had been

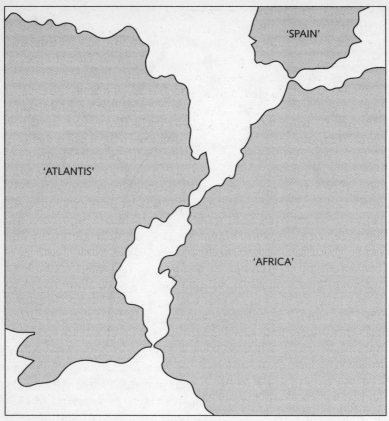

Atlantis touching Africa, after the map of Bory de St Vincent.

flooded when Atlantic waters poured into the Mediterranean, Bory de St Vincent reckoned that volcanic events in the Mediterranean had sent waters out past Gibraltar to drown Atlantis – he felt sufficiently confident to draw a detailed map. But it was the rediscovery of the physical ruins of the American civilizations in the nineteenth century that put new life into the idea of Atlantis in or near the Americas and renewed interest in the Spanish conquerors' accounts of the native American peoples. There were the spectacular pyramids of Mexico and Central America, and also the less dramatic but often still very impressive mounds of the USA from Mississippi to Illinois and Ohio. The mound at Cahokia in Illinois is over 30 metres high, with a base area greater than that of the pyramid of Khufu at Giza. Thomas Jefferson, on the basis of excavating one of the much smaller mounds, very sensibly concluded that these North American monuments were indeed the work of the native Americans, but others thought they had been made by Danes, Canaanites or – most fashionably – by the descendants of the Lost Tribes of Israel, carted off by the Assyrians in the eighth century BC. These remnants of the Lost Tribes were supposed to have somehow made their way through Asia to the Bering Strait and got across to Alaska, or more likely sailed with the Phoenicians to the Americas. This is the origin of the idea that the Phoenicians made regular Atlantic crossings to America, first touted in the mid-nineteenth century. In recent times the Lost Tribes idea has rather dropped out of 'alternative archaeology', but the associated notion of Phoenician crossings to America (especially in the guise of the Carthaginians) has been well kept up.

The notion of Atlantis as the source of all American cultures if not of all cultures all over the world was boosted, quite erroneously as it turned out, by a Flemish scholar after the middle years of the nineteenth century. Charles-Etienne Brasseur de Bourbourg travelled widely in the Americas and learned Indian languages in pursuit of his search for the origins of the Indians and their ways of life. In Madrid Brasseur found a copy of a book about the culture of the Central American Maya written by the Spanish bishop of Yucatan, Diego de Landa, in the 1560s. De Landa had started as a bigoted destroyer of pagan American culture, but came round to an interest in preserving the Mayan heritage. (It was, incidentally, he who pioneered the non-Atlantean 'Lost Tribes' theory of Amerind origins. Actually, of course, those 'Lost Tribes' were assimilated in their deportation and never trekked to the Americas via Siberia or sailed with Phoenician traders to the New World.) De Landa's belated concern for Mayan culture did not preclude a high-handed approach to his native informants that severely reduced the quality of the material in the book Brasseur rescued from obscurity. In it, de Landa described the customs of the Maya in his day with some account of their history and a claimed decipherment of their hieroglyphic writing. He was right about the signs for days and months of the Mayan calendar (which was the basis for reading the dates on their monuments) but wrong about everything else, in that he thought the Mayan hieroglyphs were a straightforward alphabet like our own when they are evidently a mixture of signs for sounds and signs for whole words (rather like the Egyptian hieroglyphs, though sound values predominate with the latter). We have to say *evidently* since, to this day, the Mayan hieroglyphs are not quite fully deciphered.

We do know, however, that de Landa's decipherment was almost entirely incorrect and transliterations from Mayan texts via his alphabet system are quite worthless. Back in 1864, Brasseur did not know that and, in any case, his 'translations' using de Landa's alphabet relied heavily on imaginative extrapolations from his knowledge of Central American Indian languages, as spoken and written down in Latin characters. Only three Mayan books in their own script survived the attentions of Spanish missionaries and it was on to one of these, the *Madrid Codex*, that Brasseur turned his method of translation. What we know as a work of astrology and divination emerged from Brasseur's hands as an account of a great catastrophe that overtook a large island in the Atlantic Ocean in 9937 BC, the survivors of which colonized first America and later Egypt. Brasseur claimed the Indian name for this lost island was not Atlantis (that must have been one of Solon's retranslations) but Mu, thus launching another long-lived piece of exotica on the world of 'alternative archaeology'. It was nothing more than a faint resemblance between de Landa's fancied Mayan 'letters' for m and u and a couple of signs in the codex that gave birth to Mu in Brasseur's brain.

Although it was soon clear that Brasseur's Mayan alphabet really produced untranslatable gibberish, his work on the *Madrid Codex* was improved upon by Augustus le Plongeon towards the end of the nineteenth century, along very much the same lines. In his translation the Land of Mu disappeared suddenly in the night in the midst of violent volcanic activity, sinking with sixty-four millions of people some eight thousand years before the original codex whose copy resides in Madrid. In other Mayan texts le Plongeon claimed to have identified the story of a princess named Moo: Moo of Mu, as it were. When forced to flee the Atlantean, or 'Muvian', colony of Yucatan after the murder of her husband, Moo sought refuge on Mu but it was nowhere to be found anymore, so she travelled on to another Muvian colony in Egypt, where she built the Sphinx as a memorial to her murdered consort. So great was the Egyptians' regard for Moo that they turned her into the goddess Isis, according to le Plongeon. Le Plongeon is the begetter of Atlantean, or properly speaking 'Muvian', notions that are still with us and of combative attitudes to orthodox scholarship that are still very much the hallmark of 'alternative' writers ('the so-called learned men of our own days are the first to oppose new ideas and the bearers of these' – one of his milder observations). So it may be worth recalling a few of his other contributions. He seriously proposed that various lines and zigzags on a Mayan lintel were representations of telegraph wires, proving that the Maya had possessed this late nineteenth-century device. He asserted that the writing on the wall at Belshazzar's Feast in the Book of Daniel was Mayan and that the last words of Jesus meant not 'My God, My God, why have You forsaken me' in some sort of Aramaic, but rather in Mayan 'Now, Now, sinking, black ink over nose', which manages to be both more colourful and bathetic at the same time. He thought the reclining Chacmool statuary of some Central American sites enshrined an accurate mapping of the east coast of the Americas from Newfoundland to Cape Horn. Robert Wauchope in his valuable *Lost Tribes and Sunken Continents* says of him, apropos of his own splenetic remark about learned men, that he himself 'opposed no new idea whatsoever, on any grounds', and we may add that for le Plongeon those ideas never needed to be consistent one with another.

Mu, the Mayan name for Atlantis as far as Brasseur and le Plongeon were concerned, subsequently underwent a bizarre relocation from the Atlantic to first the Indian Ocean, and then the Pacific Ocean as a result of the truly mind-boggling musings of the theosophist Madame Blavatsky, recounted in the six volumes of *The Secret Doctrine* published between 1888 and 1936. (She died in 1891.) The bizarreness of the relocation resides in the fact that the name of another speculative lost continent, proposed for zoological reasons, was identified with Mu and Atlantis seemingly just because it had the same two letters mu in the middle of it. The scientific hypothesis (long since abandoned) was that a land connection between the east coast of Africa and south-east Asia had once been the home of the evolution of the first primates, in the shape of the lemurs now confined to Madagascar: the hypothetical land mass was dubbed Lemuria and Madagascar was seen as its principal remnant. As all this concerned the world of a remote geological epoch it had of course nothing whatever to do with human history; none the less, in this curious fashion, Le-mu-ria established itself in some people's minds as a lost continent of the Indian Ocean and the ideas of lost human civilizations long associated with Atlantis became attached to it too. But it was Madame Blavatsky's Theosophical Society that really put Lemuria on the alternative map of speculation about human origins. Her authority for her doctrines rested on claims of a long sojourn in Tibet (for which there is no evidence) and of receiving subsequent communications from two dead Tibetan sages (for which there could be no evidence). Even the Society for Psychical Research in London branded this former bare-back rider, pianist, sweat-shop worker and Russian general's wife a fraud.

She supposedly came by her knowledge of her lost worlds from actual records (written in the 'Senzar' language) that survived the ancient cataclysm and fetched up in Tibet. 'Quotations' from these alleged records and commentary upon them make up *The Secret Doctrine*, gibberish which it is impossible to read for more than a few lines at a time, drawing on Donnelly and the unreliable late nineteenth-century Sanskrit scholar Louis Jacolliot, as well as on earlier occultists' speculations about the part played by black magic in the destruction of Atlantis. According to theosophy, Lemuria was home to the Third Root Race: reddish apelike creatures, some with eyes in the backs of their heads or four arms, who laid eggs! The Fourth Root Race made up the population of Atlantis and was more human in form. (Human beings today belong to Blavatsky's Fifth Root Race.) Blavatsky, it is interesting to note, went against the trend of more recent efforts to correct Plato's dates downwards: she thought he must have meant not nine thousand but nine hundred thousand years ago for the end of his lost civilization.

William Scott-Elliot took on Blavatsky's approach in works like *The Story of Atlantis* (1896) and *The Lost Lemuria* (1904), revealing along the way – by means of 'astral clairvoyance' – such wholly incredible wonders as '8ft tall' Toltecs and Venusians peopling a quite fantastic rearrangement of our planet's land masses. Scott-Elliot restored the notion that the Atlanteans deserved their watery fate – for dabbling in sorcery, according to him. And then James Churchward, author of works like *The Lost Continent of Mu* (1926), definitively contracted Lemuria into Mu and shifted it from the Indian Ocean to the Pacific, demoting Atlantis in the process to the status of a colony of Mu. Still, both were enormous places – Churchward's Atlantis filled practically all of the North

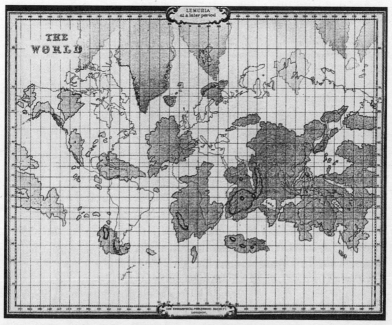

Scott-Elliot's world map, with Lemuria, Atlantis and much else that was never there.

Atlantic (from the West Indies to Madeira, from the northern coast of South America to the latitude of Newfoundland and Ireland) and his Mu was larger still (occupying most of the Pacific between latitudes of about 30° south and 30° north), with lines of communication to all the secondary centres in the ancient world. Just as Blavatsky alleged a Tibetan source for her information, the Anglo-American Churchward claimed to have learned about his Mu from tablets preserved in a monastery in India.

The self-styled Colonel Churchward is interesting for our study of the ever-evolving Atlantis Syndrome in that his ideas are in part so transparently the product of late nineteenth-century and early twentieth-century colonial ideology. For him the 'civilizations of India, Babylonia, Persia, Egypt and Yucatan were but the dying embers of the first great civilization'. As for the Stone Age cultures that were being revealed to pre-date the world's oldest civilizations in his day: 'Savagery came out of civilization and not civilization out of savagery" and 'A savage, left to himself, does not rise. He has fallen to where he is and is still going down. It is only when he is brought into contact with civilization that an upward change in him becomes possible.' From his tablets, Churchward had learned that his lost continent 'was teeming with gay and happy life over which 64,000,000 human beings reigned supreme . . . The dominant race in the land of Mu was a white race, exceedingly handsome people, with clear white and olive skins, large, soft, dark eyes and straight black hair . . . On cool evenings might be seen pleasure ships, filled with gorgeously dressed, jewel-bedecked men and women.' The idea of good-looking supermen lording it over lesser breeds and taking civilization round the world is made very explicit in Churchward.

Now it was possible to believe in two lost continents: the original huge Atlantic island version and the even bigger, older, primal vanished continent in the Pacific. Whatever the merits of the Lemuria hypothesis for remote geological times, it clearly has no bearing on the history of human civilization over the last eight thousand years or so: as handled by Blavatsky and Churchward, this extension of the Atlantis idea has wandered into occultism and complete scientific illiteracy, with a fair

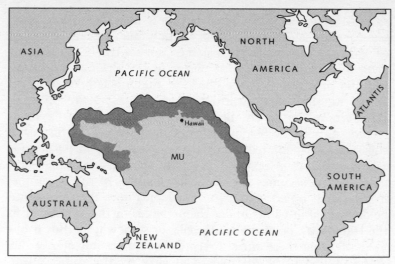

The lost land of Mu, with Atlantis peeping in on the right, after one of Churchward's maps.

suspicion of fraud over Tibetan texts and Indian tablets. Other theosophical musings have sometimes produced grimmer pictures, of mist-enshrouded lost continents peopled with impossible semi-human inhabitants, so recklessly nonsensical that we need have no more of them except to note that Atlantis in one form or another regularly features in them as a lost supercontinent breaking up over hundreds of thousands of years (theosophical time-scales of more or less human history are strikingly extended), with its last remnant properly called Poseidonis – Plato's Atlantis. The name is worth remembering for when we come to Edgar Cayce and his Atlantean predictions.

The school of thought pioneered by Brasseur and le Plongeon, then taken to extremes by people like Blavatsky and Churchward, added significantly to the checklist of features of the developing Atlantis Syndrome. Atlantis is no longer a stray ancient civilization – however magnificent – that came to grief through natural catastrophe; it is not just the source of the American Indian cultures. It is now the mother-country of colonists in other lands like Egypt (rather than aggressor against an independent Egypt as per Plato) and, when itself seen as an offshoot of Lemuria in the Indian Ocean or shifted as Mu into the Pacific, it becomes the source of all ancient civilization and the central player in the drama of human spiritual progress. It is the abode of the 'Ancient Wisdom', of which we shall hear so much more before we are finished. What's more, to go one better than Plato's ancient Egyptian records as seen by Solon but since disappeared, its history is still available (admittedly only to the select few) in mysterious Tibetan or Indian texts. Henceforth, the existence of secret ancient texts becomes one of the key features of the syndrome: if these texts aren't actually in our hands now, they're soon to be discovered in vaults under the pyramids or the Sphinx, or in the Himalayas, or at the south pole, or somewhere. (But it has to be said that these ancient records have a notably elusive side – they failed to be discovered at Giza by the millennium, though long promised by certain 'alternative' thinkers.)

Writing at about the same time as the prickly le Plongeon and batty Blavatsky but in a more reasonable vein was the man who really revived Atlantis as such (without Lemuria) as a not too far-fetched development of Plato's original concept. Ignatius Donnelly went along with the developing syndrome insofar as Atlantis was seen as the fount of both American and Old World civilizations in a Golden Age of sorts, but there were no occult accretions, no root races, no dodgy Tibetan or Indian records, no lost island-continents in the Pacific. Instead he set out to provide a wealth of evidence to show that both the Old World and the New shared numerous traits (not just archaeological) that could only be explained by a common inheritance from a vanished landmass in the Atlantic, where Plato said it had been. Donnelly takes Plato very much at face value, ignoring any possibility of myth or moral purpose in his Atlantis material. So doggedly rationalistic is Donnelly that he somehow doesn't even register the essentially myth-located start of Plato's account with the god Poseidon's mating with a mortal woman and then divinely reshaping the island. 'The early history of most nations begins with gods and demons, while here we have nothing of the kind; we see an immigrant enter the country, marry one of the native women and settle down; in time a great nation grows up around him.' To this Donnelly adds, quite incredibly, 'Neither is there any evidence on the face of this history that Plato sought to convey in it a moral or political lesson, in the guise of a fable, as did Bacon in *The New Atlantis*, and More in his *Utopia*.' To have read Plato in full on Atlantis, as we may be sure Donnelly did (unlike many a subsequent Atlantologist) and come away with no sense of Plato's moralizing is to carry literal-mindedness to extremes. Still, we should perhaps be grateful that Donnelly remained on rational ground in envisaging his Atlantis as a Bronze Age sort of place – the nearest he gets to latter-day high-tech Atlantological speculation is to flirt with the possibilities of the magnetic compass and gunpowder as Atlantean inventions.

This Ignatius Donnelly was a remarkable character – he has been called perhaps the most erudite man ever to sit in the House of Representatives. He was born in 1831 in Philadelphia, where he became a lawyer. In 1856 he moved to Minnesota to co-found an immigrants' boomtown called Nininger City (in partnership with one John Nininger), which was to be a cultural as well as an industrial magnet to settlers. He edited a journal that was published in English and German, until a financial panic the following year emptied the town and left Donnelly as its sole inhabitant. He went on to be an early supporter of the anti-slavery Republican Party, became lieutenant-governor of Minnesota and a US congressman. After leaving the Republicans and involving himself in several minority parties, he returned to a revived Nininger City to edit a liberal weekly till 1879. Three years later he enjoyed his greatest literary success with *Atlantis: The Antediluvian World*, following it up with *Ragnarok: The Age of Fire and Gravel*. These two works established many of the details of the Atlantis Syndrome and related outlooks on human history and prehistory. By the late 1880s Donnelly was at work to prove, by means of a code he believed he had discovered in Shakespeare's works, that Bacon was the real author of the bard's plays and poems, as well as of the works of Marlowe and Montaigne. In a piece of prophetic fiction entitled *Caesar's Column* (of 1891) that recalls Plato's and Bacon's use of fiction for social and philosophical purposes, he painted a picture of the USA of 1988 as a capitalist plutocracy with a downtrodden working class, predicting along the way such technological developments as television and poison gas. He died in 1901.

As far as Atlantis was concerned, Donnelly gathered together an impressive (at first sight) array of data in support of his theory of its primacy in the story of ancient civilization. Donnelly wanted to establish a baker's dozen of propositions about Atlantis:

– that there was once in the Atlantic (before 9600 BC) a large island, reaching close to the strait of Gibraltar in the east;

– that Plato's description of that island was historically accurate, and not fable (just as Heinrich Schliemann thought, at about the same time as Donnelly, that Homer's Troy was not fable either – interestingly, Schliemann himself had no interest in Atlantis);

– that Atlantis was where human civilization first arose;

– that Atlantis became a mighty nation with people enough to populate Mexico, the Mississippi delta, the area of the Amazon, the Pacific coast of South America, the west coasts of Europe and Africa, the Mediterranean region, the lands around the Baltic, Black and Caspian seas;

– that Atlantis was the original of the Garden of Eden, remembered after its destruction as having been for a long time a scene of peace and happiness – Elysian Fields, Mount Olympus, Asgard of the Norse gods;

– that the gods and goddesses of the Greeks, Hindus, Germans and Scandinavians, etc., were based on the kings, queens and heroes of old Atlantis, whose historical doings became the myths of those gods;

– that in the mythologies of Peru and Egypt in particular can be discerned the original religion of Atlantis, which was sun worship;

– that Egypt was probably the oldest colony of Atlantis and Egyptian culture the nearest thing to Atlantean life that we can now know;

– that the European Bronze Age, too, was derived from Atlantis and iron also was first made there (though, awkwardly for Donnelly, metal use came late to the Americas);

– that the Phoenician alphabet, which lies behind subsequent

European alphabets, was inspired by the alphabet of Atlantis, as was the Mayan alphabet (though we may recall that the Mayans had no true alphabet and neither, really, did the Egyptians – the Incas of Peru had no writing at all, despite Donnelly's belief to the contrary in which he was wrong even in light of the knowledge of his day);

– that Atlantis was the original home of the Aryans, the Semites and the common ancestors of both the American peoples and the Egyptians (these reddish-brown folk were apparently the most civilized of the racial groups on Atlantis);

– that Atlantis went down in a great natural catastrophe, submerged with nearly all its inhabitants – an event not seen by Donnelly as any sort of divine retribution, which could hardly be visited upon the noble fount of all later civilizations, and not explicitly related despite his title reference to 'the Antediluvian World' to the Flood of the Bible;

– that a few escapees from the disaster went east and west from their lost homeland in ships and on rafts to tell the story that would become the basis for the common Flood narratives of the Old World and the New.

To support these theses about Atlantis, Donnelly amassed a wealth of suggestive data from all sorts of sources. He did it with considerable erudition and literary flair and, in the state of knowledge at the time, with a reasonable but even then not overwhelming degree of scholarly responsibility.

He pointed to the then newly discovered Mid-Atlantic Ridge of underwater mountains, of which the Azores are the highest peaks, as evidence for a once-elevated mountain range now sunk beneath the sea. He reminded his readers that the science of geology had revealed many examples of lands once under the sea (with marine fossils to prove it) that were now raised high and dry. He noted cases in recent history where volcanic activity had destroyed islands or even thrown them up in very short order, while earthquakes had led to the submergence of shorelines. What he did not admit was that all such cases were pretty small-scale affairs: no huge island-continents like his Atlantis had ever been pulled under or flooded overnight. What he could not know was that the mountains of the Mid-Atlantic

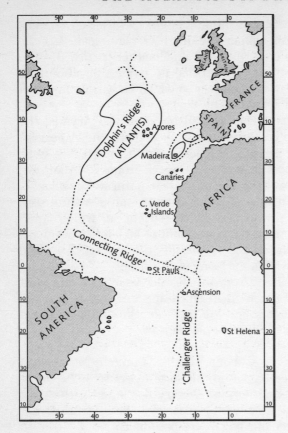

Donnelly's location of Atlantis.

Ridge are not in the process of going under as a result of the submergence of land but rather in the process of coming up as a result of mountain building under water. The Azores aren't the tips of sunken mountains still just managing to show above water, they are the highest points of a mountain range that is coming into being under the Atlantic Ocean as the continents of Africa and the Americas drift apart on their tectonic plates. (The volcanic tachylite dredged up from the Atlantic is not proof as Donnelly thought – and others after him – that this ocean bed was once above water: it can be formed underwater too. Nor do freshwater diatoms in Atlantic seabed sediments point to the former presence of terrestrial rivers there, as has been suggested

66

since Donnelly's time: they turn out to have been blown over the Atlantic from African lakes by Saharan winds.)

The above-sea continents of our planet are made of relatively light rock, overwhelmingly granite, resting on denser substrates (the tectonic plates) below them and beneath the sea, that themselves float on a semi-molten slush. The African, South American and North American plates rub shoulders at the Mid-Atlantic Ridge. In the highly unlikely event (impossible, really, in light of plate tectonics) that there was a great island-continent in the Atlantic that sank beneath the waves in about 9600 BC, we should expect to find granite on the ocean bed with very little sediment on top of it. But we find absolutely no granite and undisturbed sediments up to 800 metres thick. The fossils in the bottom layers of the sediments belong to the Cretaceous Period, over sixty million years ago. It seems superfluous to add that no prehistoric or historic archaeological material comes from the mid-Atlantic ocean bed, any more than it comes from the slopes of the Azores above water. (Incidentally, if a huge island à la Donnelly sank rapidly beneath the waters of the Atlantic, we should expect to see evidence of catastrophic wave action around the shores of the Atlantic in the Old World and the New, but we do not.)

The Mid-Atlantic Ridge, 20,000 kilometres long from north to south (and itself part of a continuous feature that runs right round the globe), is a submarine volcanic chain, with scant signs of the sort of weathered valleys and plains we should expect to see if it had ever been above water. (On the contrary, the ridge is made of comparatively young rock, as is the ocean floor generally.) It is volcanic because, as the plates of Africa and the Americas drift apart, igneous rock boils up in molten form in the rift that divides the plates, extending – as it cools and hardens – the breadth of the ridge and itself helping to push the plates apart. Not only is there none of the granite of which Atlantis would have been composed above water, there is also no trace of the plate on which the granite would have rested. (All these same arguments apply to any Lemuria in the Pacific, too, it should be noted.)

So Donnelly cannot conceivably have been right, any more than Plato taken at face value, about the size and location of

Atlantis. If you want to hold on to anything of Plato's Atlantis, then you have – as L. Sprague de Camp pointed out – to change so much of it that, once the changed items are seen to have no strict factual basis, you are left wondering why any of it should be taken seriously and how on earth you would choose which bits to believe: it's always like this when you try to tinker rationally with belief systems. We shall see in due course that a somewhat different location, but still in the Atlantic, with necessary size changes has been proposed more than once to rescue Plato's Atlantis: but we can be sure at this point that there is no rescuing Donnelly's. This stark fact might be thought to render most of his further arguments for Atlantis pretty well redundant right away, but – as with so many belief systems – the undermining of his central claim has not caused the rest of his ingeniously constructed scheme to go away, even if it fares no better in detail than the stuff about the Mid-Atlantic Ridge. Much of what Donnelly brought to Atlantis remains at the core of the Atlantis Syndrome.

He claimed that the existence of Atlantis, pretty well filling up the Atlantic between the Americas and Africa/Europe, facilitated the coming and going of flora and fauna of all kinds between the Old World and the New, in both directions, thus explaining common features of the natural world in both areas. Well, whatever they have in common for naturalists, it was not achieved by a land-bridge in the shape of Atlantis: in fact, migrations on the wing or on floating debris or carried by the wind, to say nothing of common evolutionary links of the distant past, can explain the similarities while Donnelly's Atlantis cannot explain the dissimilarities. Donnelly's claim that potatoes, maize and cotton were shared between the Old and New Worlds before Columbus is just not true (even for cotton, where Old and New World species are different); but it is interesting to note that his claims about tobacco in the Old World have recently been revived with the reported discovery of tobacco traces in a few Egyptian mummies (cocaine, too, in one particular collection, not repeated in others and not heard of since the initial announcements a few years ago). This, for the moment, is one of the minor mysteries of archaeology, and its solution need not at all be to conclude that tobacco was crossing the Atlantic in the first millennium BC: the complete lack of any archaeological context on either side of the Atlantic to demonstrate regular cultural interchange is, as we shall see later, one of the decisive factors in rejecting any idea of established commercial relations before the sixteenth century.

Donnelly made much of the apparently sudden rise of Egyptian civilization to argue that Egypt was a colony, the first he thought, of Atlantis. There are still Atlantologists today who repeat the proposition of the sudden appearance of ancient Egyptian culture, but they do not know their Egyptology. In Donnelly's day, before systematic field archaeology was much practised in Egypt and in particular before the predynastic archaeology of Egypt was known at all, it was still possible to see Egyptian civilization as a sudden arrival along the Nile. Today we have detailed knowledge of the progress towards civilization that occurred over thousands of years in Egypt, from hunting bands to farmers to political unification and the development of the hieroglyphs, building up to the beginnings of Egyptian historical times in about 3000 BC. Donnelly's version of Egypt's origins is just wrong, and so is his idea that, after brilliant beginnings, Egypt's culture declined – on the contrary, Egyptian civilization went through several cycles of decline and renascence, and judgement about the relative merits of the different periods is subjective. The very idea that Egypt did not have a long period of its own development behind it but depended on colonization from elsewhere for its beginnings is itself all too clearly a notion born in the colonial nineteenth century, when European powers were at the height of their imperial expansion, exploiting their colonies for their own benefit but telling themselves and the world that they were bringing civilization to backward peoples.

Donnelly reports that the Indians of Central America themselves pointed to an origin for the Yucatan peoples in the east, with Atlantis in his mind if not in theirs. In the end, what can folk history be worth in cases like this – how could we know? Sure, the Aztecs said they had come from an island called, wonderfully, Aztlan – but they also said that was in AD 1168 and there are several local sites that might fit the bill,

Aztlan, from Spence's *The Problem of Atlantis*.

including islands in the Gulf of Mexico, or in lake locations in the east of the country. If Aztlan was the Atlantis that sank beneath the waves in *c*. 9600 BC, where were the Aztecs in the meantime?

Donnelly was among the first to draw attention to examples that he thought (as many have done since) looked like Semitic or Negroid faces in the art of Central America – bearded or thick-lipped faces out of character with the population types of the region – in support of his idea that ancestors of today's widely separated races all lived on Atlantis (or the Atlanteans regularly sailed to their countries). Again, this is very subjective stuff: ancient carvings are not photographs but works of art done for all sorts of ideological reasons, some of which are now unknowable to us. The Olmec heads in which Negroid traits of nose and lips are regularly discerned by Atlantologists also show in the very same faces the slit eyes and high cheeks we associate with Mongoloid peoples; and eyewitness accounts of the first meeting between Cortes and Montezuma tell us that the Aztec ruler sported a well-groomed little beard. Current Atlantologists still make much of this Donnelly-pioneered material about heads, faces and figures in native American art that look a bit Caucasian or Semitic or Negroid, both as indications of regular transatlantic crossings in ancient times and as pointers to the intrinsic racial character of the original teachers of the American Indians (from Atlantis, of course). Endless repetition has not made these arguments any sounder. The Atlantologists further frequently retail supposed stories of the native Americans about bearded white gods (like Quetzalcoatl and Viracocha) coming to their homelands at the dawn of their histories. But in no case has it been shown that these stories of full-bearded white (or at least white-robed) gods pre-date the arrival of the Spaniards, whom it certainly suited to have the story of white gods put about, as precursors to their own conquest. Pre-conquest painted images of bearded gods, such as they are, usually show brown, even black or blue figures – never white.

The coincidence of shared cultural traits, between say Egypt or Babylon and the Maya or Inca people of America, impressed Donnelly as proof that they had all derived their inspiration from a common source, none other than Atlantis. In general, it seems that minds in the toils of the Atlantis Syndrome are unable to recognize that people all over the world are constantly inventive and well capable of coming up with similar ideas, or similar solutions to similar problems, in different places and – importantly – at different times. Donnelly expressly repudiates this view:

I cannot believe that the great inventions were duplicated spontaneously . . . there is no truth in the theory that men pressed by necessity will always hit upon the same invention to relieve their wants. If this were so, all savages would have invented the boomerang; all savages would possess pottery, bows and arrows, slings, tents and canoes; in short, all races would have risen to civilization, for certainly the comforts of life are as agreeable to one people as another.

But the notion of parallel inventions in parallel circumstances does not require all peoples to invent all the same things everywhere and every time – it simply shows how they sometimes might hit upon some ways in common. Like Churchward after him, Donnelly takes a very dim view of the creative capacities of 'savages':

> Civilization is not communicable to all; many savage tribes are incapable of it . . . This abyss between savagery and civilization has never been passed by any nation through its own original force, and without external influences, during the historical period; those who were savages at the dawn of history are savages still.

As with Churchward, as with Lewis Spence (whom we shall review later), as with every other Atlantological writer (whether they are always aware of it or not), the ideology of empire is clear in these remarks. Donnelly's American republic may not have shared in the European powers' acquisition of colonies, but it had imported slaves and dispossessed the original inhabitants of its land, so that even a liberal-minded writer like Donnelly was inevitably infected with disdain for the 'savages' of his world. (At one point, he explicitly compares his Atlantean empire with that of the British.) And if nobody ever invented anything for themselves to help raise them out of savagery, then 'as all roads lead to Rome, so the converging lines of civilization lead to Atlantis'. How Atlantis pulled itself up by its bootstraps is never explained – indeed it appears with Donnelly, as with the rest who think like him, to call for no explanation, like God.

That similar practices of metalworking, embalming, pyramid building, calendrical and astronomical observation, systems of writing, modes of artistic representation and so forth have been displayed on both sides of the Atlantic (or anywhere in the whole wide world for that matter) at some time is not proof that all their practitioners got their ideas and methods from a common source. The very fact that the pyramids of Egypt and the pyramids of Mexico are separated in time by two thousand years constitutes a powerful suggestion that the two lots of pyramids were quite independently developed: if you build very big and very high by simple methods, then narrowing your building as you go up is an inevitable constructional strategy. If the Old World and the New both relied on a common background in Atlantis, why was there no plough, no wheeled transport, no domesticated animal save the dog in Central America – why no smallpox, yellow fever, measles or malaria either? Why no bellows, glazing of pottery, kiln-drying of bricks, stringed instruments? Why does the Mayan calendar sport eighteen months of twenty days, unlike any of the systems of the Old World? Donnelly appears to suggest that what all civilizations have in common they must have got from Atlantis; where they differ, they must have invented their divergences in post-Atlantean days. But he is really very general in his comparisons (despite attempts, not very successful when looked into, to make detailed resemblances stick). In the end most of his examples of shared cultural traits serve to highlight differences in detail as much as general similarities: for example, the encoffined mummies of Egypt were made and laid out quite differently from the Peruvian mummies buried sitting up without chemical preservation or wrappings, and all they really have in common is the fact of mummification of one sort and another. Donnelly's shared general traits of agriculture, architecture, sculpture, writing, priesthood, ritual, transportation by road and canal (which he cannot closely compare in detail when it comes down to it) are just the necessary general traits of all civilizations – things arising out of the limited range of possibilities and inevitabilities that all civilized societies resort to. But it is in language and myth that Donnelly invests his most vivid efforts.

Linguistics was not nearly as developed a discipline in Donnelly's time as it is now and it was excusable for him to speculate about language relationships in a way that wouldn't be acceptable any more (except among Atlantologists). Thinking the Incas spoke an Indo-European language (as all Europeans except the Basques, Hungarians, Finns and Turks do), accepting le Plongeon's claim that the Mayan language was one-third Greek, and believing that the Central American Chiapanec language was anything like Hebrew, or the Otomi language anything like Chinese and Chaldean (or that these two language groups were anything like each other in the first place): all this is quite impossible in the light of modern knowledge of languages, as most of Donnelly's successors began to realize in the twentieth century. Even now, though, Atlantologists still sometimes make too much of chance similarities between words in Old World and New World languages, without recognizing the vastly different structures of the languages out of which these odd words are picked. Philology might be soundly based when it notices that the English word wolf and the Latin lupus are descended from a common source in a context of many such parallels and a similar grammatical structure, but philological practice can soon degenerate into speculative fantasy among the untutored. In Donnelly's hands, Atlantis via Aa(t)lantis and then Oluntos is soon identified with Olympus and firm conclusions follow straight on: 'We may, therefore, suppose that when the Greeks said that their gods dwelt in "Olympus", it was the same as if they said that they dwelt in "Atlantis".'

It's perhaps even worse with the speculative interpretation of folk tales and myths from different places to reconstruct historical relationships between peoples or alleged historical events of the past. That many peoples have had tales of lands now under the sea is not surprising – and we don't even have to look for too much in the way of real historical prototypes for these stories, even on a small local scale, since a vague idea of flood and submergence seems to be part of human culture in general. It may conceivably go back to shared memories of post-glacial flooding after the end of the ice age about ten thousand years ago (most of which would have been very gradual but might have involved more sudden episodes here and there – say in the Black Sea). Its appeal may even go back to our times in the salt-water womb, an experience we all share. It is interesting to note that flood stories are not common in the folk tales of Central Asia and Africa – unless derived from missionaries' Bible lessons – where disastrous floods are rarer, nor in Egyptian lore. And if we note, like Donnelly, that the Egyptians (with a bit of interpretation), Greeks and later on Celts all had stories of idyllic islands in the Atlantic Ocean, we can only recall that the

Canaries do better than the Azores or the Bahamas as obvious candidates to have inspired these legends and the pre-existence of Atlantis is not required at all to explain them. We need not be so impressed that, once Donnelly has responded with a resounding 'Yes!' to his own rhetorical question about Greek mythology, 'Who can doubt that it represents the history of a real people?', then the way is clear for him to reinterpret all Greek myth as a record of the rulers of Atlantis and to see the Titans as the real original Atlanteans. Nor that, similarly, the religious mythology of the ancient Egyptians proves their Atlantean origins too: 'They claimed descent from the Twelve Great Gods, which must have meant the twelve gods of Atlantis, to wit, Poseidon, Cleito and their ten sons.' Ye gods, is all we can say. People like Donnelly seem at times quite incapable of crediting the workings of the human imagination, despite the frequent overworking of their own.

As if Donnelly's contributions to the Atlantis Syndrome in his first book were not enough, he went on in his next (also a bestseller) called *Ragnarok: The Age of Fire and Gravel* (1883) to introduce a further element that would have a long future in Atlantis-related literature and to argue for it with an extension of his methods of folklore interpretation that is also characteristic of Atlantology to this day. (Ragnarok was the end of the world in Scandinavian mythology.) Donnelly proposed that certain gravels and till deposits to be found in North America (and Europe) were to be explained as the result of the earth's collision with a comet about thirty thousand years ago (which he now pictures as driving the ancestors of the Atlanteans to Atlantis out of North America). These gravels and boulder-clays are in fact the deposits of glaciers grinding over the ground during the ice ages (as was already known to geologists of the nineteenth century) but Donnelly interpreted them as the results of flooding after the fire caused by the comet. Donnelly's geological misapprehensions are irrelevant now. What was significant was the planting of the idea of comets colliding with the earth (later speculators have brought in the much solider asteroids as well) as agents of human destiny. Atlantis in particular has often been seen as a victim of comet or asteroid impact – very recent Atlantological writings repeat this notion, despite its clear absence from Plato's account where only earthquakes and floods (not even volcanoes) are invoked.

Donnelly chose to back up his cometary theory with recourse to more of that highly interpretative handling of folklore and legends, in this case American Indian lore and legend, that he had already employed in his 'Atlantis'. For example, an old Ute Indian story (the Utes' stamping ground was the south-west of North America) told how the sun-god in his early years – when he was on the loose to come and go as he pleased – had accidentally singed the arm of his brother the hare-god. This brother was so angry he fired a magic arrow into the sun and shattered him to pieces, so that fiery fragments rained down on the earth. The hare-god got caught up in the conflagration and, when his eyes burst with the heat, his tears put out the flames that were consuming the earth. After that, the rest of the gods determined that the sun should henceforth not be allowed to wander at will but be confined to a daily round of the sky. With this colourful tale, the Utes had 'explained', to their satisfaction, the origins of day and night and the sun's path across the heavens. And in this colourful tale Donnelly, incredibly (and it's even more incredible with his successors), saw the record of a comet (the arrow and the fragments falling to earth), a general conflagration (the burning of the world), and floods (the tears of a hare-god, no less). Donnelly assembled so many stories like this in which he thought he detected common features that he was satisfied that their overall impact demanded his explanation for them. But the pitfalls, terminally conclusive we might think, of this mode of interpretation of a ragbag of old stories, myths and legends are obvious. Unfortunately, it's not so obvious to some that the method is wholly abandoned today. Absolute farragoes of fanciful interpretation of Egyptian or Mexican mythology and folklore continue to be published, often in support of theories about ancient astronomical wisdom and usually to do with something violent and spectacular like a rogue planet or asteroid or comet. Responsibility for this tradition can be squarely laid at the door of Ignatius Donnelly – his final contribution, among so many, to the diagnostic features of the Atlantis Syndrome.

L. Sprague de Camp characterizes Donnelly with an insight

from a contemporary that might well be applied to many another toiler in the vineyard of what we now call 'alternative archaeology': as a man 'with an extremely active mind, but possessing also that haste to form judgements and that lack of critical sense in testing them, which are often the result of self-education conducted by immense and unsystematic reading'. It remains a curiosity that his books were bestsellers, for they are in large part such tedious concoctions of obscure mythological material – but then the same could be said for much more recent offerings in the same vein. At least Donnelly is almost completely free of that strain of academic-bashing that disfigures most Atlantological and related writing since le Plongeon. He must have been a securer person in himself than most of the writers in the genre he created have been since. Instead of berating the indifference of the professional historians of his day to his fancied breakthroughs in understanding the past, he concludes in a generous and expansive mood (writing in 1882):

Who shall say that one hundred years from now the great museums of the world may not be adorned with gems, statues, arms, and implements from Atlantis, while the libraries of the world shall contain translations of its inscriptions, throwing new light upon all the past history of the human race and all the great problems which now perplex the thinkers of our day?

Well . . .

4

ATLANTIS IN THE ATLANTIC

Plato said Atlantis was in the Atlantic Ocean and its eastern part, whatever the gigantic extent of it to the west, was close to Gibraltar and the coasts of Spain and North Africa. We have already seen that this location is just not possible and so, to hang on to anything of Atlantis, you have to interpret Plato in some other light. One eminently rational attempt to do that (the most rational ever proposed) involved a location in the Mediterranean at a quite different date from the time-scale confidently asserted by Plato, fixing on the eruption of Thera and the decline of Minoan civilization as sources – somehow a little garbled in transmission – for the alleged Egyptian records shown to Solon. We have seen that this theory, too, falls down on close examination: all that is left of it is the possibility that extremely vague memories of an island cataclysm and the passing away of a once impressive Mediterranean culture may have contributed (whether via Egypt or not) to Plato's imaginative invention of Atlantis.

But once the idea of *interpreting* Plato, as opposed to taking him at face value, was in the air there was no stopping speculation as to where Atlantis had really been. And some of the proposed locations are pretty surprising, even perhaps to open minds determined not to be blinkered by narrow archaeological orthodoxy.

As far back as the sixteenth century there were some fairly extraordinary proposals about the real location of Atlantis. Greenland was one of them, which at least had the merit of intruding into the right ocean according to Plato; more than can be said for sites in Palestine and modern-day Iraq that were also put forward in the same century. In the seventeenth century Sweden and South Africa joined the list of speculative locations, followed in the eighteenth by Spitzbergen in the Arctic (the author of this suggestion, Jean-Sylvain Bailly, also toyed with Mongolia, before he was guillotined in the French Revolution) and Ceylon. It is hard to imagine two more contrasting sites for the island paradise of Atlantis than Spitzbergen and Ceylon. (Of course, it is continental drift and gross climate change that account for tropical fossils in places like Spitzbergen.)

Malta, Iran and the Atlantic coasts of Morocco and Nigeria were rivals to Donnelly's Atlantic Atlantis in the nineteenth century with the latter two locations offering some plausibility as far as Plato's elephants went. There was even a Teutonic rival to the very idea of a Graeco-Egyptian sort of lost civilization in the shape of Atland, an alleged catastrophically destroyed advanced island civilization of the North Sea recounted in a Frisian manuscript said to have been discovered in Holland in 1871. In the twentieth century minor additions (there were some major ones, too, as we shall see) were added to the Atlantis roll-call of speculative locations with Britain (inevitably in the end), the Guadalquivir Valley in Spain (there had at least been a Phoenician post there at Tartessus), Brazil (Colonel Fawcett, of course) and, remarkably, the tiny island of Heligoland about 70 kilometres north-west of Cuxhaven in the North Sea. A German pastor named Jurgen Spanuth claimed in 1953 to have discovered writings in Egypt (by that very priest who told Solon all about Atlantis) and with these writings to have located an Atlantean fort about 10 kilometres off the coast of Heligoland. These priestly writings are not in the public domain of Egyptology. Heligoland was indeed a much larger island in the past (24 kilometres in diameter in AD 1300, encompassing Spanuth's Atlantean fort) which only means the fort was almost certainly built in recent historical times. Spanuth is an interesting example of the Atlantologists' compulsion to pull in everything and explain everything. For him, Plato's orichalcum (plainly a metal) was really amber, and the comet (it's often a comet) that did for Atlantis also took care of Thera and created the Exodus phenomena. The Atlanteans became the Sea Peoples of late Egyptian records.

This listing, from Spitzbergen to Brazil and from Iraq to Heligoland, by no means includes the full catalogue of some forty sitings for the original of Atlantis that have been suggested at one time or another, but anything like plausibility (which isn't saying much) remains attached to only one area today, at the western end of the Atlantic in the region of the West Indies. The first writer to posit evidence for Atlantis in this area was the journalist Lewis Spence in the 1920s, suggesting that a trace of Atlantis 'still persists fragmentally in the Antillean group, or West Indian Islands'. Spence was wise enough to see that Donnelly's linguistic arguments might not hold up and concentrated instead on the evidence of flora and fauna from the Old World and the New and, of course, on the perceived cultural similarities between different civilizations in the two regions. But he recognized that no metalworking civilizations of the sort Plato envisaged for as long ago as 9000 BC could have existed anywhere in the world at that time and he gave over his version of Atlantis to the sort of Old Stone Age hunter/artists that were coming to light through archaeology in the caves and rock shelters of France and Spain in his day. The Crô-Magnon types of early humanity with their sophisticated Aurignacian and Magdalenian flake tools, bone points, animal carvings and wall paintings were his candidates for occupancy of the vanished Atlantic island. He proposed a series of waves of migration of these first representatives of true humanity (as opposed to more simian fellows like Neanderthal Man and Java Man) from Atlantis to Europe and America, starting about twenty-five thousand years ago and ending with the loss of Atlantis about ten thousand years ago.

Spence's *The Problem of Atlantis* further suggested that the American Indians had reached the continental mainland via 'Antilia', a south-western relic of the once great island-continent, itself surviving today as the dotted islands of the West Indies. We must note that much has been altered along the way from Plato by Spence, particularly in making Atlantis a Stone Age culture. Antilia was a name used on medieval maps, before Columbus discovered the New World, for an

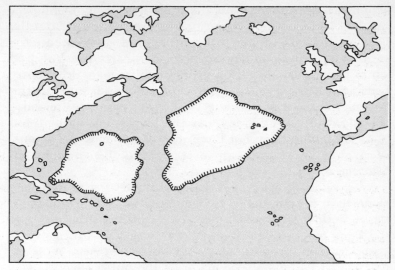

Atlantis split in two, according to Spence.

island (sometimes with seven bays or seven cities) supposed to exist somewhere out in the far Atlantic: most likely a continuation of Phoenician, Greek, Roman and Moorish sailors' lore of distant islands in that ocean. It is possible Columbus himself was partly looking for Antilia. Some pre-Columbian maps show their imaginary Antilia enough like the real Cuba in general size, shape and location (though not orientation) that when Cuba was officially discovered it was natural to apply the old name to it and, by extension, to the island group of the West Indies as a whole. But any resemblance is quite possibly a coincidence in that Antilia was clearly modelled on the shape and orientation of Portugal: Ante Ilha means 'counter isle' in Portuguese and the placing of this island on some but by no means all pre-Columbian maps makes it the western reflection of Portugal to the east. (Zipangu – Japan – is sometimes shown with much the same shape.) None the less, the presence of Antilia on the old maps may also be a result of a prior discovery of the West Indies before the officially celebrated one of 1492. Behaim's Globe (of 1492) claims that its Antilia was first seen in 1414 by a ship blown off course across the Atlantic. One pre-Columbian map of 1455 actually identifies its Antilia with Atlantis, anticipating late nineteenth-century and early twentieth-century speculations like Spence's by nearly five hundred years. After the expedition of Columbus, maps frequently became festooned with a riot of imaginary islands in the Atlantic all the way from the West Indies across to Ireland – the Isle of Brasil or Brazil was the longest-lasting of these non-existent localities, but there were also islands of Demons, of Avalon, of St Brendan, of Drogio, of Emperadada, of Estotitland, of Grocland and so on and on.

Spence's early work on Atlantis is interesting in that, like Donnelly's, it manages to eschew occultism and irrationality (more so than some much more recent offerings) but to be at the same time hopelessly misguided, even for its own day. It enshrines many a feature of the Atlantis Syndrome of attitudes and approaches and, in the matter of the Antilles, pioneers an Atlantological notion (even if Spence didn't originate it) that persists to this day. The most striking thing is Spence's constitutional inability (which he has in common with every other sufferer of the syndrome) to credit human beings with any imagination – though, in a way, he goes in for so much of it himself, again in common with his confrères.

He cannot even credit a known artist like Plato with imaginative creativity in the business of mythologizing. Like Donnelly, Spence can't see the moral in Plato's tale and so takes it straightaway for factual report of history. (It is quite lost on Spence that Plato was writing about sixty-five years after the date of the alleged conversations of the *Timaeus* and *Critias*.) 'Had his account', says Spence, 'been of an allegorical character . . . its fictional atmosphere would have been obvious.' Well, both the allegory and fiction of Plato's story *are* obvious, as we have seen, and to say that the sinking of Atlantis goes against all the rules for mythical lands which are always talked of as still around somewhere is to show no ken of the artistic and philosophical purposes of a man like Plato. As Aristotle hinted, in artistic terms Plato had to sink his Atlantis precisely because it plainly isn't around any more, and its sinking was the whole philosophical point of the story.

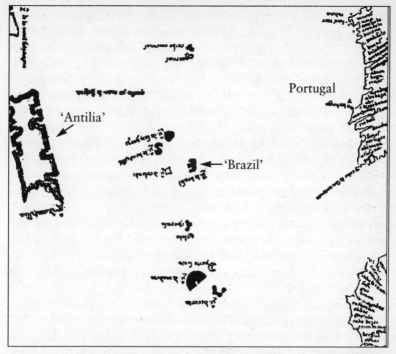

Antilia and various other phantom isles, including Brazil in the centre, from Bianco's map of 1436. Note the 'upside-down' captioning.

When it comes to his cull of myths and folktales from around the world, Spence is if anything even more reckless than Donnelly in his determination to see them all as accurate records of conquest and catastrophe, only veiled in the flimsiest way with the elaborations of inventive imagination, which he is able to strip away with no difficulty at all to reveal the historical truths they have preserved. In one incredible passage (all too reminiscent of chains of 'reasoning' still to be found in today's bestsellers of 'alternative archaeology'), Spence takes us from Antilia to another mysterious island of the west Atlantic called on an old map Yd laman Satanaxio, which Spence says one authority claims to mean 'Hand of Satan' (but another claims does not). This then recalls for him an Italian romance, of which no further details are given, about a hand coming up out of the sea near India (of all places, we might think) to snatch people away. And oddly enough 'Great Hand' is the name of a uniquely bearded Mayan god whose Mexican equivalent, 'as is clear' to Spence, possessed volcanic attributes. The next thing we know, Spence is taking it for granted that this 'volcanic' god gave his name to the oddly named island near Antilia and that all this constitutes proof that there were a lot of earthquakes in the Antilian region. 'For these and other reasons' the bold Spence feels sure that Atlantis broke up into two regions of which the easterly survives now only as the Madeiras, Canaries and Cape Verdes while the westerly lasted longer in the form of Antilia and seeded the New World with civilization, with what's left of it showing now as the Antilles. (Bermuda and the Azores are the remains of links between the two former Atlantean regions.) After this farrago, Spence has the cheek to chide Brasseur and le Plongeon for writing insubstantial rubbish about the survival of the whole island of Atlantis until 9600 BC.

In case the reader begins to wonder why I have credited Spence with an avoidance of irrationality after an example like this, I should point out that, though Spence's chain of reasoning is full of gaps and baseless assumptions, it is not conducted outside the realm of the possible (if unlikely) – what is more, his 'other reasons' for coming to his conclusion about the splitting of old Atlantis into two are rational ones, though wholly unevidenced. He correctly saw that Donnelly's comparison of Mexican and Egyptian pyramids founders on the vast time discrepancy between the pyramid building of Egypt and that of Mexico. But his theory of late Crô-Magnon inspiration from Atlantis for Old World civilizations is also stretched when it comes to applying it to the New World. A long sojourn on Antilia, after the disappearance of the east Atlantic half of Atlantis, is his way of explaining the comparatively late flowering of the American civilizations, which only arose when the Antilians were forced to move on to the Americas in the end.

It is Spence's contention that the myths of the Americas – North, South and Central – all record a true history of the catastrophic flooding of the original homeland of the

American Indians and their subsequent migration to their present homes. Like all Atlantologists, Spence can never credit any culture anywhere at any time (save in Atlantis itself) with its own development of its own way of life: for him and everyone in the grip of the syndrome it is axiomatic that all cultures got their culture (or the seeds of it) from somebody else. As we have urged before, this is a notion directly related to the imperial arrogance of the colonial powers of the nineteenth century. It is also a plain intellectual error derived from too much unthinking reliance on the idea of cause and effect and first causes, applied in a very simple-minded way. It treats a way of life as a given, fixed thing without internal dynamics of development and adaptation. It takes a way of life as an unchanging whole which cannot have evolved within itself but must be derived from some other whole outside itself. The immediate problem that all causes of all effects must themselves be the effects of other causes seems never to occur to people like Spence when once they have posited their version of the first cause – Atlantis is somehow self-caused, like God, and needs no further exploration. (The reference to religion is not unapt – both religion and Atlantology downplay human achievement. The Atlantis Syndrome owes a good deal to religious traditions of thinking.) The urgent need felt by the Atlantologists to derive all other cultures from a prior and primal culture ceases to operate once that prior culture is invoked – once they reach Atlantis, conveniently sunken under the waves (or under the south pole or in outer space as fashion and some show of plausibility dictate at the time), then the trail can be allowed to go cold and the boldest of 'alternative archaeologists' can rest from their labours, looking no further.

What they will never bother to labour at is the study in depth of the substantial findings of real archaeology. Spence did not do it in his day and his inheritors in the field of 'alternative archaeology' do not do it nowadays either. Spence was woefully ignorant of the archaeological knowledge of his time about Stone Age life (he thought for example that the Neanderthal folk had smaller brains than the Crô-Magnons) and ignored professional archaeological advice to forget a western origin out in the Atlantic for the Aurignacian and Magdalenian cultures. In a revealing passage he bemoans the attitudes of the archaeologists of his day just as the current 'alternative archaeology' writers do:

> If Crô-Magnon Man did not hail from that region, when, I ask, did he enter Europe? I consult the oracles, but, alas! 'the oracles are dumb!' They cannot answer me, and that for the most excellent of reasons – because they do not know themselves, or, if they do know, fear to speak.

With this passage it is clear that Spence not only contributed the propagandizing of the Antilian interpretation of Atlantis to the syndrome but also pioneered (with le Plongeon) an unjust and even ugly attitude to professional archaeologists that is still very much with us in the 'alternative' camp: the ready resort by Atlantologists to insinuations of ignorance, incompetence, cover-up and conspiracy to hide the truth on the part of the academic 'establishment'.

What professional, academic archaeology has achieved over the past century-and-a-half (with inevitable mistakes along the way, to be sure) is a consistent picture of human development all over the world that tries to make the best use of all the available evidence (and there is always far more of it than people like Spence appreciate), with an emphasis on the importance of context over stray finds, however striking. One Carthaginian coin on an American beach would be a stray find that might have any one of several explanations (including being dropped by a modern coin collector), while the repeated occurrence of Minoan pottery in particular levels at several Egyptian archaeological sites would represent a palpable context of associated evidence on which one could build a theory, say of Minoan-Egyptian commerce of some sort at a particular date. Something that might be an old wall underwater but might also be a geological feature is more likely to be the latter if not a single human artefact is ever found in association with it. If it occurs to you that the Sphinx of Giza might be of predynastic Egyptian manufacture but all you ever find near it is Fourth Dynasty archaeological material and never a trace of anything predynastic, then you are probably wrong. If there's just one radiocarbon date for an archaeological find, you can't build much on it: if you have a consistent cluster you can, and so you can if your one date is compatible with other lines of evidence for the find. If the same patterns of associated finds are repeatedly turned up at different sites, then you can begin to think about cultures and cultural interactions. These are extremely simple examples that do not do justice to the subtlety of archaeological reasoning over long periods of time and wide areas of terrain, but they do suggest why archaeologists make so much of context and repeatability and are not impressed by isolated instances that do not fit into any known context.

There was some excuse for Donnelly's and Spence's ignorance of the early, developmental stages of the cultures they discuss. The first steps towards great achievements are always only faintly recorded beneath the spectacular monuments that follow on; and in the early days of archaeology it was naturally the established, showy products that were studied first, before much was learned about the processes that led to them. Geology has seen a similar progress: fossils of transitional forms of evolving creatures, representing very small populations, are harder to find than fossils of well-established long-lasting evolutionary success stories – people opposed to the science of evolutionary biology still have difficulty appreciating this fact, even though the transitional fossils are nowadays often available. Even in Spence's day, some of the background to cultural developments that took place in the Stone Age, in the Americas and especially in Egypt, was being archaeologically illuminated. Spence, however, would have none of it. For him, the Aurignacians and later the Magdalenians of Stone Age western Europe had popped up fully formed from nowhere without any background in situ; the American cultures had suddenly appeared in full rig from nowhere; the Egyptian civilization had materialized in all its glory out of the same nowhere – Atlantis, of course, in all cases according to Spence. With infinitely less excuse nowadays, when the cultural evolution behind all those developments is well explored, Atlantologists and other 'alternative archaeology' exponents go on repeating the same hoary and long-demolished claims that the Olmecs of Central America or the first dynasties of ancient Egypt spring into being in the archaeological record without local precedence from whatever 'nowhere' any particular writer favours.

Just as Spence, like Donnelly, made hay with any stray archaeological find in any one place that could be compared with another somewhere else, to draw extravagant conclusions of common descent from his version of Atlantis, so he too couldn't always resist handling linguistic 'evidence' in the form of stray parallels between words in one language and another with the same bold disregard for context. Just as he thought mummies in Egypt and (quite differently made and dated) mummies in Peru must prove that mummification as a practice had been invented by one culture parental to both the Egyptians and the Inca (the Crô-Magnons, he said, who sometimes coloured their dead with red ochre), so he thought it fair game to note any old resemblance between a word in one language and a word meaning something similar in another as proof that the people using these words were all descended from a common source. Again context meant nothing to him – the languages could be constructed on absolutely divergent grammatical principles, and for that matter have next to no more words in common, just so long as odd stray words could be compared. You will find this laughably amateur sort of philologizing still carried on in very recent works of 'alternative archaeology' by some of the best known authors of the genre.

Place names and proper names especially recommended themselves to Spence as a field for his philological speculations. His most spectacular exhibit, first noted by Gomara in the sixteenth century and repeated by Donnelly, is the Aztecs' name for the homeland they thought themselves to have come from to Mexico – Aztlan, with its echoes of Greek Atlantis, daughter of Atlas. Never mind that the Aztecs also thought they left Aztlan in AD 1168, about ten thousand years after Plato's Atlantis is supposed to have finally disappeared. Spence also thinks that some of the names in Plato's account of Atlantis, like that of

PLATE VI.

Quetzalcoatl as Atlas.

Small Figure of Atlas supporting the World
on his Shoulders, to compare with the
above. (From National Museum, Naples)

A page from one of Spence's books compares Quetzalcoatl and Atlas.

Poseidon's mortal wife Cleito, can be mated up with ancient Mexican gods' names. 'Cleito – to which the name Coatlicue bears a suspicious resemblance – and Atlas, to whose name the first portion of Uitzilopotchli's name also bears a similarity.' Congratulations, Mr Spence – out of the twenty-four letters of these gods' names, eight are indeed in common with Cleito and Atlas. Spence's methods reach a nadir when he links (King) Arthur to (the Egyptian god) Osiris. 'At first sight,' he admits, 'this hypothesis may seem wildly improbable, but a prolonged consideration of the question has led me to believe in its substantial accuracy. I cannot elaborate it here any further.' (The prolonged consideration seems to have involved the thought that Arthur and Osiris both awaited resurrection away in the west, but it doesn't seem to have occurred to Spence that the land of the sunset is an obvious place for a sojourn before resurrection, and for all human cultures resurrection itself is an obvious idea that will very readily be associated with observation of sunset followed by sunrise.)

We are back with Spence's inability to recognize that inventive and creative people, who exist in all human societies, are likely to make up colourful stories to handle the universal experiences of life and death that will frequently resemble the stories of other people in other times and places precisely because human experience is universally very much alike despite superficial cultural differences. This trait of people like Spence is perhaps the chief diagnostic symptom of the Atlantis Syndrome and it is nowhere seen more clearly than in the Atlantologists' response to mythology and art. In the severest cases, they seem simply unable to conceive that people ever make things up at all with free play of the ever-creative human imagination amid all the varied scenes of human experience. (And, in a way, this is odd, as we have already noted, since the Atlantologists all make so much up for themselves in the most ingenious fashion!) To take a worst case, for a really committed Atlantologist a tomb carving of a man reclining at the base of an elaborate design of branching curlicues cannot possibly be a representation of the tomb's dead occupant cleaving to his mythology's Tree of Life (in accordance with archaeologists' knowledge of Mayan religion):

oh no, it must be a straight-faced attempt to represent something banal in our own days' terms like an astronaut at the controls of his spaceship. (Outer space is the last refuge, short of the astral plane, of the Atlantis idea.)

Atlantologists compound their initial obtuseness about human creativity with an absolute refusal to believe that any idea might be invented more than once. Even if they have to face it that the geniuses of Atlantis must have invented everything in the first place, they simply can't allow that any other human beings might have independently hit upon similar ideas in response to similar circumstances. In terms of technology, they cannot believe that pyramids might have been developed in different places at different times (despite the obvious advantages of the form when you are trying to build big structures high with simple means). In mythological matters, they not only cannot believe that similar stories (of floods and fires, for example) must inevitably be elaborated in all cultures – no, they positively fall over themselves to see strong parallels in different stories from different places that are hardly there at all. In all this, they do no justice to the creative powers of their fellow human beings and are themselves led into over-imaginative fantasies about human history.

An example from Spence serves to illustrate the common tendency of the Atlantological approach to myth. Here is his effort to see Plato's scene-setting of Atlantis in the *Critias* reflected in American myth.

Pariacaca, the demi-god who had emerged from one of the eggs . . . came, like Poseidon, to a hill-country where he was insulted by the people. In wrath he sent a flood upon them so that their village was destroyed. [We cannot restrain ourselves from the immediate comment that Poseidon came to an island, was not insulted and sent no flood.]

In the neighbourhood he met a very beautiful girl, Choque Suso, (the Cleito of Plato?) weeping bitterly. [The names have perhaps three sounds in common! Besides, wasn't it Coatlicue just now?]

He enquired of her why she wept and she told him that the maize crop was dying for lack of water. He fell in love with her, and assured her that if she would return his passion he would provide the much-needed water. [None of this is in Plato, so someone's doing some inventing.]

She consented to his suit, and he irrigated the whole land, as did Poseidon in Atlantis. Pariacaca eventually turned his wife into a statue. [Which Poseidon did not!]

Spence is pleased to see in all this the acropolis of Atlantis, Poseidon, Cleito, Poseidon's irrigation works, the setting-up of statues in the temple of Atlantis and, in a roundabout out-of-order way, destruction in return for wickedness. 'Could the resemblance be closer?' he asks, to which we can only reply, 'you bet it could' – and then wonder what kind of person could ever think there was a worthwhile resemblance there at all. But Spence is far from alone in the annals of 'alternative archaeology' with this sort of myth-bending. It thrives still, as we shall see in due course.

Spence typifies another Atlantological trait when he insists on drawing in anything and everything he comes across in his reading as further proof of his theories. The Old Stone Age cave paintings of France and Spain sometimes feature bovids among their animal representations and this is enough for Spence to show that the bull sacrifices of Plato's story were descended from Crô-Magnon practices on Atlantis. Any fortified site in the world has for him echoes of the ring defences of the capital city of Plato's island (the Aztec Mexico City ruins, in particular, in their lake setting appeal to him, though they don't especially resemble Plato's highly geometric description). A Central American picture of the god Quetzalcoatl carrying something on his back must be one and the same with Atlas carrying the world on his back. It is as though a personality like Spence's must force everything it encounters into the pattern of his theory and must believe that his theory encompasses everything: every ounce of his experience must be bent to his purpose. It doesn't occur to him that what we have from the long past of the whole wide world is too fragmentary and too arbitrarily sifted by the accidents of preservation and discovery to be fitted, every last scrap of it, into one simple scheme. Moreover, Spence was ignorant of a

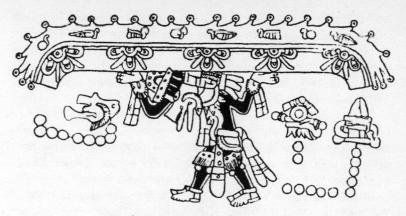

Another Mexican Atlas from Spence.

great deal of the real archaeology of his own day, which he would have had great difficulty in fitting into his scheme. And, in any case, life just isn't like that. But we shall again recognize this same obsessive will to force all available data into the favoured theory when we come to look at some of Lewis Spence's successors in the field.

At the end of *The Problem of Atlantis* Spence comes to a down-rating of Plato's date for the rise and fall of the island's heyday of civilization. Although he credits his Crô-Magnons with a fair degree of sophistication for their time, he sees that their representatives in France were not living anything like Plato's Atlantean lifestyle of 9600 BC, so he thinks they embarked on city life back home on their eastern island of Atlantis in about 7000 BC, with cities arising in Egypt about a thousand years later (they didn't, in fact, till nearer 3000 BC). Subsequently, according to Spence, Atlantis was flooded but civilization lived on in Egypt and in his westerly Antilia, from which latter location – before its demise – it spread a bit late in the day to the Americas. For Spence, though, it seems the real inheritors of the Atlantean genius fetched up in, wait for it, his homeland of Scotland! (He was at one time editor of *The Scotsman*.) His book concludes with talk of 'Scotland's admitted superiority in the mental and spiritual spheres', though England is allowed more than a look in: 'England, too, undoubtedly draws much of her sanity, her physical prowess and marked superiority in the things of the mind from the same source.' In the interest of sales, this otherwise amiable writer might have included his readers in the USA in the general flattery, but perhaps he thought he had covered the better part of them.

At the very end, Spence puts in an ominous plea – rather at odds with his previous rational (if wrong) tone – for open-mindedness towards the possibility of psychic investigations into the past. (He also wrote such works as *The Fairy Tradition in Britain* and *Second Sight, Its History and Origins*.) And it is true that later works of his take on an apocalyptic note of warning about the end of the world that aptly foreshadows another (part-time) Atlantologist's interest in psychic searching for Atlantis in the western Atlantic. But before we come to the psychic stuff, let us note that Spence has single-handedly made an enormous contribution to the development of the Atlantis Syndrome. First, he has put Antilia on the map, as it were, but above all he has so well exemplified the traits of myth-bending, as I call it, and theory-forcing in which everything is grist to the mill, with that essential dash of hostility to the world of professional, academic archaeology that his successors always evince. At least it can be said of him that his book is not dressed up with a showy apparatus of pages of notes at the back, for all the world like a work of scholarship from Harvard – he doesn't even run to an index.

Altogether more modern than Spence's palaeolithic Atlanteans were the inhabitants of the fabled island as envisioned by the American psychic healer Edgar Cayce from the 1920s up until a year before his death in the 1940s, though he put them (or the last traces of them) in much the same part of the world. His Atlanteans, as revealed in his numerous psychic 'readings' that involved Atlantis and in the works of disciples like his son Edgar Evans Cayce and Lytle Robinson, were so well equipped with aircraft, submarines, elevators, telephones, radio, photography (Cayce had been a commercial photographer), television, even something like lasers and nuclear power from crystals that it is just a wonder that they came out of the destruction of Atlantis – which they had fully foreseen – as feebly as they did, leaving their colonists in Egypt with nothing better than the bucolic lifestyles of the Old Kingdom to get on with. It is an interesting general point to note that nowadays the alleged supercivilizations of the past are invariably endowed with just about the level of technology with which the man in the street is familiar at the time when these supercivilizations are being proposed: perhaps just a bit more advanced, if anything. If there are any hints of something really more advanced, in technological areas beyond us at the present (Cayce mentioned the Atlanteans' ability to overcome gravity which came in so useful in Egypt with the pyramids), you can be sure that specific details of these advances will be thin on the ground. This rule goes for ancient supercivilizations and supercivilizations in outer space. Cayce's Atlanteans didn't have the Internet. They did, however, in truly mid-twentieth-century style, have the capacity to destroy themselves and Cayce attributed the end of Atlantis not to earthquake and flood, not to fire from volcanoes or from heaven, but to meddling with the forces of nature: apparently on more than one occasion, the last time resulting in the cataclysm that filtered through to Plato. We have to say only filtered through since, to go by Cayce, Solon's Egyptians knew next to nothing about the true achievements and demise of Atlantis. (Cayce is not thought to have read Plato, but there were Blavatskyites among his 'patients'.)

Cayce ran his healing operation from the town of Virginia Beach in Virginia. James Randi, that great investigator of psychics and all things paranormal, reckons Cayce's success rate as a healer was par for the course among such practitioners – with the usual sort of vaguenesses and get-out clauses (often expressed in verbosely illiterate language to confuse matters even more), boiling down to the recommendation of home-spun remedies that wouldn't have been out of place in a family medicine encyclopaedia of, say, the years of Cayce's Kentucky childhood.

Cayce got his psychic inspirations in trances (his utterances while asleep being recorded by helpers), which earned him the name of 'sleeping prophet' among his followers, and it seems that Atlantis quite often intruded itself into these trances from about 1924 onwards. Quite a lot of Cayce's 'patients' were revealed to be reincarnations of Atlanteans, all marked by an unusual competence in technical matters – as might only be expected if they had been used to flying aeroplanes and tinkering with television in their previous lives. Cayce himself had been a priest of the Atlantean epoch. In 1926 the sleeping prophet's involvement with Atlantis took a step forward when his medical advice helped an associate of a wealthy businessman with interests in Florida and the Bahamas. Cayce was invited to employ his powers in a search for oil and mineral resources – and pirate treasure – on the Bimini islands (there are two of them, north and east) in the Straits of Florida. Before he actually went to Bimini, a trance in Virginia Beach disclosed that Bimini really did, as hoped, contain gold and silver bullion and plate. For good measure Bimini was itself revealed as the above-water remnant of a once-great continent vanished beneath the waves. On the visit to Bimini that ensued in 1927, none of the gold and silver, bullion or plate, could be found despite further psychic confirmation from Cayce that they were looking in the right places. Fortunately, subsequent trances were able to reassure all concerned that while there was nothing wrong with the original readings the goods could not be delivered up to people motivated by a commercial desire to find treasure. Cayce never went near Bimini again.

But Bimini stayed on the sleeping prophet's mind. In 1933 he offered the slightly half-hearted prediction that in 'Poseidia' (his name for the Bimini remnant of Atlantis and its sunken environs) 'a portion of the temples may yet be discovered under the slime of ages of sea water – near what is known as Bimini off the coast of Florida'. (Other bits of Atlantis that survived the main cataclysm for a while rejoiced, according to Cayce, in the names of Aryan and Og!) Again in 1940 he prophesied (more positively) that 'Poseidia will be among the first portions of Atlantis to rise again. Expect it in sixty-eight and sixty-nine.' Put together, these predictions suggested, back in the 1930s, that evidence of Atlantis could be expected to turn up at Bimini in 1968 or 1969. Associated remarks during trance readings also suggested that Atlantean records would one day become available in Egypt and in Yucatan: in a rather vague way the Egyptian Hall of Records was predicted to come to light in tandem with 'earth changes' that would occur between the 1950s and 1998.

Cayce died in 1945. Before we leave him to his eternal slumbers, we may note the significant additions to the Atlantis Syndrome that are represented by Cayce's sort of material. Donnelly's Atlantis may have been the fount of all civilization and a wonder for its time, but it was still a Bronze Age concept overturned by natural catastrophe. Cayce's Atlantis is an all-American twentieth-century enterprise replete with the highest technology Cayce could imagine (as an American of the first half of the twentieth century) and the agent of its own destruction – not through luxurious decadence bringing down divine wrath nor through natural catastrophe but through meddling with forces of nature unknown to Plato or Donnelly: an interesting cultural shift. Its secrets, moreover, are accessible by psychic means (on a scale that even outdoes Blavatsky) and don't rely on archaeology or other branches of history and science to bring them to light; though, of course, it's always nice to have archaeology confirm them, especially where Atlantean records might be concerned. The records are not themselves a new element contributed by Cayce (Blavatsky had made much of them as already existing in Tibetan fastnesses and so on) but Cayce's Hall of Records to be found near the Sphinx at Giza has become a key feature of Atlantean daydreams.

By the 1960s Edgar Cayce's legacy had turned into a well-endowed foundation which interested itself, through its Association for Research and Enlightenment, in worldwide efforts to support the sleeping prophet's reputation for visions and predictions. (Searching for Cayce's Atlantean Hall of Records at Giza before the end of the last millennium has been one of his followers' less-than-successful efforts to shore up that reputation and we still await the submersion of Japan, the shifting of the earth's poles and the Second Coming of Christ, all predicted by Cayce.)

And so it was, on the shaky basis as we might think (ridiculous even) of Cayce's trance visions of a high-tech Atlantis reaching from Africa to the West Indies, that all eyes turned to the Bahamas in the late 1960s as the place where proof of the vanished island-continent's existence would finally come to light. All eyes in the heads of Cayce's followers, Atlantologists and 'alternative archaeology' enthusiasts, that is.

None of the extensive ocean surveillances and fly-overs mounted by the Cayce Association itself from 1965 turned up anything to validate his assertions. But a couple of airline pilots did spot something in 1968 that soon came into the orbit of the Association for Research and Enlightenment – not surprisingly, since both pilots were members of that body. What they had seen, while flying north of the large island of Andros, was a rectangular formation of some kind that they called a 'structure' and thought might represent the foundations of a building, its eastern end having apparently a walled-off area within it. The pilots spoke of their sighting to two further followers of Cayce's ideas, J. Manson Valentine and Dimitri Rebikoff, who promptly organized a dive on the site in August 1968. They explored a 35 by 20 metre feature, claimed to be aligned perfectly east to west, that was delineated by the growth of sea-grass on what they judged to be deliberately laid blocks of limestone about a metre thick. Their press release spoke of 'a kind of masonry', 'definitely man-made', and even an 'ancient temple'. A later explorer of the same site declared the feature to be not constructed of limestone blocks but rather to be made up of piles of loose rock; he further claimed that a reporter with a local paper had told him that an Andros islander had in turn told him that he had helped to build it as a sponge pen in the 1930s, for what that can be worth. It might be a little far offshore and a bit dangerous to boats in shallow waters, and other sponge pens are smaller, deeper and made of wood, but there the matter rests and if it wasn't a sponge pen, it hardly looks like one of the more spectacular productions of old Atlantis either, especially Cayce's Atlantis of submarines and television sets. No human artefacts of any kind were found in association with it. Other regular-looking features similarly demarcated by growths of sea-grass, one of them in the form of concentric circles, have been reported from time to time, but never followed up with any systematic investigation or recording before the shifting sands have obliterated them again.

More striking is the so-called Bimini Road that came to light in September 1968, also at the hands of J. Manson Valentine, off the North Island of Bimini. Straight rows of what look like large regular blocks of limestone, almost completely buried in the sand, run in shallow water roughly parallel to the present shoreline of the island for, reputedly, over 600 metres. Northwest of these lines of blocks runs a wider row of mostly smaller stones that curves back on itself like the handle of a walking-stick. The one-block depth of the original lines (occasionally there appears to be one block on top of another) militates against interpretation as a wall to hold back the sea as has been suggested, while the curving back of the second run goes against its having been a road, but – again – these features were quickly announced as artificial constructions and the name of 'road' has stuck to them in Atlantological lore. But a geologist and archaeologist who examined them promptly declared them natural in origin and belonging to a well-known feature of the Bahama shorelines: Pleistocene beach rock, which they pointed out also paves the southern shore of the island for all to see. This beach rock formation comes about when an accumulation of debris, mostly made of calcium carbonate in the form of crushed seashells, cements with sand grains as a very coarse limestone. This coarse limestone product is rather easily cracked as it lies exposed on the shore when storms break over it and waves undermine the sand bed on which it rests, to produce blocks with straight break edges that can look like artificial creations, especially when sea erosion rounds the tops into pillow-like curves. (There's an example of such artificial-looking beach rock at Madeira.)

The blocks of the 'Bimini Road' are offshore and under shallow water because they were formed some thousands of years ago when sea level was a little lower after the close of the last ice age: the walking-stick curve follows the bend of the modern shoreline, only further out to sea to the north. A radiocarbon date on shells within the limestone of the blocks came out at only about 2200 years before the present. That the blocks were produced by natural agency and not moved into position by human beings is demonstrated by the identical internal layering of adjacent blocks. No man-made artefacts

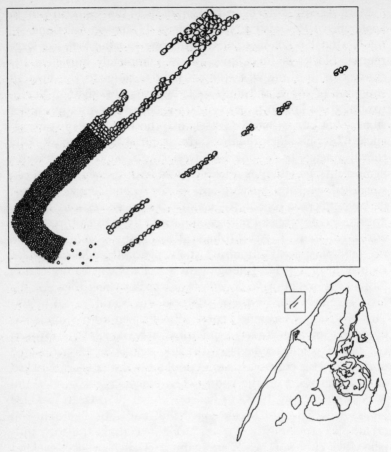

The Bimini Road off North Bimini.

were found in association with the blocks – no potsherds or tools of stone or metal – unless you are impressed by a piece of stone with a sort of tongue-and-groove cut in its edge, of indeterminate cultural character and age, which is probably a bit of jettisoned ship's ballast of the last few hundred years. Stray finds from the general area of the 'road' have been reported to include pieces of granite and marble (itself, interestingly, a form of calcium carbonate) not native to the Bahamas, for which the same explanation serves: ballast dumped in these tricky shallow waters. Columnar fragments reputedly found about 4 kilomctrcs away to the south have been fully explained as cement from rotted barrels lost in a wreck or thrown overboard. Several more locations in the same area of the Grand Bahama Bank have been said to show regular, geometric patterns of stones under the water, some of them in the hard-to-explore direction of Cuba, but nothing convincing has ever been properly recorded. One of the more fantastic claims involved an underwater pyramid detected by sonar that has never since been relocated and whose sonar tracings are all too capable of explanation as an artefact of sonar itself that can occur when an exaggerated scale of drawing is applied to a low-profile feature of the ocean bed that has been reversed over. The fact is, to put it quite bluntly, that no recorded archaeological context has ever been cited as evidence for ancient buildings in these waters. There is consequently no hard evidence to support Cayce's extravagant claims.

Between them, Spence and Cayce focused attention on the general area of the Antilles as the best (or least bad) place to look for the last traces of Plato's Atlantis-in-the-Atlantic. While both contributed significantly to the growth of the Atlantis Syndrome, neither gave the world of professional archaeology any reason to take their proposals seriously. Meanwhile, let's take a closer look at the work of the professionals.

5

HOW DO WE KNOW?

While the Atlantological speculators of the nineteenth and early twentieth centuries had been elaborating their colourful visions, sometimes without much acquaintance with the doings of contemporary archaeologists, the professional study of the past – academic archaeology, if you like – took great strides forward both in terms of its available techniques for studying human prehistory and of its discoveries about it. Prehistory is that vast period of time when human beings of some sort or another went about their manifold affairs on this earth, living and dying, working and mating, winning and losing, fighting and running and doing the myriad things that people do – without writing down a single line to record the ups and downs of their lives and whatever they may have thought about it.

For writing and written records are available to us from the past for only the last five thousand years or so out of humanity's span of several millions of years, and then only patchily, with just a few regions of the world having really old records and some only joining the community of the written word in the last couple of centuries. Until a couple of centuries ago, it looked even to educated persons in the western world as though we should never be able to learn very much at all about human affairs before the advent of historical times with surviving records. Of the prehistory of Britain (though the word prehistory had not been coined in his day) Dr Johnson declared: 'All that is really known of the ancient state of Britain is contained in a few pages. We can know no more than what old writers have told us.' He meant the Roman historians. Rome's history went back beyond Britain's, and

Greece's beyond Rome's, but until the middle of the nineteenth century any greater antiquity than theirs appeared to reside only with the Egyptians and the peoples of the Bible lands. Ingenious minds could count up the chronological intimations of the Bible and arrive at an age for the whole world since its creation of only some six thousand years, so times before history were evidently quite short and, on the face of it, called for no particular curiosity as to what had gone on in them. The Bible told the important part of that.

Even so, in that Bible-dominated world, there were some unsettling anomalies for those who were aware of them. Stray finds of fossilized animal remains or stone tools of primitive manufacture could be put down to the results of the Flood in the former case or in the latter be taken for thunderbolts, but they made some people speculate about other ages of the world and other ways of human life. In the eighteenth century exploration and the pursuit of natural history encouraged the classification of animal and plant life into related groupings that practically begged to be seen as the outcome of evolutionary relationships, on a scale from simple forms of life to ever more developed and complicated ones. Picking up on suggestions from classical and Renaissance thinkers, more than one naturalist on the eve of the nineteenth century proposed some form of biological evolution to account for the world's flora and fauna, though without any convincing mechanisms of change and inheritance. From the infant science of geology there came increasing evidence that the rocks of the earth on occasion contained the fossils of creatures no longer to be found anywhere in the world, suggesting to some both a greater antiquity for existence than the Bible allowed and a greater variety of life in the past. A stop-gap theory to try to accommodate these discoveries was the notion of 'catastrophism', which saw the record of the rocks as witness to a whole series of divine creations before the present one, each one replete with its own forms of life and each one terminated in its turn by a divinely engineered disruption (like the Flood) before a new creation was initiated. (It may be as well to mention at this point that eighteenth-century geological catastrophism – and its modern versions in Atlantological speculation – have nothing to do with the recent vogue for 'Catastrophe Theory' among mathematicians dealing with the description of systems showing abrupt and apparently discontinuous change.) Advocates of geological catastrophism in the late eighteenth and early nineteenth centuries usually excluded human life from all but the latest bout of creation, though some contemporary discoverers of human remains – both bones and stone tools – felt sure their finds took humanity back into entirely earlier phases of creation than the one in the Bible in which humanity featured as a very special element.

The interpretation of the rocks and their fossil sequences as products of catastrophic convulsions was already being challenged at the end of the eighteenth century by the 'uniformitarian' theory that saw the geological record as predominantly the result of the slow and steady workings of such non-catastrophic processes as sedimentation in lakes and seas and erosion by wind and rain, of the sort we still see unspectacularly at work in the world today. Uniformitarian geology did not ignore the more dramatic forces of volcanic and seismic upheaval that can occasionally produce rapid and violent change, but it interpreted the biggest part of global geology in terms of very slow natural processes working over huge periods of time. Uniformitarianism was crucial in preparing people's thinking to accept an immense antiquity for the earth and for life on it, though what was thought immense in 1800 was but a fraction of the huge span of time we assign to earth history today. If you grew up on 4004 BC for the creation of the world, then twenty million years must have seemed like a very long time!

In the middle of the nineteenth century, the case for the great antiquity of human life became compelling with the unarguable discovery in northern France of stone artefacts of vast geological age in the same levels as the fossil bones of extinct animals like the mammoth and woolly rhinoceros. Even when people clung to the catastrophist geology that envisaged a series of previous creations before the present (biblically characterized) one, they were now faced with proof of humanity's not so special attendance in a former scheme of creation. When these discoveries were considered in relation to uniformitarian geology, then the stage was set for the acknowledgement of the true antiquity of humankind.

Darwin's brilliant but essentially simple concept of evolution by natural selection completed and established the revolution in thinking about the past that had been under way for a century before his publication *On the Origin of Species* in 1859. He made the idea of a long process of biological evolution finally compelling by showing how it could have gone on by simple natural means. Before the science of genetics was developed, he couldn't show exactly how random inheritable mutations occur in the constitution of living things between generations, though he did demonstrate with a wealth of examples that such random mutations do occur. They have no end in view, they are not to a purpose; most of them are of no use or are positively deleterious to the well-being of the offspring that display them. If such changes are seriously damaging to the creatures that carry them, then those creatures will do badly in life and leave few or no offspring of their own. If they chance to be notably advantageous to their carriers, even in a small way, then such creatures will prosper that bit more and have more and better-equipped offspring like themselves. Human beings had been selecting domestic animals to breed for their desired qualities for ten thousand years before Darwin saw that nature blindly does the same thing on a gigantic (and gigantically cruel) scale for herself. Human beings have bred the dog into a startling variety of forms by wilfully selecting animals from varied litters to have offspring with valued characteristics, bit by bit breeding towards extreme forms (and, let it be noted, deselecting animals with traits that were not required) – nature has done the same thing remorselessly to every line of living things on this earth, only without the wilfulness and solely in response to the changing circumstances of the world in which her creatures have to live. What can live in any given situation will live, and what can thrive better will thrive and, crucially, breed more successfully. Darwin may not have known about the mechanics of mutation, nor of the precise processes of inheritance by sexual reproduction, but he established the fact of evolution by natural means and thereby consolidated the concept of the extreme longevity of life on earth. It was immediately obvious that human life, too, came within the scope of Darwin's theory: that human life had also evolved (by natural means, moreover) and might be expected to have a considerable antiquity of its own.

A few people had believed in the antiquity of man before Darwin, and finds of flint tools and even human fossil bones in geological deposits of evidently great age, or in association with the bones of extinct animals, were remembered after Darwin. Neanderthal Man came to light just before Darwin's work was published and new finds were made in numbers as the nineteenth century progressed. But it wasn't just the extreme antiquity of humankind that was being revealed.

Human prehistory of comparatively recent times was also being illuminated. The 'ancient state of Britain' and other north-west European lands, which Dr Johnson had thought for ever unknowable beyond a few scraps recorded by the Roman historians, proved to be capable of investigation after all, when approached in a new way. The Danish scholar Thomsen devised, twenty years before Darwin, a classification scheme for artefacts and weapons of evidently pre-Roman provenance that carried an evolutionary implication for human culture as well as for physical humanity. He proposed that the use of stone preceded the use of metal in the progress of toolmaking; moreover that bronze metallurgy came before iron. With this 'Three Age' system, discoveries in the ground could be roughly allocated to different periods, even if the dates of these periods were still unknown. It became apparent that, again roughly speaking, the system worked stratigraphically in the ground: if a deep hole yielded up both stone and metal finds from the distant past, the stone ones tended to underlie the metal and, for that matter, the bronze to underlie the iron.

In this way the concept of the Stone Age, the Bronze Age and the Iron Age (which in Europe shaded into historical times) came about. The Stone Age was later subdivided into Old and New Stone Ages (Palaeolithic and Neolithic) and later still a Mesolithic period was inserted between them; the Palaeolithic era was itself assigned its Lower, Middle and Upper Palaeolithic phases; and indeed the whole system has been elaborated and revised repeatedly over the century-and-a-half of its use, while retaining its basic usefulness to this day. Within the various subdivisions of the system, it was soon possible to start constructing evolutionary 'typologies' of finds, with the help of stratigraphy, in which changes in tool types over time could be plotted – say from simpler to more complex versions (though it could also go the other way at times) – to form a scheme against which new finds could be measured even in the absence of stratigraphy. Typology became one of the key concepts of nineteenth- and twentieth-century archaeology.

The Three Age System had the beauty of not requiring tools of stone or metal to be found in every archaeological context. Other items, known from other sites to be associated with certain types of tool, could also be assigned a place in the scheme – by virtue of that known association. To begin with, of course, it was very difficult or impossible even to guess at the real dates in different parts of the world of practically any of the system's phases and subdivisions. None the less, its usefulness as a means of relative dating of archaeological material was immediately clear: sometimes it is almost as useful to know what comes before and what comes after as to know precise dates for things.

As the nineteenth century progressed, light was thrown on more than the remote prehistorical state of affairs in regions like north-west Europe outside the realms of the known ancient empires of the Romans, Greeks, Egyptians and biblical peoples. Other civilizations and cultures that were perhaps hinted at in a shadowy way in the biblical and classical sources, or were entirely new and unknown, started to come to light. Egyptian history came to be much better known with the decipherment of the hieroglyphs. The archaeology of the Mesopotamian empires of the Bible, like the Assyrians and Babylonians, emerged from the soil of the lands of the Twin Rivers, and the first hints arrived of older peoples like the Sumerians who preceded them. In the Americas the sometimes very impressive mounds of Ohio and the Mississippi were explored and excavated, while the spectacular ruins of the Mexican, Central and South American civilizations could not fail to give pause for thought (some of it pretty extravagant). In the latter part of the nineteenth century, a grand evolutionary scheme of human culture took shape, prompted both by the wealth of archaeological discoveries that were being made and by the encyclopaedic knowledge of the world's existing peoples that came to western scholarship in the wake of colonial expansion. It seemed that somewhere in the world one could still find the Stone Age alive and kicking in the form of hunter-gatherer communities. Elsewhere farming peoples lived settled lives essentially like the Neolithic or Bronze Age cultures of the archaeological record. And in yet other places civilized people – to the extent that they enjoyed political organizations of some complexity and employed written records to administer their states – held sway, rather as the first civilizations of Egypt and Sumer must have done.

It looked as though the present world preserved an evolutionary chronology of human progress from what came to be labelled 'savagery', through 'barbarism' to 'civilization'. That not all people in every part of the world had attained civilization (let alone western civilization) suggested to many in that colonialist era that civilization was a precious invention of the few, diffused only to such among the lesser breeds as could respond to its glories, while many could only soldier on with the crude simplicities of their hunting ways of life or, at best, achieve a barbarous simulacrum of civilization, having to make do with their chiefs and joss-houses instead of kings, presidents, parliaments and cathedrals. It took only one more leap of the imagination to conclude that civilization had only ever had one source in all the world (mysterious old Egypt was a favourite) from which it had been spread – by something like the soldiers and missionaries of the late nineteenth century – to all its other foci around the globe. This was the notion of 'diffusionism' as an explanation of the archaeological record, dubbed hyperdiffusionism in such an extreme form. (Its capacity to blind is well illustrated in the way that the impressive ruins of Zimbabwe could not be seen as the work of any but 'white men' from the ancient Near East, or Arab craftsmen or Portuguese, never as the work of native Africans of the fifteenth century, as archaeology showed it to be in the 1930s.) Hyperdiffusionism is still with us, not among professional archaeologists but rather among speculators of the 'alternative archaeology' persuasion, in the footsteps of that arch-hyperdiffusionist Donnelly.

For all its diffusionism, the archaeological thinking of the late nineteenth century was by no means without its achievements. Its broadly evolutionary basis, its synthesis of discoveries from all round the world, its use of ethnographic observation on the current scene to illuminate the past: all these traits give it in retrospect a serious and substantial, indeed monumental, character that archaeology in the first part of the twentieth century rather eschewed. In place of nineteenth-century archaeology's pursuit of the big themes and big schemes (even if they were to some degree the wrong themes and schemes), the twentieth century's – at least as far as prehistory went – was more concerned with the chronology and detailed characterization of the individual cultures it unearthed. (Culture is archaeology's word for the total picture built up by repeated occurrence at a number of sites of a clearly associated set of artefacts inferred to represent the handiwork of a single, distinctive society of people.) This reaction against the grand pretensions of the nineteenth century was a necessary one which accomplished much useful work, especially when techniques of excavation were refined along the lines first developed by the best of British diggers in the late nineteenth century. Previously unknown civilizations came to light in the early twentieth century when the Minoans of Crete and some other Aegean islands (to whom we have already referred in connection with Plato's story) were rediscovered, along with the Indus civilization of modern-day Pakistan. The spectacular cave art of ice age Europe came to be better and better known. Important work went on in the Americas, too, especially in the southern regions of the USA.

The chronologies of the cultures that archaeology was unearthing before the Second World War, and indeed the overall chronology of global cultural evolution, remained to a large extent a matter of best guesswork where the only hope was to relate whatever was found, if it possibly could be, to the few known cases of well-established chronology that were available. In practice, this often meant Egypt as far as the Old

World was concerned. If your finds could not be related to Egypt by finding, say, Egyptian pottery in an excavated level in Crete or Minoan pottery of a certain sort in a well-dated context in Egypt, or if your site pre-dated Egyptian history or was too remote from Egypt to have any sort of reliable interchange with it, then you were often in the dark as to the absolute dating of your finds, though a relative chronology of local application might well be possible. (Egyptian chronology had been achieved by a most ingenious chain of scholarly reasoning involving various surviving Egyptian records, which were incomplete and flawed in interesting ways, and astronomical calculations based on the idiosyncracies of the Egyptian calendar system – I have described the process in my previous book, *Riddles of the Sphinx*, published by Sutton Publishing in 1997.)

At the end of the Second World War a dramatic step was taken towards the goal of a universal absolute chronology for all archaeological situations. This was the development of the dating technique variously called radiocarbon or carbon dating and C14 dating. This method was the vanguard of a whole array of current techniques based on various sorts of radioactive processes. It promised, within limits, to offer an objective method of dating archaeological contexts that would free the archaeologists from reliance, even where that was available, on Egyptian history or any other known historical framework. By the end of the 1960s C14 dating, extended and refined, sounded the death-knell for any lingering hyperdiffusionism in archaeological thinking when it demonstrated that certain cultural phenomena of western Europe, previously often attributed to Egyptian influence (such as the construction of massive stone edifices like megalithic tombs), actually pre-dated similar developments in Egypt. (The speed with which general acceptance of this upset in thinking came to the world of academic archaeology rather undermines the conviction of Atlantologists like le Plongeon and Spence that professional archaeologists are wilfully blind to all new interpretations of the past.)

Along with the revolution in dating ushered in by the C14 technique, there came to archaeology after the Second World

War a fresh emphasis on the importance of environmental evidence for archaeological interpretation. Human beings have always lived their lives, and made the things they leave behind them in the archaeological record, in environmental contexts of the greatest significance for them. Staying alive at all in some environments has been a major achievement, and the world about us has always both set limits to our doings and also afforded the means to do what we can do. Study of environmental evidence in connection with archaeological finds can not only help to date them (to known climatic phases, for instance) but also to characterize the way of life of the people who produced them in the first place. Modes of subsistence and patterns of settlement can be investigated, with the possibility of exploring theories of economic and social change. In the wake of this new emphasis on environmental studies, archaeology came to enjoy a closer relationship than before with various specialisms in the natural sciences and to tilt towards a more scientific ethos in general, which the school of 'New Archaeology' in the 1960s espoused with enthusiasm. From the 1960s on, archaeology became again – as it had been, on a lower level, in the nineteenth century – a global study with pretensions to the objective explanation of social evolution. Interest in the mechanics of human progress revived: the evolution of big-brained *Homo sapiens* and our conscious mind, the beginnings of toolmaking, the origins of language and art, the causes of the farming revolution after the last ice age, the development of urban life and social stratification, the invention of metallurgy and writing, the universal human impulse towards religion and ideology in general – all these big issues came into archaeological thinking. Dr Johnson would have been astonished, to say the least!

For what archaeology has achieved, since it emerged from undirected antiquarian curiosity in the late eighteenth century, is a methodology whereby a wealth of data prompting philosophical reflection about human existence can be extracted from the surviving fragments left behind, mostly in the ground, by the previous activities of our ancestors. Most of this surviving evidence is so unprepossessing that even today many people might be tempted to think, like Dr Johnson himself, that no knowledge could be got out of it. Like him, many people would not even recognize its existence. For every tomb like Tutankhamun's, for every Terracotta Army, for every Stonehenge there is an array of less spectacular sites and a mass of unglamorous evidence in the form of flints, potsherds, wood fragments, bits of metal, animal bones, pollen grains, stains in the soil and generally humdrum debris from the past that, properly interpreted, is usually of greater significance than the few flashy finds. It is so very important to note that when we speak of 'finds' in archaeology, finds sometimes of the greatest significance, we may be talking of broken bits of pottery, for example, that would perhaps make no impression at all on a layperson. A 'find' is not necessarily, and not usually, some spectacular item that would impress anyone who saw it. It is the triumphant achievement of archaeology, as it has developed over the last couple of centuries, to have been able to make so much of the so little that has come down to us from the past, especially from prehistoric times when there are no records to give us a start. Without the methods and interpretations of archaeology, the prehistory of the human race would be a near-total mystery.

Clearly, there can be little or nothing to show for a great deal of what went on during the thousands upon thousands of years in which thousands upon thousands of human individuals were living and interacting with each other. Much of what humans do leaves no traces behind it in the first place and only the most imperishable of human products – along with the most imperishable features of their environments – can be expected to survive, and then only in a patchy fashion and subject to the vicissitudes of different circumstances and downright accidents. And as to what does come through from the past, there is always the problem of finding it: some things obtrude themselves on our attention from time to time, like Roman remains coming to light in the foundations of city blocks, but systematic archaeology needs something more than that to build up its evidence of the past. Knowing where to look and having a strategy for looking are both very important for archaeology. Settlement pattern studies have profited from such procedures as aerial photography and fieldwalking over the landscape to pick up on surface features that guide us to look for ancient sites. To consider Atlantis specifically for the moment, it is worth noting that the sea is on the whole a pretty unpromising medium in which to go looking for the remains of any hypothetical very old civilization. If such remains were covered by deep sediment (as they might well be after many thousands of years), then they might be fairly well preserved but they would certainly be hard to find even with sonar. If they were not buried in sediment, then the destructive capacities of the sea would surely have been brought to bear on them over the long period of their drowning. Basalts and porous limestones are subject to chemical and biological attack in sea water and most metals so long submerged would be very difficult to recognize after all these years. But perhaps the Atlantologists can take heart – according to the perverse modes of thought of which we know them to be capable, the very absence of any evidence for Atlantis on the ocean floor could easily become 'proof' of the long submergence of the place.

What is vitally important for all archaeological investigation and interpretation is context. All finds, whether considered as individual items or as whole assemblages of material from particular sites, need a context in which to understand them. This is why raids on archaeological sites to pull out some spectacular (and valuable) piece are so destructive of knowledge. The context of these pieces is lost to them: the other items with which they were associated, the stratigraphic level from which they came, the floral and faunal remains around them that might have told so much about the environment in which they were deposited, perhaps carbonized fragments along with them by which they might have been radiocarbon dated – all these lines of evidence and more are lost when looters hack some coveted artefact out of its context. Raids on the past are not confined to physical ones with spades and pickaxes. There is an intellectual sort of looting, too, where archaeological finds are treated out of context and used in aid of fantastic theories about the past, such as this book is all about. Often the finds employed in this way are stray and anomalous ones, made a long time ago or in dubious circumstances or both, never having had any context in the first place – but it is not at all unknown for genuine archaeological data to be ripped out of their real cultural and chronological contexts and abused in this fashion.

Archaeology is the business of finding as much as we practically can of what has come down to us from the multifarious epochs of the human past, extracting from what we find the maximum possible information in all directions and then interpreting what we think we have found at any point in the development of the study in terms of our interest in the development of human life in all its aspects on this earth. No mean ambition, and it is impressive to note what has been achieved – as we shall see in the next chapters. For the moment, it may be useful to establish a bit more about the methodology that serves the ambition.

Sites for investigation are found, as we have already seen, by means of aerial (and now satellite) photography and by fieldwalking to log surface finds – also by their proximity to other known sites or in the course of commercial development and sometimes, of course, by accident. They are looked for, too, in order to answer questions that have arisen in consideration of other sites. Once the archaeologists are interested in some spot, there is a whole battery of techniques that can be called up in aid of their searches before they ever dig: probes with cameras (especially video cameras), ground-penetrating radar, metal detecting, soil resistivity testing, magnetometer survey, acoustic mapping, soil chemistry – the whole paraphernalia roughly equating with what a popular television archaeology programme calls 'geophys'. When excavation ensues, it is the importance of stratigraphical sections and grid planning that comes to the fore, to record the precise location of all finds in relation to the vertical and lateral extent of the site in its physical context of soils or sands. The aim is to provide a record so good that not only the current excavators of the site but all who come after them and study their record will be able to derive information from it. Finds, not just of human artefacts but of environmental features too, must be as fully described and plotted as possible, with any necessary laboratory work on them, before the computerization of the record.

Dating is never far from the minds of archaeologists, both in the field and in the study. The question of date arises inevitably and all the time, both in relative terms of what comes before and after what and in absolute terms of what, after all, is the precise date in years of any particular find or, more to the point, any associated group of finds. Ancient civilizations with calendars and records are few and far between and their chronologies are hard or impossible to extend to other ancient peoples; in any case such methods of dating do not take us very far back. Absolute dates can potentially be derived from tree ring counts in wooden finds, pushing back to some ten thousand years ago (and, incidentally, helping to calibrate radiocarbon dates). But wooden items with tree ring details that can be correlated to established ring patterns through the ages are not to be found in many archaeological situations, and in any case we really need absolute dates that can take us back tens of thousands of years and more, so as to bring order to the archaeology of times beyond the end of the last ice age. This is why radiocarbon dating came as such a welcome development to archaeology in the 1950s. This method, which relies on measurement of radioactive decay in the carbon component of all living things after death, has – in common with all the related methods that have followed it – its limitations and comes on its own terms, as it were. C14 can only date organic materials directly, so using it to date other discoveries requires the greatest attention to context and association of finds. There are possibilities of date-distorting contaminations which have to be avoided. The method comes with a statistically quoted margin of error, so that dates are given with a plus-and-minus range within which there is a level likelihood (usually 65 per cent) that the true date falls: in other words, say for a particular example at 500 ± 80 years BC, any date between 580 and 420 BC might with a 65 per cent likelihood be right. There have been refinements to narrow this margin but it can be seen that for late historical periods radiocarbon dating is not always sufficiently finely discriminating to be very helpful. On the other hand, for remoter prehistoric times the method is invaluable. As with stray finds, one-off carbon dates are not impressive: but whole arrays of dates from a certain level or from similar levels in several sites support each other. And a mosaic of dates, dotted in stratigraphies that can be correlated in different places, can help to date whole archaeological sequences even if dates are not available at every point. Relative chronologies (either stratigraphic or typological, where a sequence of, for example, evolving tool types or pottery styles is known) can be converted into absolute chronologies with the determination of some absolute dates (by C14, etc.) in some places. This is a physics-based extension of the older method of trying to tie in non-historic and prehistoric finds (i.e. from peoples without records and calendars of their own) with the known history of record-writing and calendar-keeping peoples like the Greeks, Egyptians, Chinese and Maya. The physics-based methods, of course, take us much further back in time – some of them very far indeed, like the Uranium Series, Electron Spin Resonance, Fission Track and Potassium-Argon or Argon-Argon techniques. (Note that these methods don't usually date human remains or artefacts directly, but rather the natural contexts with which they are associated – context is always vital.) The relative chronology of ice age times, with its known alternations of glacial and interglacial phases (and of relatively colder and warmer stadials and interstadials within the glacial phases), has been established on the basis of geological deposits, floral and faunal sequences (which chart the evolving natural history of these changing times), and the analysis of deep sea cores from the oceans' beds (among other factors). The various radioactivity-based methods mentioned above have converted this relative chronology of the ice age epoch into an absolute chronology stretching back well over a million years: in fact several million years, into the era of the early phases of human evolution, before the ice ages began.

There are other methods of dating in the offing that work along different lines from the radioactivity techniques, some of them still experimental or not yet sufficiently accurate or wholly reliable (a promising one uses the alterations to rock produced by cosmic ray bombardment to date the time elapsed since rock surfaces were first exposed, for example by carving). DNA research has been employed, on the basis of genetic variations among modern populations that are deemed to occur at a constant rate, to try to date the major phases of human evolution since half-a-million years ago. The study of present-day language families has, in a rather similar way, been suggested as a means of discerning and dating the movement of peoples in prehistoric times, but since a person or a group of persons can always change their language (like the rest of their culture) in a way that they can never do with their genes, the prospects of this particular approach don't perhaps seem imminently bright.

Modern archaeology has, then, a powerful apparatus of scientific techniques at its disposal to help it with its enquiries into the human past. It has developed, moreover, since its antiquarian origins a sophisticated rationale of its own aims and approaches, possibilities and limitations. Before, in the next chapters, we contemplate a sort of thumbnail sketch of the current consensus of academic archaeology about what happened in the past, it will be helpful to consider what archaeology can tell us about the prehistory and early history of the human race. It can, for example, tell us a good deal about where people were living at various epochs of the human story and how they got their livings. It can tell us about the sort of tools and weapons they made and shelters they lived in; what sort of food they could obtain and how they handled it. It can tell us something of the interactions of different human groups in exchange of goods, trade and conflict. It can tell us – subject to the paucity of surviving fossils from the small populations of the remote past – about the physical evolution of the human line from small-brained apemen to big-brained modern types (and something of the likely population sizes involved). It can suggest lines of thought about the times of vast change in human experience when the first signs of personal decoration and works of art arrive in the archaeological record, or when in some places the inveterate practices of hunting and gathering finally gave way to domestication of plants and animals to initiate the farming way of life. It can offer evidence of gender differentiation and degrees of social organization in ancient communities and chart the development of hierarchical arrangements with top people in big houses and lesser folk in smaller ones. It can register expansion of settlements and growth of urbanization in some regions on the eve of written history. It can hint, at least, at some of the religious beliefs and ideological inclinations of the various communities of the past. Every human society (since, presumably, the emergence of the modern mind of modern *Homo sapiens*) runs on ideology: that constant urge towards subjective and imaginative interpretations of the human condition which makes such an enormous contribution – for better and for worse – to all our lives.

Its capacity to throw light on the processes of variety and change in the long course of human existence on this earth is the real glory of archaeology, much more so than the occasional finding of gold-stuffed tombs or sunken palaces or gaudy temples. However fascinating and rewarding such finds may be, they are only part of the raw material that forms the basis for thinking to some purpose about our human past.

6

OUT OF AFRICA

At the start of the twenty-first century, archaeology has come into a well-established body of technical methods and intellectual approaches to apply to its study of the past. They are not things that can be learned overnight: like all specialized and scholarly fields, archaeology is an immense study. You can't hope to master it on the basis of the sort of amateur interest that pretty well everyone feels about human history, any more than you could hope to casually master the fields of relativity and particle physics and dispute with their professional practitioners – though of course there have been people who have presumed to do so. It may not sound tactful to the exponents of 'alternative archaeology', of which Atlantology forms a core piece, to say so but it is presumptuous of them to wade into matters in which they have no depth of knowledge, especially when their dabbling involves denigration of the professionals, as it almost always does in the end.

Of course, academic archaeology isn't always right about the past, in detail or in general (it doesn't aspire to eternal truth, only to the advancement of knowledge), and its interpretations change with further discoveries and further thought. There are, moreover, schools of thought within it with different and competing interpretations. But its knowledge has been hard won and its interpretations are subject to constant scrutiny and evolution. Anyone at all interested in the history of the human race, and particularly perhaps persons with a bent towards alternative notions of the past, would do well to take on board some acquaintance with the general outline of the human adventure as conceived by the archaeologists in the present state of knowledge and thinking. There is a broad consensus as to how that adventure unfolded, though some parts of it are relatively obscure still and some are open to disagreement. It is a very colourful story, with several key areas of great intellectual interest, as we shall try to highlight. And it takes us back a very long way, to begin with.

The evolution of humanity out of its primate ancestry has been accomplished by the same Darwinian mechanisms of random mutation and natural selection as have fashioned the rest of the living world. The primates are an order of the mammalian class of animals with some very distinctive attributes. They have qualities of vision, agility, brain capacity and manipulative ability that taken together mark them out from the rest of the animal world. The earliest proto-primates of the fossil record were mouse-sized creatures that lived on insects, or slightly larger animals that probably ate leaves and fruit. By about 55 mya (million years ago) the earliest primates resembling anything in the world today, like tarsiers and lemurs, were flourishing in North America. These were the first of the line to show that noteworthy primate trait of having bigger brains in relation to their body size than is usually the case in the animal world. Such relatively big brains indicate cleverness in some direction or other. Among the early primates, the cleverness was probably dedicated, in association with colour vision and dextrous paws, to spotting and taking high-quality food like ripe fruits and fresh leaves, against the visually noisy background of a clutter of branches and foliage, especially at night — for the eye sockets of the early primates indicate that they were nocturnal creatures. High-quality food sustained the nervous activity of these creatures' clever brains without entailing the sort of large and elaborate gut that some other animals need to get nourishment from poor food.

As well as serving their cleverness in securing food, the biggish brains of the early primates also found their place in the management of social dealings within the little bands of the various primate types. Most primates (there are exceptions) live in social groups; and among animals of all sorts, it is the socially living species that are almost always the clever ones. Socially living primates are the really clever animals, with humans as the cleverest of all. Society brings benefits like mutual support, cooperation in joint efforts and shared defence against enemies, but it also brings potential problems of quarrelling, competition and increased risk of disease. Both the benefits and the problems of social life need management and it is probable that the demands of group living played as big a part in the evolution of primate cleverness (and primate brains) as did stereoscopic vision and manipulative agility in the branches. In the end, with the human part of primate evolution, it played probably the bigger part.

Among the earliest evidence of monkey-like creatures in the geological record are the fossils of *Aegyptopithecus* from the Faiyum lake deposits of Egypt, at about 35 mya – many related forms flourished to about 31 mya. Their small eye sockets indicate that these were no longer such nocturnal creatures and details of their teeth in some cases already point towards the evolution of apes and humans, though some of them had tails like monkeys. Today's monkeys and apes, in their social groupings (the orang-utan is less sociable), display a great mental capacity for negotiating their way through mutual interactions, with cooperation or selfishness as it suits, forming alliances and breaking them off as opportunity offers, buttering one another up and cheating one another by turns. To continue to use such anthropomorphic terms, we might say that they seem able to guess at their fellows' intentions and disguise their own when there is advantage in it. A great deal of brainpower is needed to handle social relations with this degree of complexity and sophistication – there must be good memory of past experiences and some capacity to predict consequences in the future. Again, in human terms, we can talk of an imaginative ability to enter into the 'minds' of others at the same time as knowing one's own. If not of conscious minds like ours, we can speak of high intelligence among our primate relatives (and ancestors): a peculiarly social sort of intelligence, dedicated to social interaction, which forms the basis for the evolution of a social sort of consciousness. This is a topic of great philosophical interest for students of the early reaches of archaeology (in its broadest interpretation) where the big questions of human evolution are involved. In response to what environmental and social pressures and opportunities did primate intelligence and the first glimmerings of consciousness evolve?

Between about 35 and 25 mya global temperatures were steadily dropping (though not to as low as they are today). This cooling of the world, that brought noticeably colder conditions to northern latitudes, saw increased aridity as its chief effect in tropical and subtropical regions, with shrinkage of forest and woodland in places like North Africa. By about 23 mya East Africa's forests were home to many sorts of ape, without so many monkeys (who were probably continuing to thrive in the less forested areas). *Proconsul* is the best known of the early East African apes, showing a progression from *Aegyptopithecus* towards the apes of today: among the various *Proconsul* species muzzles were shorter than among the monkeys and brains were large both relative to body size and in absolute terms. Shoulders and elbows showed signs of development towards the suspensory, tree-swinging habits of modern apes, though the long arms of the living apes (and to some extent of our own ancestors, too) were not yet in evidence.

The world's climate warmed a little after about 25 mya, to peak at about 16 mya, but there were further drops in temperature at about 12, 10 and 7 mya, after which a really severe drop heralded the long epoch of fluctuating ice ages and interglacial episodes, all basically cold, in which human evolution has occurred (and in which we still live, with permanent ice in Antarctica). The factors leading to this climatic deterioration include: changes in the heat output of the sun, which goes up with sunspots and down with less stormy times in the solar atmosphere; variability in the intensity of the sun's heat at the surface of the earth caused by shading by interstellar dust or volcanic dust in the earth's atmosphere; changes in the earth's reception of solar heat as a result of the overlapping effects of variations in the earth's orbit around the sun and the angle (and wobble of that angle) of its axis to the plane of the solar system. There are cycles in most of these factors that mesh together in interactions too complicated to model with any certainty, and vulcanism is a rather random influence. But, as we have seen, the geological record of the earth has preserved detailed evidence of the alternation of ice ages and interglacials – in cores from ocean beds and from the polar ice-caps, in lake sediments, in deposits of wind-blown debris (called loess) blown off the lifeless regions close to the glaciers, in sequences of pollen grains and animal bones from geological and archaeological sites (some indicating warm and some cold conditions) and in old raised beaches that record changing levels of the sea (for ice ages lock up precipitation in glaciers above sea level at the same time as cold contracts the volume of the world's oceans). When data like these are correlated all over the world and dated by the sorts of physics-based methods we mentioned in the previous chapter, then a very useful chronological framework for the evolution of humanity can be constructed.

After about 16 mya, when things began to cool once more in the northern latitudes, southerly climes again grew drier. Increasing aridity in East Africa started to put selective pressure on the region's early ape inhabitants. They began their long retreat into the continent's shrinking tropical forests where they hang on today, though thanks to Africa's collision with Europe and Asia as a result of continental drift some of their relatives were able to spread out into the woodlands of southern Europe (for a time) and Asia. Times of great environmental change favour the rapid evolution of small but diverse populations of living things.

One of *Proconsul*'s relatives or descendants gave rise to the common ancestry of the African apes and the human line between about 10 and 7 mya. Remains from Kenya indicate the presence of a creature with molar teeth rather like the present-day gorilla's within this range of time. Today's African great apes share about 98 per cent of their genetic make-up with our own – the gorillas a shade less, the chimps a shade more – and studies of genetic divergence between ourselves and chimpanzees suggest a date of something like 6 or 7 mya for the separation of our lines of evolution, since when we have gone our separate ways to arrive (despite that 98 per cent or so of shared genetic material) at such very different creatures as we are, both in appearance and behaviour. The genetic differences, particularly in the area of control gene functions, result in a very different process of development in each human being from that of each chimpanzee: even so, we can perhaps acknowledge – given the genetics in common – that natural selection had not so very much work to do to get from something like a chimp to something like a human being. For all their differences from us, there are elements of great ape life that do show some faint resemblances to the life of modern, or recently vanished, foraging communities of humans. Although plant food is the chief item of their diet, chimps do eat meat occasionally (young monkeys, for example) and sometimes acquire it by means of cooperative hunting operations in a way that no other primates do except ourselves. They employ no weapons in the hunt nor tools to cut up their meat, but they do use sticks to poke out grubs and, occasionally, stones to help break up their plant food. They will sometimes hang on to such stones for their usefulness, though they never fashion them into tools by knocking bits off them. It is in the area of social relations and social strategies that they reveal their most human-like traits. In fact, chimpanzees have brought the social skills of the primates to heights only exceeded by humanity itself: they manipulate and deceive one another and are very alert to the possibilities of being themselves deceived. The rest of their lives – their food gathering and tool-using, their sexual activity, their parental duty (in the case of females) – may evidently be conducted by instinct with a time-honoured automatism, but real inventiveness is brought to bear on their social dealings. The scope to prosper and gain advantage in social relationships (ultimately, to mate more often and successfully by living better and longer and more actively) was at an immense selective premium in the evolution of the higher primates, especially of the human line.

Our common ancestor with the great apes of about 7 mya was not, of course, itself a chimpanzee, though it must have resembled one more than us: a sort of unspecialized chimp, quadrupedal but without the very long arms and knuckle-walking that the chimps and gorillas went on to evolve when they fully adapted themselves to a different ecological niche – the forest – from the one our ancestors thrived in – the savanna. The common ancestor was still arboreal in habit, though not too evolved in the direction of the living apes to be unable to scuttle on two legs occasionally over more open ground: an already big-brained (for body size), probably black-coated, fruit- and insect-eating (and maybe tool-using) forest species that soon split into the chimp and human lines.

The earliest hints in the fossil record of that human line date to between 5 and 6 mya. Ethiopia has turned up a very early find, of at least 5 mya, that looks ancestral to later East African developments. From Kenya comes a lower jaw fragment that stands close (at about 5.5 mya) to the separation of the chimp and human primate branches. About a million years later, again from Ethiopia, come some remains of a creature called *Ardipithecus* that shows real signs of an affinity to the human line of descent: teeth (rather apelike) and jaw fragments and some other skeletal parts are accompanied by a piece of skull which preserves the basal hole through which nerves pass into the spinal column. In chimps, this hole is not positioned right under the skull but rather to the back end of it because, moving about on all fours, chimps do not carry their heads balanced on their spines but rather thrust forward and needing strong musculature to keep their heads from hanging on their chests. The hole in the skull fragment of *Ardipithecus* is quite well forward under the weight of the skull, in a way that suggests that evolution towards bipedal walking was already under way.

Better known than *Ardipithecus* is the genus first named in South Africa in the 1920s, *Australopithecus* (meaning 'southern ape'). *Australopithecus* was no ape as we know apes and was not confined to South Africa. A species of this genus called *A. anamensis*, from Kenya at about 4 mya, takes human evolution across the line that finally separates our ape ancestry from our subsequent human lineage. While the layout of the teeth of individuals of this species still shows an apelike squareness (rather than our own parabola), the leg bones display clear evidence of bipedal locomotion. Environmental indications for this time in East Africa point to a woodland situation with some bush. After this time climatic changes began to impose still drier and less wooded conditions on our remote East African ancestors. Grasslands spread at the expense of wooded areas and the fossil record demonstrates several instances of faunal evolution in adaptation to the new circumstances. Elephants and rhinos, for example, developed teeth better suited to grazing and chewing than before. The early species of evolving humanity were also cases of adaptation to grassland life.

Some time after about 4 mya *A. anamensis* appears to have given way to another species we call *A. afarensis*, whose most famous representative is the individual known to the world as 'Lucy'. This species is represented by the remains of enough such individuals to make a fuller account of their physical character and way of life than was possible with any earlier phases of human evolution. Males were much taller than females, at about 1.5 metres against 1 metre, and very much heavier, perhaps more in connection with a protective and defensive male role in the dangerous open grasslands than with gorilla-like rivalry for harems. Brain size, at between 350 and 500 millilitres, was in the ape range but quite large for body size, housed in skulls with projecting muzzles and sloping foreheads. Canine teeth were smaller than those of apes, but molars were bigger, for chewing harder food from the grasslands. Short legs and long arms point to a still part-arboreal way of life, though details of the pelvis, thighs, knees and feet are indicative of bipedal walking. At a place called Laetoli in Tanzania, where fossil remains of *A. afarensis* have also been found, some preserved footprints of this species have been followed for 27 metres, seventy prints in all belonging to two individuals (perhaps male and female or mother and child) who strolled side by side (with a third walking in the steps of the larger individual) one day some 3.6 million years ago. Halfway along they appear to have stopped for a while to look to the west. This is the first, incredibly old, instance in a long line of poignant moments that dot the archaeological record of our past. The footprints show that these creatures' big toes were in line with the rest, like our own, and not opposable like an ape's, and they brought their feet down with a positive strike as we might expect of practised walkers.

Bipedalism, along with brain enlargement, is one of the most interesting topics of this remote epoch of archaeology. There have been many suggestions to explain the adaptive value of upright posture with walking on two legs. When any thick pelts that our ape ancestors had retained were shed to promote heat loss in the shadeless savanna, then upright bipedalism would have reduced the amount of skin area presented to the heating and damaging direct rays of the sun. Bipedalism also gets the head up, away from the heat-radiating ground and into cooler breezes. Standing upright made it possible to peer over the grasses of the savanna at natural enemies or potential prey. Going on two legs may even have evolved in the first place not so much to get around in the open but to cross unwooded ground as quickly as possible and make it back to the shelter of the shrinking woodland patches of the time. At all events, adaptation to a certain amount of life on the savanna opened up a new ecological niche for a specialized breed of apes (which is what our ancestors were) to exploit.

Standing up and walking, furthermore, freed the hands to carry stones and throw them when danger or the chance to kill some small animal arose. The hands, already clever organs with a long primate evolution behind them, were also freed to evolve into ever better agents of manipulation in concert with improving mental performance by better brains. With upright posture, those brains now found a new world to look into with their long-evolved primate acuity of vision: the savanna world of great depth in distance and great variety of detail dotted around it at different depths, from the small rodent underfoot to the lion troop under distant trees.

Bipedalism must also have altered the visual appearance to one another of the evolving super-apes, particularly perhaps where sex was concerned. The big penises and full breasts of the human line may have evolved in step with bipedalism, changing the nature of sexual attractions and helping – in the very long run – to promote more personalized bonds between adult males and females and their offspring. With more in the way of full-frontal encounters of every kind, bipedalism would in general have enhanced the subtlety of all social encounters, promoting ever more mental agility on the social scene and extending the range of facial and vocal signs that underlie the development of language. Bipedalism marks the turning point at which apes and humans decisively parted company.

A new sort of *Australopithecus*, generally comparable with *A. afarensis* of East Africa, has recently been discovered in

South Africa at about the same date range of 3.6 to 3.2 mya. A slightly later species named *A. africanus* is well known from South African finds and seems to show an evolutionary advance over *A. afarensis* in its smaller canines, bigger molars, flatter face, higher forehead and less marked sexual dimorphism between males and females. The relationship between all the various sorts of *Australopithecus* identified in Africa makes a tangled web, where the last word in the way of classification remains (and with new discoveries will always remain) to be said. But there is a broad division between the slender forms like *afarensis* and *africanus* and a more robust set (robust in the skull and jaw, that is) that evolved later as a specialized adaptation to chewing hard vegetable matter. It was from the slender sort of Australopithecines that the genus *Homo* was to arise. We are, all of us in the world today, the sole surviving species of that human genus: *Homo sapiens sapiens*, in full classification.

The earliest appearance of this human genus is represented, at about 2.5 mya, by fragmentary fossils from Kenya, Malawi and South Africa. At 2.3 mya in Ethiopia further fragments of *Homo* have been found in the same geological context as some of the oldest manufactured tools we know, simple flakes of basalt and chert and the cores they were struck from. (Whether any of the Australopithecines made – or even used – tools is not known for certain, but extremely crude tools have been turned up elsewhere in Ethiopia with a date of up to 3 mya.) Less fragmentary than these *Homo* finds from before 2 mya are the remains, from both East and South Africa, of a species called *H. habilis*, of around 1.8 mya. The cranial capacity of *habilis*, at some 700 millilitres, shows that this species had very definitely left the ape range behind as far as brain size is concerned (though still at only about half the average size of modern people). In fact, *H. habilis* shows a considerable range of types in its surviving fossils and may, especially with further discoveries, be separated into two or more different species in future. Some of the specimens exhibit the rather long arms of *A. afarensis*, but teeth are more human, faces flatter, foreheads higher and skull bones thinner.

The origins and consequences of toolmaking constitute

another of those key areas of interest for the archaeology of the earliest part of the human story. The oldest distinct toolmaking tradition known (after those very crude essays in Ethiopia) is called the Oldowan; it was based on the bashing of pebbles to produce both flakes that could cut and cores that could chop. Finds of broken animal bones in association with some of these early tools suggest their use on the meat-bearing parts of animals, either caught or more likely scavenged from other creatures' kills. Evidently the low level of meat eating seen among today's chimpanzees had been exceeded by *H. habilis*, providing a convenient source of energy-rich nutrition to fuel an active life on the savanna. Both catching small prey and scavenging under threat from carnivorous rivals required mental alertness and cooperative endeavour: so nature continued to put a premium on brainpower. Toolmaking to a regular and socially shared pattern also called for good brains capable of a sequence of operations in line with some sort of 'vision' of the finished product, however automatically and unconsciously it was carried out. The Oldowan tools were still pretty crude items and it took all of a million years for them to evolve into anything better, but they mark a great progression in human evolution. Ground living, toolmaking and meat eating are the trinity of adaptations that made early humanity out of former apes. And it happened at a time when there was as yet no use of fire, no building of shelters that we can see, no burials of the dead, certainly no production of works of art, probably nothing we would recognize as real language and no human consciousness as we know it – perhaps just the beginnings of a very socially restricted sort of imaginative awareness built on general primate potential as the size of early communities grew and the scope of cooperative activity was extended, with attendant frictions and opportunities.

A more sophisticated pattern of toolmaking evolves in the African archaeological record at about 1.5 mya with the core-tools, called hand-axes, of the Acheulian tradition: the flakes knocked off to make them were also used as tools. The Acheulian tradition employed a much more complex sequence of knappings to produce its fully bifacially worked hand-axes, and so required a more detailed vision in the mind's eye (whatever those distant minds were like) to motivate and guide the process of manufacture through its sequence of steps. It is likely that evolving brainpower in physically enlarging brains was needed to bring this greater complexity about, laying more groundwork for the ultimate emergence of a more conscious awareness of mental operations. It may be that regular toolmaking through a fixed sequence of steps planted the seed of our deep-seated conviction that our world proceeds as a chain of causes and effects and according to purpose. Interestingly, some of even the earliest tools show evidence of manufacture by right-handed individuals and the brains of some *habilis* specimens evince the asymmetry associated with handedness (which is not markedly present in any other primates than humans). Brain asymmetry also appears to be involved in the human use of language, and toolmaking and language share certain traits of structuring out of procedural steps. So it is quite likely that the archaeological record of increasing complexity of tool production also charts in a very general way the progress of language sophistication from very simple (and, again, probably socially restricted) usage towards more flexible utterance. It is a sobering thought, in this light, that Oldowan tools changed very little over a million years and the Acheulian was to continue in some places (albeit with growing diversity) for more than a million more. Still, we can tentatively relate the appearance of the Acheulian with some likely progress in the development of language among our ancestors, which can be further illuminated by study of the chimpanzees' capacity for vocalization and sign recognition and by the study (where the fossils permit) of mouth and throat anatomy in the remains of early species of humanity. The question of the origins and early development of language use constitutes another of those areas of great philosophical interest for the archaeology of remote Stone Age times.

At least one of the *habilis* specimens we have shows signs of evolution towards the next distinct species of early *Homo*, who first figures in the fossil record at about 1.75 mya. A wonderfully complete skeleton of this *Homo ergaster* is represented by the remains of the 'Nariokotome Boy' found near Lake Turkana in

East Africa. This youth of about 1.6 mya was only some eleven years old at the time of his death, but was already over 1.5 metres tall, with a brain size of 880 millilitres. Fully grown, he might have reached 1.75 metres with a cranial capacity of 900 millilitres, already well on the way to the modern human ratio of brain to body size. In about 1.5 million years brain size had doubled from the time of the late Australopithecines to only about one-third less than that of people today. This increase is partly related to an overall increase in body size, which reached its modern level (and for the most part its modern configuration) with *H. ergaster*. But it is also related to the evolutionary usefulness of the brains that were enlarging: these people were cleverer than their predecessors – better scavengers maybe (perhaps even hunters in a small way), better toolmakers, better talkers, better members of society, as it were. Remember, improvements don't have to be so very dramatic all at once to confer a crucial margin of survival and breeding capacity on their carriers, which natural selection will perpetuate into future generations; this is how new species come about over hundreds of thousands of years, and sometimes quite quickly when pressure of circumstance favours them.

Details of teeth in *ergaster* specimens indicate an increase in meat eating over chewing of vegetable matter; details of nose and ear chart progress away from ape towards human characteristics; details of the larynx put *ergaster* midway between Australopithecine and modern human forms, strengthening the supposition that language use could have been developing at this *ergaster* phase of human evolution.

Homo ergaster is the name given to the species representing this phase in Africa. But by now human beings were spreading to other parts of the world. There is some evidence that already in the time of *H. habilis* and the Oldowan tool tradition people had spread into Europe and also into Asia. It is possible that the distinctive eastern Asian versions of both human types and toolmaking habits were the result of a very early emigration from Africa before the full evolution of *H. ergaster* and of the Acheulian had taken place back home. Certainly the *Homo erectus* specimens of Java and China and elsewhere in Asia are not quite like the *H. ergaster* people from Africa, while broadly belonging to the same stage of physical evolution, and Acheulian hand-axes are not so prominent in their part of the world, with rather simpler cores and their flake products as a rule. In the Far East both *H. erectus* and his simple stone tool kit (we don't know what went on with perishable materials like bamboo, for example) continued without much change for a very long time, perhaps down until nearly 100,000 BP (Before the Present).

In Africa and Europe *H. ergaster* evolved over time into new species. After the *ergaster* (and broadly similar *erectus*) phase, most of what there was to show for further evolution concerned the skull rather than the postcranial skeleton, which had already reached more or less its modern form. *Ergaster* skulls are heavily made with large and rugged faces in front of their relatively small brain cases. These traits were not shed overnight but reduced as brain size continued to grow. From a site called Gran Dolina in Spain, at about 800,000 BP, have come remains (of hand and foot bones, teeth, jaws and cranial pieces) that show some advance on the African *ergaster* specimens; at about 500,000 BP from Heidelberg in Germany, the Mauer jaw looks still further evolved, and the shin-bone from Boxgrove in England belongs to the same sort of creature at about the same date. (It was at about this time, too, that the Acheulian hand-axe tradition reached Europe: before that tools were of a more Oldowan simplicity.)

The use of fire and the building of shelters is not unambiguously demonstrated in Africa in the *ergaster* epoch. In Europe, particularly when really cooling times came on after about 800,000 BP, fire and shelter surely became essential requirements if life was to be sustained at all. Caves were the obvious choice for shelter and we do find evidence from this time in France and Germany (and in Syria) that built structures of walling or emplacements for wooden poles were sometimes used to improve on the natural shelter of the caves. Fire is attested in western Europe as far back as about 400,000 BP: the first certain occurrence of deliberately tended fire in the archaeological record. Fire made more than a merely material contribution to life (keeping people warm and thawing their winter scavenged meat, with smoking if not cooking to add to the joys of existence): the fireside gave light, too, by which the daytime activities of life could be extended and, above all perhaps, it promoted social life as the scene of meat sharing, mutual grooming and caring for the young. With no hard archaeological evidence beyond the appearance of hearths in the stratigraphy of cave deposits, we can only speculate as to how fire was first conserved from naturally occurring conflagrations and later on generated by the sort of friction devices we associate with scout camps. Certainly, the mastery of fire is further testimony to the growing cooperative intelligence of early humanity.

In Africa, too, progress beyond *ergaster* is demonstrated by several finds. From yet another site in Ethiopia comes the Bodo skull of about 600,000 BP, with the biggest face on any known human fossil, showing prominent ridges over the eyes and a mid-line keel on top of the head (for anchoring heavy musculature) that would not be out of place on an Asian *erectus* skull. But Bodo's nasal area and forehead are much more modern in form, as are the places on the underside of the skull where the jaw articulated. Interestingly there are cut-marks on the bone round the eyes, on the cheeks and forehead and at the top and back of the skull that point to defleshing at the end of the Bodo individual's life, for they never healed. Cannibalism or some other sort of postmortem procedure suggest themselves quite powerfully in this case, as they do with some of the numerous *erectus* remains from Zhoukoudian in China at about 450,000 BP. Cannibalism in recent history has rarely been undertaken for its nutritional potential, but almost always as a ritual of some sort. There is precious little to suggest ritual activity or belief in these remote reaches of human evolution, but the possibility of cannibalism – along with occasional finds of semi-geometric doodlings on pieces of bone and lumps of colouring materials – does hint at the first glimmerings of human imagination. There is not, however, the least suggestion of the making of any items of personal decoration or any works of what we could even remotely call art.

The Bodo skull is just the sort of cranium we would expect to go with the Mauer jaw and Boxgrove shin and, taken together with other related finds in the same age range, it can help us to identify a new species, called *Homo heidelbergensis*, as the successor of *H. ergaster* in both Africa and Europe. In Europe *heidelbergensis* went on over several hundreds of thousands of years to evolve into the Neanderthal folk. As early as 400,000 BP a skull from the French Pyrenees (found along with fragments of some sixty other individuals) shows incipient Neanderthal traits, with a cranial capacity, at about 1160 millilitres, well up on *ergaster* but still short of Neanderthal and modern human averages. The stone tools found in association with this skull are of the mostly axeless flake variety called Tayacian which is the forerunner of the Mousterian tool kit typically found with Neanderthal bones in later times. The skull from Petralona in Greece has a still bigger brain at 1220 millilitres and shows, despite its lack of distinctive Neanderthal features at the back, the double brow arch of the later full Neanderthalers and their broad nasal opening with inflated cheeks.

The same sort of transition from *heidelbergensis* to a later form is evident in Africa, too – in the shape of the skull from Broken Hill at Kabwe, formerly known as 'Rhodesia Man'. Here the signs are of a human type on its way from the Bodo pattern to an early form of *Homo sapiens* with no development of the distinctive traits that separate the Neanderthal people of Eurasia from ourselves. At first sight, the Kabwe skull looks pretty alien to our modern selves, with its enormous brow arches as its most unmissable feature. But its general shape, with a cranial capacity approaching the modern average at 1300 millilitres, does anticipate modern humanity, particularly in its steep-sided aspect seen from the back and its fullness at the rear when viewed from the side. It dates to perhaps as far back as 300,000 BP. The arrangement of the voice-box is thought to suggest a better capacity for forming a wide range of sounds for potential use in speech than is seen in any earlier human fossils – or in the Neanderthalers, whose ability to discriminate between certain consonantal sounds is in question.

It is to Africa that most of the evidence now points for the evolution of the fully modern sort of humanity we call *Homo sapiens sapiens*. An array of fossils, genetic evidence from the modern peoples of the world and discoveries of artefacts of a technologically progressive kind all combine to make Africa again, as it was at the very dawn of our line, the focus of human evolution. The first really significant advance in toolmaking after the hand-axe seems to have been initiated in East Africa at around 250,000 BP, though it is named after the Paris suburb where it was first noticed. The Levallois technique represents, for the times, an impressive sophistication of tool manufacture in that it required rather more forethought about the intermediate steps needed to achieve the desired end product: a flake of stone whose outer surface has already been so well prepared by preliminary flaking work on the core from which it will be struck that, once it is knocked off with a final hammer blow, it will require next to no further retouching for use as a projectile point or cutting and scraping tool. Making a hand-axe, you could see the product gradually taking shape in your hands, prompting each step along the way; the Levallois point only jumped out of the mind's eye into tangible finished form with the final blow. This technique is not just a technical improvement on what went before, it is also a conceptual advance – linked to the appearance, at roughly the same time, of the first archaic representatives of true *Homo sapiens*. We can reasonably speculate that the sophistication of all this was mirrored in some advancement in the use of language, with a better sense of unfolding logic through time as 'sentences' were built up.

The Levallois technique was not adopted everywhere (for one thing you needed a liberal supply of good stone to make it worthwhile) but in most parts of the then inhabited world – away from the Far Eastern realm of *Homo erectus* and his not very evolved descendants, with their Oldowan-style tool kits – there is a noticeable general improvement in toolmaking with more variety of types and a more efficient exploitation of the raw material. This was the era of stone technology known as the Middle Palaeolithic, to distinguish it from the Lower Palaeolithic times of the Oldowan and Acheulian. Later on, after about 75,000 BP, there are spells (but only spells, which come and go) of an even more forward-looking stone technology in both South and East Africa. For the first time as a major component of any human tool kits, narrow blades were being struck off specially prepared cores instead of broader flakes. These blades made better knives and were adaptable to other more complex tool types like awls and burins, and they could be miniaturized for special uses in a way that flakes could not. Blades are the hallmark of the Upper Palaeolithic cultures of Europe in the age of the Crô-Magnon cave artists of fully modern type who came after the Neanderthalers from about 40,000 BP onwards. And, indeed, in Africa at rather more than twice that date there is evidence for the early appearance of more or less fully modern physical types. From the Klasies River Mouth and Border Cave sites in South Africa have come very modern-looking fossils dated to between 115,000 and 75,000 BP (Klasies River Mouth also has blade technology slightly later on); from Tanzania, the Sudan, Ethiopia and Morocco come further specimens with distinct modernizing tendencies (high cranial capacities, flat faces, chins) in a range that goes back to at least 160,000 BP.

The fossils and the blade episodes are complemented by a growing body of genetic work that suggests an origin for *Homo sapiens sapiens* in Africa. Genetic sampling of all the present-day populations of the world (which represent a single species, fully interbreeding, with only the most superficial variations – however striking to us) has established that the highest degree of variation in our mitochondrial DNA is to be seen in Africa. The implication is that modern people have lived rather longer there than anywhere else, thus allowing more time to develop a few variations on the basic mtDNA configuration we all share. It has been possible to calculate a likely date (not agreed by all workers) in the range of 200,000–100,000 BP for the emergence of that modern configuration – which agrees well with the fossil evidence from Africa.

MtDNA has also been investigated in the case of the Neanderthalers. The original find from the Neander Valley in Germany has yielded enough mtDNA for us to say with some assurance that this particular Neanderthaler and, by implication, the whole lot of them were not closely related to any modern human beings and are unlikely to have interbred with our ancestors very much, if at all. They seem to have parted company with our line as long ago as *Homo heidelbergensis* of 500,000 years ago. In the present state of our knowledge, it looks as though African *heidelbergensis* became archaic *Homo sapiens* who became *Homo sapiens sapiens*, while European *heidelbergensis* became *Homo sapiens neanderthalensis*, who eventually died out. The Neanderthalers had, on average, bigger brains than our own, but they were rugged people, evidently physically adapted in the end (the earlier ones less so) to the extreme cold of the first part of the last ice age, after about 120,000 years ago. They held their own, hunting as well as scavenging – their wooden spears have been found – in the very harsh conditions of ice age Europe, without bone needles to sew their garments (their front teeth show they chewed animal hides to make their clothes) but with fire and constructed shelters to improve their caves and other living sites. Their tools are of Middle Palaeolithic character, without blades, and they produced no items of personal decoration or works of art worth mentioning (a few lines and scratches are imputed to them). They did on occasion deliberately bury their dead and there is some not altogether unambiguous evidence that they may have carried on a bear cult, impressed perhaps by the human shape (only more so) of the fierce cave bears of their time. (At the very end of their career on earth, some Neanderthal bands adopted elements of a more sophisticated way of life in the form of blade technology and personal decoration, but by then the Crô-Magnon people were in their midst and most archaeologists believe the Neanderthalers were influenced by them.)

The Neanderthalers were a northern people, used to the cold. But at times during the early phase of the last ice age, some Neanderthalers went south into the Levant, where an intriguing situation arose *vis-à-vis* the earliest emigration of fully modern types out of Africa. The Neanderthalers may have been there first, but at around 90,000 BP or so (perhaps a little earlier) there is ample evidence for the presence of *Homo sapiens sapiens*. These were moderns without a modern culture: they were using exactly the same Middle Palaeolithic tools as the Neanderthal folk did (and as did most other people in the world – up to this time blade use was only a sporadic affair). About the only traits that might distinguish them from their Neanderthal contemporaries are suggested by some evidence that they occasionally buried their dead with food offerings and they seem to have hunted more efficiently, with an eye on the seasons rather than scraping along with whatever they could get at any time. By about 60,000 BP the Neanderthalers were back in the Levant (if they ever went away) with their identical Middle Palaeolithic tool tradition. The Upper Palaeolithic with blades arrives in this region – in a full-blooded fashion, never to give way to Middle Palaeolithic again – in about 46,000 BP: the first place in the world where we can log this important change.

It is another of those key areas of philosophical interest in archaeology to ponder why the physically modern sort of humanity, first appearing at least a hundred thousand years ago, manifested almost no different behaviour worth writing home about from any of its predecessors and contemporaries for tens of thousands of years. With the exceptions of those sporadic blade appearances and slightly superior hunting strategies, and maybe a few instances of grave goods, there is nothing that hints at the glories to come in the career of big-brained *Homo sapiens sapiens*. (We should mention some impressive bone harpoons, from an otherwise Middle Palaeolithic sort of site in Zaire, that have been claimed to date back to 80,000 BP or so – they constitute one of those instances of a single find, not corroborated elsewhere, that have to be left in abeyance until further work is done. If they are as old as suggested, they do indicate that their presumably *Homo sapiens sapiens* makers were finding new avenues to explore with their fine big brains.) Why the Upper Palaeolithic culture – of blade-based variety in stone tools, of extended range of manufacturing materials including bone and antler, of bigger populations, of better modes of subsistence, of furnished burials, of personal decoration and art – did not arrive sooner than it did is a question of great moment, since it goes to the heart of the matter of human mental evolution.

It has been suggested that, for all their modern appearance, the skulls of early *Homo sapiens sapiens* contained brains in which a bit more rewiring, as it were, remained to be done by genetic mutation under the pressure of natural selection. The whole history of the human genus is plainly one of accelerating mental prowess, probably driven in the first place by the requirements of social cleverness but subsequently of great value in the struggle for survival in its application to toolmaking and foraging. It is possible, at the same time, that the brains of *Homo sapiens sapiens* were as good from the start as they are now and that their cleverness was first applied in the social sphere, while complex developments in language use to furnish minds like our own perhaps required a long time to mature. So the fully modern mind only came together after about 50,000 BP, as far as we can see, as a conscious force integrating mental departments that had not previously been available to introspection via interior monologue and discourse with others. This is heady stuff, particularly where the perennial problem of human consciousness is concerned, but we mention it to show that real archaeology has an important part to play in the discussion of something right at the heart of what it is to be human. A rather deeper matter, we venture to think, than speculative lost worlds under the sea and reminiscences of old Atlantis revealed to sleeping prophets.

7

INTO HISTORY

It begins to look as though the likely spread of modern humanity out of Africa started at an early date. We have already seen moderns (not doing anything very modern) in the Levant at about 90,000 BP. A site on the Red Sea at about 125,000 BP suggests itself as the sort of jumping-off place from which the moderns might have set out coastally via the Gulf of Aden and the Arabian Sea and on to the bay of Bengal and Sumatra, Java and Australia. We know they were in Borneo by 40,000 BP and Australia by at least 35,000 BP (some think considerably earlier). Parts of this expansion would have required travel by raft or boat, something with which we can well credit these moderns since there is evidence that even *Homo erectus* reached islands of the Far East that were always separated by sea crossings.

In the Far East the moderns appear to have supplanted lingering populations of a not highly evolved *erectus* type, without genetic evidence in the world today to suggest any interbreeding. Traits going back to *erectus* times have been identified by some anthropologists in more recent fossils from this region, to suggest the presence at least of an older local component in later times, but the theory of parallel evolution of local races in different parts of the world through *ergaster/erectus*, archaic *sapiens* and *sapiens sapiens* phases is in retreat for the present. In fact, the racial variations of modern humanity are very superficial: we remain globally an essentially tropical species that has adapted to less amiable climates not by physiological change (the Eskimos, for example, show a bit of that, but on nothing like the scale of the Neanderthalers) but by resorting to cleverer behaviour: better tools, better clothes, better hunting strategies, better social arrangements. By resorting, in other words, to fully human culture – that vast repertoire of experience, memory and imagination that is freed from crude genetic inheritance, to be shared and transmitted by its own cultural means, through language and learning.

Full blade technology had arrived in the Levant by about 46,000 BP, when a warmer interstadial of the last ice age offered the opportunity of a passage into Europe to the moderns. We can chart their spread across Europe, where we know them as the Crô-Magnon people, at a series of dated sites, with them in place in France and Spain by about 36,000 BP. It was for a short time after that date that they coexisted with the last of the Neanderthalers, some of whom they appear to have influenced for a while in the direction of blades and personal ornaments. In the Europe of the ice age interstadial, they found a home colder than the Europe we know today, and set to turn much colder again as the final phase of the last ice age came on, peaking at an extremity of cold at about 18,000 BP. Cold it may have been, but it was teeming with wildlife for them to hunt, and on the riches of their subsistence the Crô-Magnon people were able to build a way of life of quite astonishing novelty in the long story of evolving humanity up to their time. Indeed, their art stands comparison with anything that has been done since in that line.

The oldest evidence for personal decoration comes from East Africa (in the form of eggshell beads) at about 46,000 BP. The Crô-Magnon folk show it in abundance. The arrival of clear evidence of personal decoration is of great significance in the human story. (Earlier people may have painted themselves with those lumps of ochre and other potentially colouring materials we sometimes find in their debris, but we don't know for certain.) Ornament of the person is a sign of personal and interpersonal consciousness: a good indication that minds essentially like our own had evolved by about 50,000 BP. The Neanderthalers had certainly practised deliberate burial of some of their dead, but their graves were never indisputably furnished with grave goods and their dead were not decorated with ornaments, nor indeed with colouring materials in the way that is attested in the burials of modern types. There are elaborate burials of moderns in Australia at 26,000 BP, while some of the burials of Upper Palaeolithic people in Europe have yielded quantities of decorated items, notably at a site near Moscow where thousands of mammoth ivory beads, along with perforated fox canines and ivory armlets and bracelets, delineated the tailored clothing in which these dead were buried. Here, at Sungir about twenty-five thousand years ago, we can see perhaps the beginnings of social division and hierarchy, with top people buried in style, which we can also track in variations among the sizes of huts built of mammoth bones at other east European sites. The Upper Palaeolithic people were living in larger groups, interacting over much greater distances, than their predecessors had ever been able to do, with the first indications in the archaeological record of social differentiation among members of the community. It is another of archaeology's valuable contributions to our thinking about our place in the world that it can throw light on the origins of complex society, from its beginnings among the hunters of the Upper Palaeolithic into the era of the first farming communities and on to the earliest urban civilizations.

The art of the early moderns is the most startling thing about them. After millions of years of human evolution with nothing more than a few scratches and peckings on stones and bones, we now find the most wonderful works of art: at going on for 35,000 BP in Europe, 30,000 in Africa, and before 20,000 in Australia. In Europe there is wall art and there are small art objects engraved or carved on bone and ivory and modelled in clay to be baked. Some of the polychrome cave paintings of France go back before 30,000 BP and one of the most striking pieces of carving – a lion-headed human figure – dates to about the same time in Germany. The motivation and meaning of this art (which went on for some twenty thousand years!) has been endlessly explored with many theories to account for it: hunting magic, fertility magic, shamanism, totemic symbolism, sexual dualism, ethnic assertion. What can be said for certain is that the art of the ice age testifies to the full emergence of the imaginative human mind. The mentality that produced the art was the same one that made the better tools, devised the better subsistence strategies, lived the better organized lives.

Even during the rigours of the ice age, the moderns – instead of retreating before the more atrocious conditions as all their predecessors had done – were able to extend the range of humanity into areas never inhabited before. The plentiful game of the frozen steppe of Siberia, which could supply the dietary calories needed to sustain life there if only you knew how to exploit it, enticed hunting bands further and further east, in the direction of the Americas. The low sea level of glacial times created a broad bridge to Alaska from where an ice-free corridor between the ice sheets of the Rockies and of northeast Canada could let the hunters pass south into warmer climes. (They might also have been able to go by boat along a coastline not unremittingly covered by glaciers until they reached warmer waters.) The ice-free corridor was certainly open in time for the first really reliable evidences we have of human presence in North America, at about 13,500 BP. (Two thousand years later, if not before, people were all over both the northern and southern parts of the Americas.)

Flint points from sites in Siberia at about 14,000 BP can be correlated with broadly similar products in North America that are almost as old – indeed there is an Alaskan site, where a bone needle was found, that dates to about 13,800 BP. The American points are thinner than the Siberian ones, in a way that more closely resembles a phase of flint-knapping in Europe which flourished for a few thousand years around 20,000 BP. This situation has led to speculation that people may have travelled up the Atlantic coast of France (extended by the low level of the sea) and around the edge of the Scandinavian ice sheet that connected with the ice of Greenland and Labrador to reach the east coast of the USA below the North American glaciers. This is a far-fetched idea with no real evidence to support it and the dates do not match up on the two sides of the Atlantic. Claims are made for archaeological evidence of human presence in Virginia at 15,000 (or even 18,000) BP and in Pennsylvania at 20,000, but these claims are contentious, as are ones for even older dates in Central and South America.

DNA evidence has been held to show that people may have been in the Americas for up to thirty thousand years and there is a guess (it can be nothing more) based on the family tree of native American languages that human occupation might go back some twenty thousand years. DNA also points to the area of Lake Baikal in southern Siberia as the closest genetic parallel in the world today for the gene patterns of the native Americans. The extent to which the racial types of today's world were established some twenty thousand years ago is very much open to question, so that while the indigenous populations of the Americas do in general resemble those of Siberia we must always expect considerable variation among the human remains we find in the archaeological record, just as we still find some variety within populations today. Not much can be built on the odd discovery of a skull here and there in America with traits that look a bit like, say, an Ainu or a Polynesian, or a Crô-Magnon or a Viking (whatever they are all supposed to look like). This is not to rule out the possibility of several waves of immigration into America, and not all of them from Siberia either, but we have very little to go on since human remains are very few and far between from the early reaches of American archaeology, though artefactual evidence becomes solid after about 13,000 BP.

The complex geological record of the glacial and interglacial epochs that have dominated the climate of the world over the past million years or so makes it clear that ice ages have come on quite slowly but gone out quite quickly, over as little as two or three thousand years. They have not, however, gone out smoothly, but experienced a series of hiccups with short cold snaps punctuating the general trend to warmer times. The general trend was at the same time towards wetter conditions in the more southerly regions that saw no frost and snow (except at high altitudes) during the ice ages but rather an aridification. With warmer and wetter times sea levels rose after each ice age as glaciers melted and the volume of the warmer oceans expanded. With postglacial conditions, ecological zones shifted, both generally northwards and up to higher altitudes. At the close of the most recent ice age, from about 12,000 BP, the tundra that had reached into north-west

Europe shrank back towards Siberia and the fauna it supported went with it (or into oblivion in some cases). The Upper Palaeolithic way of life that had thrived so vividly in Europe followed the retreating game for a while, but at home finally developed into a much less archaeologically spectacular, while economically quite successful, mode of subsistence that we call Mesolithic, carried on in the spreading temperate woodlands and around the coasts.

Further south, especially in the region of the Levant and its hinterland where the abundance of ice age life in the north had never been equalled, things changed too – in the end, more dramatically. Well before the ice age was out, between about 17,000 and 15,000 BP, there had been a phase along the upper Nile of a form of subsistence that foreshadows the next great revolution in human affairs after the emergence of modern-minded *Homo sapiens sapiens*: farming. (It has been called the Neolithic Revolution, since in Europe at least it is usually associated with the New Stone Age of polished rather than just knapped stone tools.) By the Nile there had evidently been quite extensive harvesting of wild grasses, to judge by the gloss on some flint sickle blades that is the characteristic result of such activity. Grindstones attest to the preparation of cereal grains harvested in this manner. This was not agriculture with any deliberate domestication of plants, and it fizzled out without turning into agriculture along the Nile at such an early date, but it was a testament to the modern inventiveness of the people who pioneered it and a portent of things to come.

In the postglacial world of the Levant and the region behind it to the east, five thousand years or so later, the experiment in harvesting was renewed. The moister conditions after the end of the ice age promoted the denser growth of wild wheat and barley and harvesting could now go on here on a large scale, alongside the hunting of gazelle that had long been the basis of the economy. If one wonders why this sort of harvesting had never been initiated at the end of any previous ice age, one has only to remember that modern-minded *Homo sapiens sapiens* had not been around in those times to think it up. It depended on a certain climatic situation, on the availability of suitable wild plants and on how well people were doing without it, but above all it depended on the wit to see the opportunity for it.

Intensive harvesting gradually turned into agriculture in the area called the Fertile Crescent, arching from the eastern border of the Nile Delta up the coastal hinterland of the Levant into the region of the Taurus Mountains in Turkey and down again to the western flanks of the Zagros range and the Persian Gulf. Among the archaeological remains of some groups of hunter-gatherers in this region at about 11,000 BP (or, to switch to the conventional dating scheme, 9000 BC), excavation has turned up sickle flints and mortar stones that, as along the Nile some thousands of years before, bear witness to the collection and preparation of grass seeds. These 'Natufian' people seem, indeed, to have deliberately sown some of their seeds, kept back for the purpose, away from the places where the grasses were growing naturally. This represents an interference with nature on a truly revolutionary scale: for to be able to preserve seed-heads for transport to other sites, less easily shattered heads (and wild forms shatter very readily) must have been purposefully selected. Thus began the human selection of living things to breed for human purposes, doing deliberately and with a human end in view what nature had been doing all along without purpose and with no end to it. It was Darwin who saw how natural selection has blindly guided all evolution and his insight partly rested on observation of humans' selective breeding of plants and animals.

By 8500 BC real cultivation was going on in some places, with the addition of lentils and peas to the cereal plants like wheat and barley. And what could be done with plants could also be done with animals – indeed, in the case of the dog, had probably been done already, at the end of the ice age. By 8000 BC the beginnings of animal domestication took in sheep and goats, later on pigs and cattle, whose wild prototypes were also to be found in the general area of the Fertile Crescent. The immediate aim of this domestication of animals was to have tame supplies of meat on hand – benefits like milk, wool and traction came later on.

With more animals under control, without having to travel to hunt them, and more plant food supplies located according to human convenience, the possibility of settled life in villages with their own fields, compounds and stores was available to human communities as rarely before. (It takes exceptionally easy access to abundant foraging – usually fishing – to make settled life available to non-farming folk.) At the same time fields and stores, with ever more domesticated plants and animals, led on not just to convenient produce but to more abundant produce too. At around 8000 BC the loose stone walls and towers of prehistoric Jericho indicate not just permanent settlement but large-scale engineering and maybe even defensive measures. For the potential abundance of the farming way of life has its drawbacks as well as its benefits: what starts as convenience, perhaps life and death convenience in some situations, turns into dependency and drudgery. Hunter-gatherers don't hunt and gather all day every day – farmers usually have to be out in their fields and byres for most of their time. A good farming location becomes property to be looked after and defended. The need to regulate farming work, especially as villages grow, and to manage stock and stores of food gives great scope for those primate traits of jockeying for power and taking advantage that had already found expression in the first developments of social differentiation seen in some of the houses and graves of the ice age. Chiefs and medicine-men, for want of better words, were already on the human scene: farming would give a great boost to their ambitions.

By about 7000 BC the Near Eastern world of this early version of the farming revolution contained many more villages. If they were not built of stones like Jericho's unique walls, they could at least contain two-storey houses and some shrine-like structures with plaster statuary and plaster-covered human skulls, indicating religious activity and the likely presence of priestcraft in some form to oversee it. At around 6500 BC the spectacular site of Çatal Hüyük in Anatolia, with its crowded houses and 'shrines' of mud-brick and plaster, its cultic wall paintings and its fertility figures, shows how far farming life had taken people in just a few thousand years.

The first agricultural manifestations of the Near East were lacking in one area of technology traditionally associated with farming: the making of pottery. Pottery makes its first localized mark in the archaeological record in Japan and on the nearby

Asian mainland at about 10,000 BC, as a product of a non-agricultural foraging people. (The Upper Palaeolithic people of Central and Eastern Europe had baked clay figurines, but made no pots – ceramic technology is one of those things that get independently invented at different times.) The point about pots is their use as rigid containers, for which there is more demand in a settled farming community than among nomadic hunters. They are practical items but the ease of their manufacture (once you can fire them in kilns at very high temperatures) leads to a wealth of styles and decorative traditions that make one people's pots very different from another's and also keep on changing with time – for this reason pottery, even as broken sherds, is so useful to archaeologists in tracking trading relationships, migrations and chronologies. (We recall that the dating of the Thera explosion involves pottery styles.)

Pottery appears in the Near East at about 7000 BC and soon afterwards in Europe too, as the first farmers of the region brought agriculture into Greece and the Balkans. Farming was adopted in Europe partly as a matter of migration of farming people out of Anatolia, bringing their way of life with them, and partly of conversion to the new way of life of indigenous mesolithic foragers. As with everywhere else where farming became established, Europe was transformed by this great change in human affairs: by as early as 5800 BC, a start was being made (in Brittany) on the great megalithic tomb constructions that – especially after about 4500 BC – collectively housed the dead of the early farmers of western Europe down to about 2000 BC, in association with circles and alignments of stones that outlasted the tombs. At much the same time as it first reached into Europe, farming also spread east from the Fertile Crescent across to the Indus Valley of north-east India. It was adopted in Egypt, rather late in the day, by about 5000 BC, ushering in an archaeological sequence that builds – particularly in its decoration of pottery, design of stone utensils and styles of burial – into the recognizably proto-Egyptian culture of late predynastic times after about 3500 BC. In other parts of the world the farming way of life was espoused at other times and on the basis of quite different ranges of plants and sometimes of animals, suggesting in most cases independent invention of the practices of agriculture and pastoralism, as we shall see.

The same ability to manage high temperatures in kilns that made pottery possible also facilitated the smelting of metals for the first time. Some use of finds of pure copper for cold hammering preceded the development of metallurgy but the systematic smelting of ores to liberate copper needed very high temperatures and, again, high intelligence to devise the process. Traces of other minerals naturally occur with copper ores and their presence hardens the copper smelted out of them. But tin works best in association with copper, to produce hard bronze, and tin does not naturally occur with copper, so the application of much cleverness of observation and planning was necessary to bring about the Bronze Age, with complex casting of implements and weapons. Bronze was in regular use in Anatolia and the Near East after 3000 BC, in Europe a few hundred years later and in Egypt – after many centuries of copper smelting – by about 1500 BC. Bronze manufacture was independently devised in the Far East at around 2000 BC, while copper technology was developed in Peru only some two thousand years ago, along with the use of gold at about the same time (it was being worked in Bulgaria some four thousand years before that). In North America copper was only worked cold and iron use was unknown in the Americas till the time of Columbus, its smelting having been pioneered in Anatolia in about 1500 BC, with widespread adoption in the Old World after 1000 BC, though its application in China seems to have been an independent invention of about 600 BC and it only reached sub-Saharan Africa (along with copper) after about 500 BC.

Another of the great turning points in human affairs on which archaeology can shed light is the origin of civilization itself all around the world. The archaeological record tracks the appearance, again at different times in different places, of the complex of related traits that make up civilized living – cities with large populations, grand buildings, royal or priestly power structures (or both), interdependent relations with non-urban surroundings, artistic expressions of political and religious ideologies, and some system of writing to keep records and administer the state. Archaeological thought can try to discern the patterns of progress towards civilization that have been followed in different circumstances and so seek to establish the general principles according to which civilized life arises.

Populations enlarged by successful agriculture and requiring a high level of organization to sustain their successes must tend towards civilization, with urban centres where leaders oversee courts and bureaucracies and guilds of craftsmen, all of whose city life is supported by the resources generated by farming and, to some extent, by trade with other cities. Larger groupings, with more and more people thrown together in communal interdependency, call for practical organization and strong ideology to unite and coerce the populace: for statecraft and religion. In detail, the social arrangements that emerge to handle these requirements can vary quite widely, in accordance with the ever fertile human imagination's capacity to come up with ideas.

Cities may be small, walled and contained, dominating a quite restricted surrounding area and interacting with a number of other city-states close at hand, as happened in Mesopotamia in the early centuries of civilized living there after about 3500 BC. Or they may be sprawling affairs like Memphis by the Nile with a reach of power over an entire region, as was the case with unified Egypt after about 3100 BC. In Mesopotamia it was around priestcraft and temple administration that life centred, until kings gained control of the temples in early dynastic times, without putting on the pretensions of divine kingship until much later. In Egypt, though temple administration was vital to the state, the kings were gods from the first, albeit ruling (ideally) in keeping with the tenets of cosmic justice. Egypt was a rather self-contained land in those early days, with trade rather less important than it was to the Mesopotamian states – some idea of their trading wealth is afforded by the grave goods (including people) buried with their rulers at Ur around 2500 BC; they were certainly powerful, even if they were not the god-kings of Egypt. The prestige of the latter is amply demonstrated in the construction from around 2600–2200 BC of the line of pyramids close to Memphis, as gigantic tomb complexes for the kings of the Egyptian Old Kingdom. The ziggurats of

Mesopotamia, by contrast, were pyramidally stepped platforms for temples to the gods. All this impressive architectural achievement bears witness to the dependability of the complex social organization and ideology called into being by highly intensive farming and consequent population growth.

City life arose in the region of the Indus Valley at about 2600 BC and, in the form of palaces, on Crete around 2000 BC, with cities and state apparatus appearing in China a century or so after that. As in Egypt and Mesopotamia, all these epiphanies of civilization were accompanied by some use of writing: not much in the Indus case and we still cannot read the inscriptions on the seal stones from that region; nor can we read the early efforts of the Minoans on Crete. Our ability to read the writings of the Egyptians and Sumerians is owed to veritable triumphs of scholarship in the nineteenth century, while the decipherments of the later Cretan script and the very much later hieroglyphs of the Maya in America are achievements of the latter half of the twentieth century. The use of signs, perhaps for counting and even some moon watching, was pioneered (as with so much else) by the Upper Palaeolithic hunters of the ice age, but the need for elaborate records and administrative measures only arose in the complex societies of the first civilizations.

The people of Lower Mesopotamia (whom we call the Sumerians) were the first we know of, at around 3300 BC, to start to use picture signs and then sound signs to record the words of their language – a system so successful that it could be subsequently adapted to the Semitic languages of later peoples coming to power in Mesopotamia. The Egyptians began to use their quite different hieroglyphic system just a little later on, perhaps having picked up on the idea of writing from the Sumerian example, but applying it along their own independent lines. (The two separate courses towards civilization that were followed in Egypt and Mesopotamia are quite well known to archaeologists and though there may have been a period of influence from Sumer on the eve of Egyptian history, it is clear that Egyptian civilization was a home-grown production that went on to maintain its essential integrity until conquest by foreign powers in the first millennium BC.) In fact, writing systems all over the world are usually quite different in different places, with for the most part no signs or even basic approaches in common. By 2300 BC the different systems of the Egyptians and the Mesopotamians were able to handle not just labellings and listings, as they began life to do, but to record affairs of state in a quite elaborate way, with narrative and religious texts in evidence. All this marks the beginning of history in these parts of the world.

The Aegean civilizations of the Late Bronze Age from about 1900 to 1250 BC, of which the Cretan palaces like the one at Knossos are the most striking products, either evolved by themselves as trade grew all around the eastern Mediterranean or were influenced into being by the older civilizations of Egypt and the Near East. The palaces were rambling constructions, with cut stone masonry and drainage systems, that included stores and workshops and shrines on their ground floors and residential quarters (with baths) and grand reception areas in their upper storeys, with wonderfully lively wall paintings that rival and surpass the wall art of the Egyptians. The Minoans of Crete wrote in two so far undeciphered scripts, but later writings – in the Linear B script – have turned out to be in an early Greek dialect but not in the Greek letters we know from later times. Greeks from the mainland had evidently come to power in Crete before the end of palace life on the island. The Greek culture of this time is called Mycenaean after one of its principal sites. By 1500 BC warrior élites had emerged in Greece; they buried their chiefs in elaborately furnished graves with such spectacular items as the gold face-masks famously discovered by Schliemann at Mycenae in the late nineteenth century.

After 1400 BC there were Mycenaean palaces in Greece, with rich decoration and written records in the Linear B script they had adopted from Crete. The language they were speaking was a forerunner of the Greek dialects of classical and Hellenistic times, one of that family of closely related tongues called Indo-European, to which also belong the Germanic, Italic, Celtic, Slavic, Persian and northern Indian languages, including Sanskrit, Hindi and Urdu. Of course, languages have no hard and fast linkage with cultures or peoples and they are difficult to trace back into prehistoric times before the use of writing, but glottochronology and efforts to track language groups into archaeological contexts can be fascinating – in the case of Indo-European languages, a relationship has been proposed with a culture of semi-nomads from the Russian steppes who spread into Central Europe before 3000 BC, if the first farmers didn't already speak them.

In Bronze Age Europe at the time of the Mycenaeans no other communities were using writing to record their languages, but their way of life was essentially similar to that of the contemporary Greeks. Their warrior élites buried their dead in round barrows in Western Europe (rather than collectively in long barrows as people there had done before) with a wealth of grave goods that parallels the Mycenaean burials. Stonehenge, which began life as a neolithic monument, belongs in the form we know it to this time. In the Near East of the time Indo-European speaking (and writing) Hittites and others contested with Assyrians and Babylonians speaking languages of the Semitic group, and with Egyptians who spoke a language largely Semitic but with a distinct North African component. A world of international diplomacy has been uncovered with the discovery in Egypt of an archive of letters between the rulers of the day. And trade, of course, flourished even when diplomacy sometimes failed: it is the occurrence of Egyptian material in particular at other people's sites that is so useful in dating everybody's history around the eastern Mediterranean in the centuries leading up to about 1200 BC.

This trade and diplomacy, and a good part of civilized life altogether, were severely disrupted at about 1200 BC as a result of political turmoil and population movements of the day. The trouble focused on a disparate throng of pirates and adventurers (with their families) who harried the eastern Mediterranean world and its sometimes already rocky empires for a number of years. They are known as the Sea Peoples. Most of them were of Aegean origin but some perhaps came from as far away as Sicily and Sardinia. Although beaten off by the Egyptians, some of them settled along the southern coast of the Levant to become the Philistines of biblical history at about the same time as the Israelites emerged from the fringes of fading Canaanite culture in the hill country west of the Jordan River, a mostly local development with perhaps some influx of refugees from Egypt and elsewhere. (Like other peoples of the ancient world they went on to endow themselves with a largely mythological account of their origins and early history, but their account has been a longer-lasting one than most.)

It may be that the story of the fall of Troy as remembered and embellished by Homer relates to the troubled times of the Sea Peoples. A sort of dark age separates the world before 1200 BC from the renewal that occurred among the Greeks about four hundred years later, when the bardic forerunners of Homer began to sing of Troy. When the Greeks took to writing again it was not in the old Cretan script called Linear B, poorly adapted to the Greek language, but in a proper alphabet they took from the Phoenicians during the eighth century BC. The Phoenicians, like the Israelites, had their roots in the Canaanite culture of the Levantine hinterland. They were at the forefront of the revival in international trade that began after 1000 BC, with early trading posts on Cyprus and Crete and the important foundation of a colony at Carthage on the North African coast opposite Sicily in the eighth century BC. The Semitic-speaking Phoenicians inherited and simplified, by about 1000 BC, a basically straightforward alphabetic script that was derived ultimately from the Egyptian hieroglyphs but immensely easier to employ and to adapt to other languages. Via Greek, all modern western alphabets descend from this source. (The Hebrew and early Arabian scripts were also developed from the same basis.)

The society and general outlook of the Greeks was something new in the world, and in most of the Greek communities that spread from the mainland around the islands and across to the west coast of Anatolia citizens enjoyed a freedom of self-expression and an independence of thought unrecorded among any previous peoples – and most since. When in the fifth century BC they fought their linguistic cousins the Persians, who had mopped up what was left of the old empires of Anatolia, Mesopotamia and Egypt, it was as freely associating citizens against an oriental despotism. (Women and slaves were not citizens, however.) Athens, where Plato was to grow up, was to the fore in that

The Acropolis of Athens, Plato's home city. (*Sonia Halllday Photographs*)

Minoan ships in a fresco rescued from the destruction of Thera.
(*Photo: AKG London*)

Volcanic eruption at Santorini in 1926. (*G. Goakimedes*)

Ziggurat at Ur. (*Robert Harding Picture Library*)

The author examining hieroglyphs. (*Sally Horne*)

Pyramid and chacmool at Chichén Itzá. (*Powerstock Zefa*)

Egypt's oldest pyramid, at Sakkara. (*John Ross*)

A bovid painted during the last ice age in the Lascaux cave.
(*Ancient Art & Architecture Collection Ltd*)

Ruins of Knossos on Crete. (*Sonia Halliday Photographs*)

The badly damaged Sphinx and pyramids at Giza. (*John Ross*)

The lion gate of the Hittite capital at Hattusas in Anatolia.
(*Sonia Halliday Photographs*)

The lion gate at Mycenae on mainland Greece. (*Sonia Halliday Photographs*)

The gold 'Mask of Agamemnon' from Mycenae. (*Robert Harding Picture Library*)

The 3.5 million-year-old footprints at Laetoli in East Africa. (*Author*)

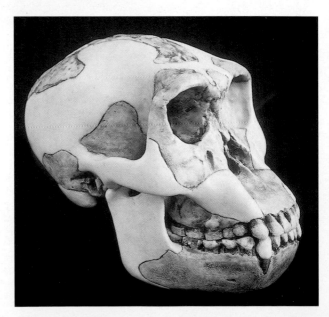

A specimen of *Australopithecus*. (*Author*)

A finely made hand-axe from France. (*Author*)

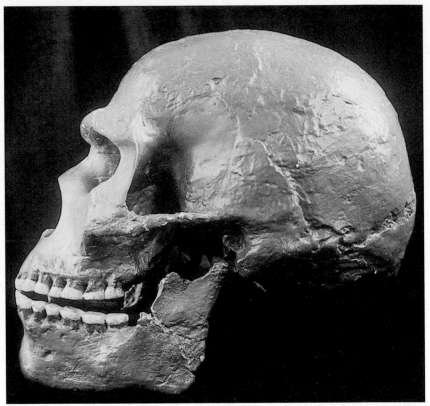

A rugged example of early *Homo sapiens sapiens* from the Levant. (*Author*)

(Opposite) A sphinx in reverse (lion-headed, human-bodied) from ice age Germany – about 30,000 years old. (© *Thomas Stephan, Ulmer Museum*)

The tomb slab of Pacal at Palenque in Central America. (*Mary Evans Picture Library*)

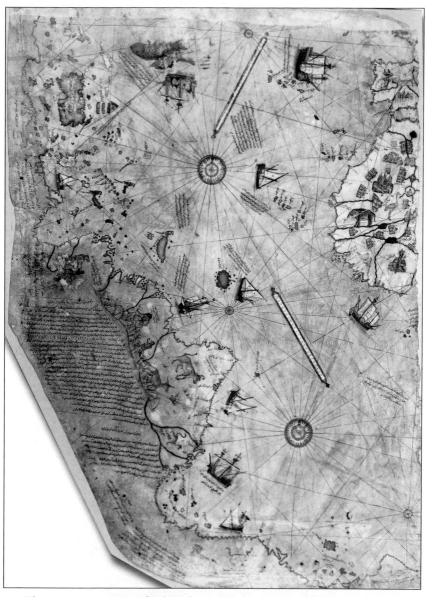

The contentious map of Admiral Piri. (*Topkapi Palace Museum, Istanbul*)

The cyclopean masonry of the fortress at Cuzco in Peru.
(*Robert Harding Picture Library*)

A gigantic Olmec head from Central America. (*Robert Harding Picture Library*)

Aerial view of the mysterious Nazca lines. (*South American Pictures*)

One of the many temples at Angkor Wat. (*Robert Harding Picture Library*)

The Gateway of the Sun among the ruins at Tiahuanaco.
(*Robert Harding Picture Library*)

struggle, which echoes in his story of the long-ago conflict between the Athenians and the invaders from Atlantis.

The history of the world is not, of course, at all the same thing as the history of Europe, the Near East and western Asia. In the Far East agriculture was developed along different lines from the agricultural styles that began in the Fertile Crescent. Rice farming began in northern China at about 7000 BC and by 6000 BC there was farming with pottery in Pakistan. Many people went on for a very long time, however, with a foraging way of life, like the Ainu of the northerly islands off the coast of eastern Asia, who fished and hunted their way into the nineteenth century. But, as elsewhere in the world, the farming revolution led on in some places to urbanization and civilization. The Indus Valley civilization flourished from about 2600 BC and Chinese civilization got under way from about 2000 BC, with writing from about 1800 BC (the start of the longest-surviving writing system in the world, still in use today). By 1500 BC bronze technology was employed in Thailand, where steps had perhaps been taken as early as about 7000 BC towards a farming way of life, though it can be very difficult to distinguish between wild and domesticated forms for the small samples of beans and peas identified.

There is evidence of early cultivation on New Guinea by at least 4000 BC, an independent focus with its own range of domesticates. Australia to the south went on, from some thirty-five thousand years ago when (at the latest) it was first inhabited, with a foraging way of life and a 'stone age' technology of some sophistication, as well as some of the world's earliest art at the start of a very long-lasting artistic tradition. The islands of western Polynesia were inhabited soon after 3500 BC and those of Micronesia by about 1000 BC – there are some very impressive stone-built burial enclosures on Pohnpei that date back to the ninth century BC. Hawaii saw human occupation from about two thousand years ago, with Easter Island inhabited from about AD 300 (the best part of its famous statuary dates from AD 1000 up to comparatively recent times), and New Zealand from about one thousand years ago.

In the Americas the human story followed much the same course as it did in the rest of the world, with the appearance of various farming communities alongside much continuation of the foraging way of life and, in some places, the eventual emergence of city life with complex political structures and written records. In Meso-America (Mexico and the Central American area in general) foraging went on as the principal mode of subsistence well beyond the end of the ice age. Wild maize seems to have been of no particular attraction to the foragers until after about 5000 BC when they started to harvest it on the Gulf coast. They were harvesting it in the highlands by 4000, with signs of deliberate cultivation from about 3400 BC. Even then it was a while before it became a significant feature of their diet that they developed by selective breeding in a settled farming situation. There are some signs of the domestication of squashes as early as 8000 BC, with things like beans, chillis and avocados following on, but in this part of the world it was, according to the archaeological record, a slow progress of gradual resort to more farming and less foraging over a long period, with the dog as the only domesticated animal.

In the southern part of North America adjacent to Mexico farming with maize, beans and squashes was introduced in places at about 1500 BC. In some parts wild grasses and other plants were collected and annually managed on such a scale that 'cultivated' forms were developed without farming as such. Cotton and tobacco were added to the repertoire, but North America saw no domestication of animals beyond the dog and the turkey, and foraging always played a big part in the economy. Thus farming as such can only be said to have existed in parts of the south-west and the south-east of North America. In the region of the Mississippi Valley, the rise of complex society on the basis of the mixed economy of farming and foraging can be plotted with the appearance of earthworks denoting communal efforts under some guiding ideology. The earliest of the earthworks date back to about 1700 BC, but only start to really impress after 750 BC, with more elaboration through the following centuries. The real glories of towns and mounds in this part of south-eastern North America only appear after about AD 700, lasting until around 1500. Cahokia is the best known such town, housing in its heyday perhaps thirty thousand people: Monk's Mound was built there in stages between about AD 900 and 1150, with a large building on top in a basic style seen also in both Central and South America. There is a lively artistic tradition among these people, as with the farmers of the south-west, and both areas were clearly communicating at some level with the civilizations of Meso-America, to which we shall come.

In South America there are indications of wild crop management, but not real cultivation, as long ago as 10,000 BC. Cultivation of potatoes and other tubers might go back to about 8500 BC. By 5000 BC wild forms of cassava, maize and some other plants that were later domesticated are in evidence in the archaeological record at sites on the Pacific coast. There is no reason to think, given the total discrepancy in the range of plants involved, that progress towards domestication here or elsewhere in the Americas was anything but a local affair, owing nothing to farming developments anywhere in the Old World. Pottery-making appeared in the valley of the Amazon at about 5000 BC, again as an independent invention of a technology of worldwide usefulness to settled folk. (Interestingly, the world's oldest mummies come from a coastal community in Chile, whose people were not farmers but semi-settled gatherers of seafood. Stuffed with clay and grass and plastered over, these mummies go back to about 7000 BC and stopped being made at about the same time as the Egyptians started making theirs around 3000 BC.)

Pottery was being manufactured in Ecuador by 3000 BC and by 2500 the plants previously collected in wild form had been so transformed by selective breeding that we know true agriculture was in full swing. Cotton, beans, gourds, maize, grains of various sorts and potatoes and other tubers had all been domesticated from Ecuador down to Peru, and cultivation goes back to 2000 BC at sites in Brazil. Meanwhile llamas for meat and transport and alpacas for wool had been brought under domestication in the Andes by 3000 BC.

From about 2500 BC a mixture of hunting, horticulture and trade supported a society in Peru which built earth and rubble mounds around open courts with constructions of adobe bricks on top, at sites on the coast and in the highlands behind. Finds at these sites include cotton textiles, burials and unbaked clay figurines (with as yet no pottery), suggesting some ritual use for these presumed temples. As in the Old World, the role of ideology in cementing and motivating settled societies is illustrated by archaeological discoveries. (Even among prehistoric peoples who left no written clues about their beliefs the presence of those beliefs can be demonstrated by archaeology.) Pottery was adopted in the Andes only after about 2200 BC, along with agriculture by large-scale irrigation, after which the farming way of life really took off there.

At about 1300 BC in the Moche Valley of northern Peru we encounter clay sculpture in low relief and at about the same time in central Peru we find incised design on stone – with a rather characteristically American scene, in the latter case, involving severed heads and dismembered bodies, that prefigures the cultic depiction of sacrifice of war captives to be seen among the later civilizations of the Americas. There are Andean sites of this period with sunken courts in stone and terraces and stairs, with pyramid-like platforms for temples and palaces. Social life was evidently becoming ever more complicated, with more command over its resources, both raw materials and human effort.

Strongly characterized cultures, more widespread on the ground, appear in the Andean archaeological record around 800 BC. The Chavin culture continued with the temples and courts of earlier times, but added underground galleries (fully developed by about 300 BC) with stelae showing creatures that combine traits from big cats, serpents, humans and birds of prey. The Moche at about the same time likewise continued with the platform mounds, creating in their 'Pyramid of the Sun' the largest such structure in the Americas. Rulers could be buried in great style in clothes decked with gold and silver beads, with some of their human retainers buried with them (in much the same way as the rulers of Ur in Mesopotamia two thousand years earlier). The Paracas people were burying their rulers in textile finery, too, at around 400 BC – their local successors were the Nazca, who created most of the famous Nazca Lines between about 200 BC and AD 700.

In around 500 BC came the rise of the great city of Tiahuanaco by Lake Titicaca, where intensive farming on constructed terraces fed a workforce capable of creating the huge stone-faced platform of the city and its other great buildings, along with some striking monolithic human statuary. To the north-west of Tiahuanaco, another highland great power operated out of Huari. Both these centres collapsed by AD 1000 when, after a few centuries of smaller regional power bases, the Incas arose to absorb them all in the fifteenth century – only to lose it all to the Spaniards in the next century, in the aftermath of an Inca civil war. While they lasted, the Inca, from their capital at Cuzco, ruled over a great empire of thousands of settlements with an administrative system like a cross between ancient Egypt for its taxes, imperial Rome for its roads and Stalin's Russia for its mass deportations of peoples to keep them under control. Their achievement is the more remarkable when they had no system of writing: just knotted strings as *aides-mémoires*.

Progress towards civilization came a little later in Meso-America than in the south. The Olmecs in the humid region at the bottom of the Gulf of Mexico are the first people we know, at around 1300 BC, to develop a strong cultural style that spread beyond their homeland. Their way of life rested on a subsistence of hunting, fishing and small-scale agriculture which they carried on alongside trade to the east and west of them. With their trade went a spread of their distinctive imagery (of the jaguar, in particular), and presumably of the ideology that drove it, into the wider Meso-American world, like a seed of later cultural developments in the whole region. The Oaxaca Valley of Mexico was near the Olmec heartland and evidently was in contact with Olmec life: settled communities were growing up there by 1000 BC. Rubble and earth mounds with platform tops put in their first appearance in Meso-America at about this time. Later on, truly urban complexes grew up in Mexico in city-states like Cholula (where the foundations date back to before 1000 BC), Monte Alban (after 500 BC) and Teotihuacan, with monumental architecture including pyramids during their Classic Period between about AD 200 and 700. The beginnings of Meso-American pyramids go back a few centuries BC, about two thousand years after the heyday of Egyptian pyramid building. The American pyramids are of a different (stepped) form from the developed Egyptian pyramids and, in their early manifestations, have no burials under them, being built as temple platforms. The layout of the religious complexes of which the pyramids form parts were undoubtedly of cosmic significance and the tunnels beneath some of the pyramids show astronomical correlations as well as local topographical alignments. Cholula's pyramid is the largest in the Americas in terms of volume, and was enlarged in about AD 700, at a time when the other old urban centres of Mexico were in decline.

Further south and east in Central America, in the Yucatan Peninsula, the cities of the Maya arose after about AD 200. In these first centuries of the Common Era, archaeological evidence in the form of pottery from the various regions of Meso-America suggests that local life was going its separate ways in different places. But at the same time places far apart were sharing in a common cult of the god Quetzalcoatl, whose acquaintance we made with Donnelly and Spence. He was an old Meso-American deity who first shows up in the archaeological record at Teotihuacan and went through many guises, as gods do, before establishing himself as the feathered serpent we associate with Mexican religion. Thanks to the widespread cult of Quetzalcoatl, ceremonial centres as distant from one another as Chichen Itza of the Maya in Yucatan and Tula of the Toltecs in northern Mexico could show great similarities of design with feathered serpents, reclining Chacmool figures and column statues of warriors in common.

Like the Zapotecs of Monte Alban, the Maya became established in Central America as conquerors who indulged themselves and their gods in the blood sacrifice of enemy captives. Various cities held sway among them at different times, at places like Copan and Palenque, where a famous pyramid contained – like the pyramids of Egypt – the burial of a ruler (called Pacal, who died in AD 683, nearly three thousand years after the last of the pyramids of Old Kingdom Egypt). The precise date of this named ruler's death is known to us because the Maya had writing in hieroglyphs like the Egyptians (though the hieroglyphs had nothing in common), and a calendar system rather better than that of the Egyptians!

The hieroglyphs of the Maya, now largely translated, can be traced back to about 200 BC but were mainly recorded after AD 200. The calendar of the Maya can be counted back to a date of some 3114 BC, simply because Mayan priestcraft structured it that way in much later times as part of their pretension to control all of time, and not because it was developed then.

The Maya collapsed in about AD 900, for internal social reasons or as a result of ecological factors or a combination of these and other forces. But the cult of Quetzalcoatl lasted into the time of the Aztecs in Mexico. The Aztecs probably hailed from northern Mexico (wherever their Aztlan homeland was supposed to be) and came south as mercenaries, who married and allied their way to power at their island city of Tenochtitlan on Lake Texcoco in the fourteenth century. Under the tutelage of their chief deity Huitzilopochtli, god of the sun and war, they were enthusiastic exponents of the ideology of human sacrifice till they went down to the Spanish in 1519.

Such then, in the meanest of thumbnail sketches which will make archaeological specialists wince at its simplifications and generalists weep over its omissions, is the broad outline of the story of human life on earth, tailored especially to take in the parts of that story that are involved in the speculations of the Atlantologists and 'alternative archaeology' enthusiasts. For they set out to overthrow whole tracts of this version of the past that has been so painstakingly put together by a host of scholars all around the world on the basis of the most detailed knowledge available and with the aid of all the best technical resources. Some of the seekers after Atlantis are only modest heretics with limited ambitions to tinker with only bits of the standard story, as we shall see in the next chapter, but others are out to tear great holes in it and replace its rational enquiry into the processes of change in human history with vast romantic speculations of very dubious pedigree.

8

ATLANTIS ABOVE THE WAVES

The Thera hypothesis, which has not yet lost all its adherents, has been the most developed attempt to provide Plato's story of Atlantis with a plausible inspiration that can be squared with orthodox archaeological knowledge. As we saw in Chapter 2, the volcanic explosion of Thera and the collapse of Minoan civilization cannot in the end (some might think even at the outset) be made to explain Plato's material in any detail. Santorini and Crete are not a huge island in the Atlantic Ocean, Minoan civilization did not thrive in 9600 BC (nor did the Egyptian and Athenian varieties), Knossos was nothing like the capital city of Plato's Atlantis, while his Atlantis was not overthrown by a volcano. Even when all sorts of ingenious, and unevidenced, 'corrections' are made to try to account for these giant divergences, it turns out that the Theran volcano did not in any case bring Minoan civilization to its end, which occurred for other reasons after a palpable recovery from any effects of the eruption. The most that can be said for Thera is that some memory of its destruction, whether or not it was passed through the Egyptians, may have contributed in a small way to Plato's literary invention.

We have seen that, since the discovery of the New World in the late fifteenth century and particularly since the speculative thinking of the nineteenth century, the idea of Atlantis has burgeoned into a set of notions that Plato never entertained – notions about an original fount of all civilization, a source of technological innovation, a sump of ancient wisdom. Most continuators of the Atlantis idea persevere with notions such as these, looking for a veritable supercivilization of the forgotten past – unknown to conventional archaeological thinking – to be discerned in the world's multifarious mythologies and in whatever can still be interpreted as problematic or mysterious in the archaeological record.

Just a very few authors still try to find explanations for Plato in conventional archaeological contexts. The geoarchaeologist Eberhard Zangger proposed in 1984 in his *Flood From Heaven* that it was really the story of the Trojan War, coming garbled to Plato through Solon and his Egyptian informants, that Plato found himself writing up at length – until the penny dropped and he gave up (in mid-sentence as we recall) when he saw the futility of the exercise. This does not, of course, do much justice to what we know of Plato's intention to make scientific sense of history through myth nor to his moral purpose in writing of the vices of the latter-day Atlanteans and the virtues of the old Athenians. In detail, Troy on the Anatolian coast below the Dardanelles is even less like Atlantic Atlantis than Crete was and none of the ancient Troys of the stratigraphy of the mound at Hissarlik sank beneath the waves as a result of an earthquake, or for any other reason. It may be that Homer's description of Troy (its situation on a plain and its hot and cold springs, for example) influenced Plato just a little bit, as did the general idea of an old war between Greece and a foreign enemy, but really no more than that can be said. Zangger is an intelligent writer and modest about his theory so we will harry him no further, especially since his idea has not found favour in either archaeological or Atlantological circles.

Two further attempts to relate Atlantis to something within the bounds of archaeological possibility have been made by the (slightly) unorthodox archaeological writer Peter James. His first venture into Atlantological speculation was made in the 1970s, with the theory that Plato had built on Phoenician sailors' stories of islands out in the Atlantic (where perhaps – in places like the British Isles – they had also picked up on legends of flooded lands), combined with 'distant memory of the builders of the great megalithic tombs and stone circles of north-western Europe'. He pointed out that this megalithic tradition was initiated, according to radiocarbon dating, before the founding of the first dynasty of ancient Egypt and goes back beyond 4500 BC, with some signs of an eastward spread that might be reflected in Plato's account of Atlantean penetration into Italy. But James's talk of the 'civilization of the megalith builders' is rather misleading, since they left behind no evidence of such traits as city living or writing that we regard as essential components of civilization. James thought that he had squared a megalithic 'civilization' of the fourth millennium BC with Plato's tenth millennium BC Atlantis by invoking the matter of exaggeration in the Egyptians' estimate of their own history – he was content that his megalith builders of north-west Europe pre-dated the foundation of Egyptian civilization (with real cities and writing) in about 3100 BC.

In his boldly subtitled *The Sunken Kingdom: The Atlantis Mystery Solved* of 1995, James rather disarmingly admits to the inadequacies of his 1970s theory (while, naturally, having none of it as far as his latest one goes). There were, he says, 'a worrying number of loose ends'. The megalithic culture came to no sudden, catastrophic end and there were no Athenians of any sort in 4500 BC. 'Finally, there was a basic implausibility' in the idea that memories of the megalith builders ever reached Egypt and were preserved there, to be colourfully passed on to Solon. Hindsight is a wonderful thing and James has no difficulty now in spotting the deficiencies of his old theory. It has to be said that he is astonishingly blasé about the deficiencies of his current speculations. Still he is able when he reviews his old idea to use it to plant doubts about the whole Egyptian connection in Plato's Atlantis material. As we shall see, he needs to be rid of the Egyptians in order to bring on his new explanation of Atlantis.

James is sound on archaeological detail, sophisticated in his understanding of Plato's purposes (which marks him out from virtually every other contemporary writer on Atlantis) and very fair to all the tendencies of Atlantean explication including the far-fetched. But, because he is going to get round to grinding an axe of his own as his book progresses, he finds himself from the start giving Plato too much of the benefit of the doubt as to the likely factual content of his Atlantis story and downplaying the mythopoetic and moral aspects of Plato's work, at least at the beginning. He needs to do this in order to make it worthwhile to put forward yet another factual sort of explanation for the genesis of the story. Thus he makes a suggestive case for believing that Plato was sincerely attempting to write a factually plausible (if not factually true) prehistory of his culture in the form of a conflict between Atlantis and Athens, in order to show how a once golden age of divinely ordained living, which, for Plato, must have once existed in one way or another, had degenerated into a silver age of change and decay, of the sort Plato actually lived in (like the rest of us). But he underestimates Plato's indifference to really hard fact in favour of mythologizing in ways that might help men to live better lives, if only they could be persuaded to believe in the myths. This is something Socrates explicitly advocates in one of Plato's dialogues. James cries up any possibility that Plato might have been in possession of some factual knowledge of prehistory: he notes, for example, the surviving walls of Mycenaean Athens on the Acropolis and thinks Plato would have known them too and what they meant. He mentions the evidence (which Zangger played an important part in bringing to light) of earthquake destruction at Mycenaean Tiryns and subsequent flooding there when the earthquake diverted the course of a river, as things Plato might once again have known something about, even though they happened about seven hundred years before his time.

James rightly emphasizes that Plato was, according to his lights, trying to think scientifically about the history of the world and to establish general scientific principles about the past. He urges us to revisit Plato's idea of cyclical catastrophism as a now necessary antidote to the prevailing outlook of uniformitarianism whose origin he attributes to Plato's successor, Aristotle. James's book achieves a real measure of intellectual stimulation in this section which is worth looking into further in the light of what we have learned about the history of archaeology as an academic study.

Until the early nineteenth century, as we have seen, most naturalists and geologists inclined to the model of catastrophism to accommodate their growing knowledge of the record of the rocks. As it became apparent that lower and so older strata contained the fossils of creatures unlike the animals of the world today, many scientists concluded that the earth had experienced a series of catastrophic destructions in the past, followed by new creations of fresh lines of animal (and plant) life that thrived until they too were overthrown in the next cataclysm. The French naturalist Georges Cuvier was the most renowned advocate of this theory, which James traces back in large part to Plato's scientific outlook. But Cuvier was always adamant, in a way Plato was not, that humankind belonged only to the latest epoch of creation and human fossils would never be found in association with the remains of the extinct animals of previous bouts of creation. In this way, he accommodated the biblical tradition of Creation, as the final and only human-orientated act of divine genesis. Plato's successor at the academy he founded was not of a predominantly catastrophist turn of mind: Aristotle, according to Peter James, initiated what nineteenth-century scientists called – specifically in relation to geology – uniformitarianism, arguing that the world we know is not the result of a long series of drastic events but rather the product of the slow working of processes we are familiar with today. Aristotle's outlook was already well established in astronomy from the Middle Ages through to Newton (only in the twentieth century modified by ideas like the cosmic 'Big Bang'). The geologists of the first part of the nineteenth century made uniformitarianism the standard model for their science too, though evidence of the ice ages of comparatively recent times imported a measure of catastrophism back into geology. And, of course, Darwin's theory of evolution by natural selection brought uniformitarianism into natural history, as we saw earlier in this book.

In archaeology, catastrophism has expressed itself as a greater emphasis on notions of, for example, invasions of new peoples into old peoples' territory, bringing rapid cultural change without antecedence in the invaded region. It is a catastrophist approach to Egyptian prehistory to see the beginnings of Egyptian culture as a sudden arrival of all sorts of distinctive traits in predynastic Egypt, without local development. A more uniformitarian approach is to chart the local processes of cultural evolution evidenced by archaeological finds in Egypt to show how Egyptian culture in fact emerged at home. In archaeology, the catastrophist persuasion is called diffusionism, since it sees innovation as always introduced from elsewhere; archaeological uniformitarianism has been called 'independent invention', to emphasize the possibilities of human creativity at any time and in any place. In the nineteenth and early twentieth centuries archaeological thinking was often stuck in the diffusionist mode: theories of cultural innovation in one somehow privileged centre, from which civilization was diffused to lesser peoples, were popular. We recall that it was often believed, until the second half of the twentieth century, that the megalithic cultures of western Europe must have been inspired to build in stone by the example at least, if not as a result of colonial expeditions, of the world's first settled civilizations in Egypt and Mesopotamia. Radiocarbon dating showed in the 1960s that the oldest western European megaliths pre-dated those civilizations. Peter James, with his first Atlantean theory, was attempting to reverse the direction of diffusion on the basis of those dates – speculating that Plato's Atlantean invasion of the Mediterranean region went back to megalithic influence going east to Italy and somehow being remembered from prehistoric times in Egypt. James is thus seen as something of an inveterate diffusionist. Other archaeologists have concluded that the megalithic achievement represents an independent development of some social sophistication and technical innovation quite separate from Egyptian and Mesopotamian progress.

In general, archaeologists today favour the idea of independent invention in several separate centres of farming, metalworking, writing, pyramid building, mummification and a host of other less striking cultural traits, especially where widely divergent dates (as for example with pyramids) in far-flung locations are concerned. One reason why archaeologists resist all Atlantological speculation is that it represents an outmoded hyperdiffusionist idea of cultural evolution: and, of course, it only postpones the problem of explaining innovation by pushing it back to another time and another place suspiciously removed from the possibility of investigation by being sunk under the sea or locked in the ice of Antarctica (we'll be coming to that one). Even Atlantis solves nothing if you go on thinking about it.

Diffusionism is a special case of catastrophism. An intrusive cultural package, diffused by invasion or missionary zeal, represents in its new location a disruption and new beginning like one of Plato's cyclical bouts of destruction and renewal. Peter James wants to make a case in his *Sunken Kingdom* for a rehabilitation of Plato's catastrophism in science in general, and in geology and archaeology in particular: he wants us to ease up on Aristotelian uniformitarianism and independent invention. There may be something timely in his plea – even scientific thought has its cycles of fashion (catastrophes and renewals at times, no doubt) and fashions can be rather obsessively followed while they last. Newton's essentially Aristotelian universe has been superseded by Einstein's, and some palaeontologists (not all of them) have espoused the idea of dinosaur extinction by meteorite impact or colossal volcanic disruption; so perhaps, for example, the Late Bronze Age of Europe and the Near East is due for a fresh look with an eye on the possibility of natural disaster (as at Tiryns) as a factor in its close. (Though when James entertains the idea of cometary intervention, other archaeologists are bound to pause.) He thinks most scientists like uniformitarianism just because it's safe and cosy, and dislike catastrophism because it holds out the threat that they might themselves be hit out of the blue by a meteorite or an earthquake. But the truth is that uniformitarianism promises the possibility of generally explaining the world in well known and familiar terms, according to understood processes working in a regular way. In contrast, with catastrophism everything becomes a special case in which less well understood and even freakish events of unpredictable outcome dominate the scene, threatening to let in outlandish and untestable hypotheses that offer little chance of a satisfying general explanation. This is not to say that catastrophic scenarios have no place in science or archaeology, only that they ought to be something of a last resort. (The trouble with Atlantology is that it constitutes one long last resort.)

James is not an Atlantologist in the pejorative sense and his reflections on Plato produce some useful ideas. He suggests, for example, that a conflict arose in Plato's development of the Atlantis theme when he first saw the end of Atlantis as the result of one of his endlessly repeated cycles of destruction, understood in an objective, scientific way – and then went on more and more to picture it as an act of well-deserved divine retribution brought on by the Atlanteans' moral failings. Perhaps, James thinks, this conflict of interpretations became too unwieldy for Plato to go on with.

Sadly, the sophistication of James's reflections on Plato and Aristotle rather deserts him as he comes to his own new theory of Atlantis. Having satisfied himself that Plato was embarked on real history, or prehistory, with his tale of the loss of Atlantis and old Athens, based on real knowledge of Mycenaean Athens that he could not have obtained through the Egyptians, James wants to jettison altogether the Egyptian transmission of the tale to Solon. In this, of course, he is at one with those who regard the whole tale as fictional from start to finish, Solon and all. He, however, does not regard it in this light. He wants to reject Egyptian transmission in favour of transmission to Solon through another cultural milieu, so as to preserve some core of the story as real history. He notes those instances of Plato's drawing on Herodotus, he notes that Herodotus nowhere mentions Atlantis, he notes the Egyptians' well-known indifference to the doings of foreigners. So Solon must, for James, have got the story from some other source during his travels away from home – and Plato must innocently have thought he got it from Egypt because the Egyptians were supposed to go back so far beyond everyone else. At this stage, James has the grace to call what he is about to propose 'a long shot', though by the time we reach the end of his book it isn't at all obvious that he really rates it as modestly as that.

To set the stage for his new proposal about Solon's source, James first resorts to a little myth-mongering that wouldn't be out of place in the pages of Lewis Spence. He asserts, no doubt correctly, that the mythical Titan Atlas – despite his identification with the western mountain range at the edge of the Atlantic – was also closely associated with Anatolia and the east Aegean islands along its coast. He emphasizes the general debt of Greek mythology to the mythological systems of the Hittites of Anatolia and the people there before them. He finds a rough equivalent of Atlas in a Hittite story and in Hittite iconography. 'We are inescapably reminded of the Greek Titans,' he writes, in pure Spence. And so, with Atlas securely established in Anatolian lore to his satisfaction, James turns to speculate about that daughter of Atlas, the island of Atlantis. Prompted by Zangger's Trojan theory of Atlantis, James turns up the Greek geographer Strabo's remarks about earthquakes in Anatolia that swallowed up villages and shattered Mount Sipylus in the reign of a king with the name of another figure from Greek mythology, Tantalus. Earthquakes and a name that could be rearranged as 'Atlantus' alert James to gigantic possibilities.

He is soon satisfied that the career and fate of Tantalus in Greek mythology matches the downfall of the overweening Atlanteans – but it cannot be said the resemblance is compelling as Tantalus was presumptuous rather than greedy and his punishment was to be eternally 'tantalized' with unreachable food and drink under a suspended rock instead of being drowned like the Atlantean miscreants. In any case, Atlas as first king of Atlantis was not at all the cause of the indefinitely later downfall of his remote offspring. James attempts to buttress his identification of Atlas as Tantalus by examining their mythological family relationships and seeing them both as gods holding up mountains, or at least depressed by rocks, relating their names in both cases to the Greek root *tlao*, to bear.

Strabo, who died sometime after AD 23, mentioned by name no city on or near Mount Sipylus but Pliny writing a few years later supplied a name for a city on the site, without mentioning its destruction except to say that it now lay under a marsh: the city's name was Tantalis – even more rearrangeable as Atlantis. Pausanias at about AD 120 compared the fate of this city near Mount Sipylus with the loss of Helice on the Gulf of Corinth (which as we have seen undoubtedly influenced Plato) in 373 BC, as having experienced the same sort of earthquake followed by collapse into the earth and flooding – under a lake in this case (presumably Pliny's marsh). James, of course, sees the shadow of Atlantis in all this.

Mount Sipylus as identified today stands about 50 kilometres inland along the River Gediz, which flows into the Aegean Sea north of Izmir. This region was the ancient kingdom of Lydia, whose last ruler was the fabled (but historically attested) Croesus, of immense wealth. Tantalus was a much earlier, and not historically attested, king of Lydia. The historical Lydian capital city was Sardis, a little further inland than Mount Sipylus, and Mycenaean pottery has been found there, bringing it into the orbit of Greek protohistory. The Hittites of inland Anatolia in the second millennium BC recorded the name of people they called the Ahhiyawa, whom most scholars today identify with Homer's Achaean Greeks of the Trojan War (or Mycenaeans as we call them archaeologically). So for James a further parallel with Plato's story is established: the possibility of conflict between ancient Lydia and Greece. He can't resist speculation that the story of the Athenian hero Theseus's expedition to Asia Minor may also reflect such a Late Bronze Age conflict; and he throws in a Lydian tradition from a time slightly later than Solon that Lydians founded the kingdom of the Etruscans in Italy and a son of Tantalus got to Palestine – to recall Plato's claim of the Atlanteans' invasion of Italy and menacing of Egypt!

There follows a good read of James's adventures in locating the long-lost ancient city of Tantalis close by modern Mount Sipylus, which he identifies in the Hittite archives as Zippasla. He finds no lake or even marsh today, though he avers that there was a small lake at the foot of Sipylus not so long ago, pumped out for extra farmland. He finds no ancient city either, nor the faintest relic of it, though there are Hittite monuments in the vicinity including a carved figure of a mother goddess that gazes down on his one-time lake from the side of the mountain. In the absence of any remains, it is possible to speculate that an ancient city might have been collapsed by earthquake into a chasm that filled with spring water and later became a marsh. James considers such a fate enough like Plato's description of the end of Atlantis to justify a hypothesis that Atlantis was based upon Tantalis. One could apply the Atlantic test at this point to disqualify this new candidate out of hand, as well as pointing out the obvious topographical dissimilarities between Plato's Atlantis, island and city, and any conceivable features of a Lydian city in the terrain around

Mount Sipylus. Such cavils would reduce James's suggestion to the level reached already by the Thera theory: it would remain possible that either or both made a minor contribution to Plato's imaginative processes, if he ever heard of them. The signs are that James rates his notion higher than that.

In James's scheme of things, Plato would have heard of Tantalis through Solon as he says, but Solon would have obtained his information not from the Egyptians but from the Lydians at some other point in his travels. And Herodotus does indeed relate that Solon also visited Lydia and conversed at Sardis with its last king, Croesus. So James is able to take his long shot and speculate that Solon learned about the destruction of Tantalis at Sardis, picked up those Italian and Levantine hints of Lydian history, even became impressed by nationalistic claims on the part of Croesus and his cronies for the great longevity of Lydian history. Solon would have seen the connection with Atlas and himself made the shift of the story to the west, where the Atlas mountains arise, before ever Plato got to work on his material. (James notes that Plato elsewhere mentions Tantalus with no suggestion at all of relating him to Atlantis.)

And so a book that starts well and continues thoughtfully ends in a riot of speculation, with not a shred of archaeological evidence to support it. Even if such evidence came to light, we would really have no more here than another contributory factor to Plato's essentially imaginative creation. It is hard to believe that anything about Mount Sipylus that Solon got from Croesus down the road in Sardis and then relocated to the far west could ever have been mistaken for real history by Plato (who in any case had to supply the Egyptian connection for himself). What Peter James has contributed to our body of diagnostic features of the Atlantis Syndrome is the attempted rehabilitation of catastrophism as a concept worth taking seriously in exploring the past history of mankind. Atlantology is, unsurprisingly since it started with Plato, a catastrophist notion. But many Atlantologists use their chosen catastrophe (volcano, earthquake, flood, cometary impact, sudden glaciation, dabbling with the forces of nature) as a casual device to shuffle off their particular version of Atlantis and explain its current unavailability for archaeological investigation. Unconsciously perhaps, there is a romantic appeal about a one-off cataclysm that removes a one-off ancient supercivilization. There's very little appeal, though, in such an idea for orthodox archaeologists, with – as James sees it – their Aristotelian and uniformitarian prejudices. His special contribution to the Syndrome is to try to make grand-scale cyclical catastrophism respectable again, though it might be thought that a landslip in old Anatolia makes a rather feeble showing as an example of the workings of a universal scheme of such cosmic pretensions.

Another attempt to find a terrestrial and relatively (only relatively) unsensational home for Atlantis was made by a writer named J.M. Allen in 1998, in his also boldly subtitled *Atlantis, The Andes Solution*. This book's dedication is yet bolder, 'To the people of that great continent, presently called South America, and formerly called: ATLANTIS'. What follows is, however, markedly less bold in its intellectual sophistication and archaeological *savoir faire* than James's work. Allen's background is the air force and aerial photo interpretation, later on working in cartography. His relief models of South America and the Bolivian Altiplano, illustrated in his book, are a credit to him.

And, as the title of his book suggests, it is to South America and the Andes that he looks for his location of Plato's Atlantis. Picking up on earlier Atlantological speculation, Allen interprets the name 'Atlantis' as being made up out of the Mexican Aztecs' word for water – 'atl' – plus 'antis', the original form of 'Andes', which Allen says means copper in the Quechua language of the Andean Highlands. ('Antilia' was also derived from 'antis' according to Allen, with the addition of the Romance languages' root for island, to mean Copper Island.) A hint of what is to come, and one of Allen's blessedly few descents into myth-mongering, is offered us when he confidently declares that the Golden Apples of the Hesperides were really lumps of copper.

Allen goes on to talk about his long-held interest in ancient units of measurement (one of the bees so prevalent in the bonnets of 'alternative archaeology' enthusiasts) and about his search for a location with Plato's Atlantean dimensions in the Americas. He has fixed on the Altiplano of Bolivia as the site which matches Plato's stated measurements for the plain of

Atlantis and its surrounding topography. It isn't entirely plain sailing, however, with Plato's rectangle of 2000 2 3000 stades, since the usual equivalency of about 185 metres per stade brings out the plain of Atlantis about twice the size of the Altiplano's very roughly rectangular and level area, which Allen tells us is 'the largest perfectly level plain in the world'. This problem is soon resolved to Allen's satisfaction by, in this instance, halving Plato's stadia to about 92 metres in today's terms. The rationale for this appears to be that Solon used the familiar Greek word stadion to translate something from the Atlantean original (via Egyptian) that was a unit of only half the extent. With this convenient correction, Allen is able to embark on an equation of Atlantean and Andean topography: the mountains are there, ringing the plain; the plain isn't far from the ocean (the Pacific, however, not the Atlantic); there is a sea of sorts to represent Plato's Atlantic on the eastern edge of the plain in the shape of the shallow Lake Poopo; there's even a short stretch of a feature to be seen on a satellite photograph that Allen interprets as part of Plato's great encircling canal. He sets a lot of store by this 'canal', as we shall see.

Allen is pretty naïve about Plato's text, reading only in translation and impressed to find different translators offering slightly different details for him to pick and choose from. He especially clings to Donnelly's version which includes not only earthquake and flood but also rain as agents of the end of Atlantis. Allen seems to need a lot of rain to fill up the irrigation channels he pictures on the plain and the great canal he believes to surround it, so as to flood through his Atlantis City on the edge of Lake Poopo and thus raise the level of the lake to swallow up the town. Just the town for Allen, not the whole island of Atlantis as per Plato, which Allen identifies with the entire continent of South America. (Later on, returned to something like its present shallow state, Lake Poopo becomes for Allen Plato's unnavigable Atlantic shoals – a startlingly implausible idea given Plato's plain speaking about the ocean just outside the Pillars of Hercules.) As one who has read Plato in his original Greek, I am able to settle the matter of rain for Mr Allen here and now – Plato does not mention it in connection with the sinking of Atlantis. Nor does he mention any volcano, though Allen more than once writes as though Plato specifically identified an extinct volcano as the core of the acropolis of the city of Atlantis. For Allen, though, all in all 'it is very obvious that the land called by Plato "Atlantis" is the same which today we call "South America"'. Just as Plato's measurements seem to Allen to need adjustment, so does his chronology. Picking up on suggestions made more than once before in connection with Atlantis, Allen thinks the Egyptian records or their Atlantean originals must have meant lunar months and not years, so that the war between Atlantis and the Mediterranean world comes down to about 1200 BC and thereby turns out to be recorded in the Egyptians' depictions of their battles against the Sea Peoples. Allen's surmise is that a survivor of the battles against the Sea Peoples, taken prisoner by the Egyptians, told the tale of Atlantis to his captors, who passed it on to Solon about six hundred years later – despite what Plato says of the Egyptian priests' boasts about the extreme longevity of their records.

With only the city of Atlantis submerged (in Lake Poopo) and not the entire huge island of Atlantis (in the Atlantic) as Plato asserts, it was possible according to Allen for the Phoenicians to carry on routine commerce with South America after the power of the Atlanteans was broken, bringing back metals in particular by a route across the Atlantic, round the Cape of Good Hope and up the Indian Ocean to the Persian Gulf and Red Sea. (He is convinced that Plato's orichalcum was in fact the naturally occurring alloy of gold and copper found only in the Andes and that the Incas' use of metal cladding on some of their walls is just what Plato was talking about for the circling city walls of Atlantis.) Allen offers absolutely no archaeological evidence for Old World commerce with the Andes, either in the form of Phoenician or Carthaginian material in South America (and the Altiplano in particular) or of demonstrably Amerind material in the Old World – other than the cocaine mummy claims we have already mentioned. In general, the importance of archaeological context seems lost on Mr Allen altogether and he presents himself as innocently baffled by the failure of academic archaeologists – in Cambridge especially – to jump at his speculations.

So impressed is Allen with his own identification of the Altiplano with Plato's description of the irrigated plain of Atlantis and its stade-wide encircling canal that he writes, rather incredibly, that 'it only remains to discover on site evidence of a channel 600 ft wide to say without any more doubts that here indeed is the proof that the city and civilization of Atlantis existed in these parts'. Later on he refers to finding such a stretch of canal as 'ultimate proof, short of locating the city itself, of the truth of Plato's story'. These chaps frequently have a bizarre notion of what could ever constitute proof of such things. Just one length of channel will evidently do for Jim Allen, with no call to find any archaeological artefacts at all, let alone any coherent archaeological context, to say nothing of the lost city itself in Lake Poopo. (He does later on talk briefly of 'large-scale canalization' elsewhere on the plain but illustrates this contention with a section of a satellite photograph so hugely enlarged to blurry disintegration that it might show anything at all. He also shows old pictures of the Aztec capital in Mexico with its canals and islands to bolster the idea of Atlantean town planning in the Americas.) Let us note, too, that Plato's one stade for the width of the conjectured channel does not appear to be in need of the halving brought to bear on his dimensions for the plain it is supposed to surround: this channel is going to be one regular Greek stadion in overall width.

It will not perhaps surprise my readers to hear that Allen does indeed go on to find his Atlantean canal with the required 185 metre (approx.) width – or rather a short run of it (in relation to the 10,000 stades-worth of Plato's full encircling channel) somewhere to the north-west of Lake Poopo. It is the feature he spotted on the satellite photograph and he duly finds a run of it on the ground in circumstances he describes with a lot of local colour. Its width, so closely matching Plato's claim, he determines by a combination of pacing and visual estimation on site. In fact, the satellite photograph he includes in his book by no means shows the sort of straight, regular 'canal' of uniform width we would expect of Plato's Atlanteans and Allen's brief investigation on the ground does nothing whatever to establish the feature's artificial origins. To me it looks as much like a geological feature as any canal. Its extent

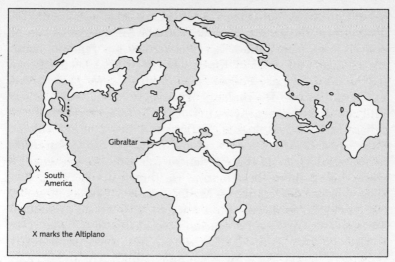

Gibraltar →

South America

X marks the Altiplano

How to put South America opposite the Strait of Gibraltar, like Plato's Atlantis, according to J.M. Allen's projection.

is not clear and no associated archaeological evidence of any sort is brought on.

That is about it, really. The cartographer in Allen allows him to show a world map with a projection so chosen as to tilt and fold away South America so that it looks a bit more like a large island across from the Strait of Gibraltar than usual, but not very much so; he also offers us another map with South America turned through 90° counter-clockwise, so that the Altiplano seems to nestle in the crook of the Pacific seaboard facing south, as Plato said the Atlantean plain did, though of course in reality the Pacific is to the east and not south. Allen's justification for this is an old map of Peru disorientated in this same fashion. As we shall further see, map-bending is a not unknown proclivity of the Atlantologists, as is pole-shifting: Allen, like many another Atlantologist, thinks the north pole was once in the Hudson Bay region, putting the Altiplano on the equator at the time and making it a champion place to live, complete with Plato's elephants. Oh, and Thera gets a look-in, as a possible Mediterranean base of the Atlanteans for their assault on Greece and Egypt, and perhaps Troy was another. A good idea of the general sophistication of the argument can be derived from Allen's ready acceptance of a few remarks about the linguistic affinities of the languages around Lake Titicaca (to the north of Lake Poopo) culled from a *Lonely Planet* travel guide to Bolivia. He makes surprisingly scant use of Lake Titicaca and the nearby ruins of Tiahuanaco, generally so venerated by Atlantologists. El Dorado is invoked and Colonel Fawcett, and Allen seems at one point to find something meaningful *vis-à-vis* the Garden of Eden in the presence of giant snakes along the Amazon. He thinks the vaguely boat-shaped geological feature on Mount Ararat in Turkey might be 'the fossilized remains of an ancient reed vessel', and that Tartessus was really a Phoenician port on the River Plate.

This is very thin stuff, though not over immodestly presented. I don't think Mr Allen understands real archaeology at all, which is a pity even if it exonerates him from wilful misrepresentation of real archaeological procedure – which is more than can be said for all the exponents of Atlantology. His contribution to our overview of the Atlantis Syndrome is perhaps to underline how readily something like Plato's story can be skewed into very superficial approximation to some known situation in history and geography, in fact to a number of quite different and mutually incompatible situations. James says Anatolia, Allen says Bolivia, others say Thera or a host of alternative locations. As might be said of competing belief systems in general, these theories cannot all be right – but they could very likely all be wrong.

9

THE ICING ON
ATLANTIS

Perhaps the ultimate catastrophist vision of Atlantis, beyond which it will never be possible for Atlantologists to go on this earth, is realized in another work of 1995 (the year of Peter James's plea for catastrophism), called *When the Sky Fell*, by a Canadian couple with the beguilingly Atlantean-sounding surname of Flem-Ath, Rose and Rand Flem-Ath.

In the Flem-Aths' book, we are faced with none of the philosophical sophistication of Peter James and with no complex, subtle reflections on Plato's purpose and the conceivable sources of his work. Practically from the start, seemingly on the basis of Plato in the *Critias* rather than the *Timaeus*, they invoke the oddly precise date of 9600 BC as the key and all-important point in time on which everything in their work depends: geological upheaval, biological disaster, movement of peoples and technological innovation. This date of 9600 BC is reiterated throughout the rest of their book (except for an appendix at the end, as we shall see). I say they invoke this date 'practically from the start' because, in a manner familiar from other Atlantological writings, they go in four pages from more modestly talking of a date of 'roughly 11,600 years ago (9600 BC)' to 9600 BC without qualification at the next mention. After that, there's no 'roughly' about it for the rest of the main text. In fact, the Flem-Aths never really do substantiate the precision of this date, but it seems to rely on Plato's not very clear dating of the war between Athens and Atlantis in the *Critias* (though something like 9420 BC would be easier to deduce from that work) rather than on the suggestion of a date after 8600 BC in the *Timaeus*. They frequently write as though 9600 BC were a well-attested geological date of some sort for the cataclysms, mass extinctions and archaeological developments they deal with throughout their book, but it is not obvious on what evidence such a date can be arrived at.

The Flem-Aths lean very heavily on the work of an American history teacher named Charles Hapgood, who devised an unorthodox geological theory from the late 1950s which he called 'earth crust displacement'. He proposed that the earth's crust is subject at intervals to sudden slippages in one piece over the interior body of the planet, rather as though the peel of an orange could be separated from the segments inside and turned about without connection to its innards. Hapgood seems to have envisaged this slippage as a naturally occurring phenomenon, as a result of uneven weight distribution of the planet's polar ice and land-masses as it spins on its tilted axis and orbits the sun in a less than perfect circle – others have added comet or asteroid collisions as further triggering factors. It has to be said that 'earth crust displacement' has found no favour with professional and academic geologists. Something a bit like it has been proposed again in recent years, but in terms of a very slow movement over millions of years of crust and mantle together in relation to the central core, with no effect whatever at the earth's surface, let alone a cataclysmic one.

Hapgood's best-known work is his *Maps of the Ancient Sea Kings* of 1966, in which he developed the theme of a lost seagoing civilization of the prehistoric past, whose detailed knowledge of the global geography of its time is reflected in certain puzzling maps of the sixteenth century. In particular, Hapgood thought one of these maps (we shall come to them presently) showed Antarctica partly free of ice, as he conjectured it would have been prior to an episode of sudden earth crust displacement that moved it over the south pole, more or less overnight. Hapgood thought this happened at something more than ten thousand years ago, though we know of no evidence in any rock samples from the past twenty thousand years of palaeomagnetic orientations that would support this idea. At all events, it is clear that a once unglaciated Antarctica will be the Flem-Aths' choice as the location of their version of Atlantis: since shifted, flooded over and then frozen, with some survivors fleeing to the ever temperate highland zones to the north. Though not in detail related to it, this notion is reminiscent of the crackpot 'World Ice Theory' of Hanns Hörbiger, who thought most of the matter in the universe was frozen water, which exploded at intervals when it fell into hot stars: his version of Atlantis also got frozen up. Hörbiger saw human history as a cycle of such cleansing cataclysms, followed by Aryan-style renewals, and his theories were very popular with the Nazi Party, whose members might justly be called persons of a remorselessly catastrophist outlook.

The so-called thinker among the Nazis, Alfred Rosenberg, inclined to a pre-Hapgood version of the wandering pole idea in his *Der Mythus des 20 Jahrhunderts* of 1934, locating the original home of the Germans on a cold, pure, semi-arctic lost continent which had somehow made them the men they were today. Interestingly, much the same idea had already been floated in the romantic racist novels of Edmund Kiss, who got his Aryans to their arctic haven from Atlantis itself. Purportedly 'scientific' ideas are sometimes inspired by fiction. Under Goebbels, German archaeologists were actually encouraged to go looking for Atlantis, with no luck of course. Rather more directly in line with the Flem-Aths' vision of Atlantis in Antarctica was the work of another pre-Second World War writer, the Frenchman René-Maurice Gattefossé, who proposed an Arctic pre-Atlantis from which civilization spread to Plato's Atlantis and the rest of the world, inspiring megaliths like Stonehenge and the cyclopean architecture of the Incas. Gattefossé plumped for changes in the earth's axis rather than Hapgoodian crust displacements.

Hapgood shades into Plato at the end of the Flem-Aths' first chapter and they start their next with a colourful and circumstantial account of the aftermath of catastrophe; it reads like a continuation of Plato's Atlantis story but is in fact based on his general suggestions about how small bands of survivors might gather themselves together after any one of his

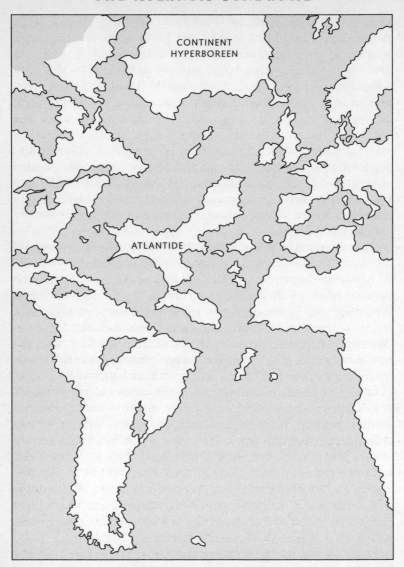

Gattefossé's version of Atlantis.

cycles of destruction. Plato mentions no survivors at all of the Atlantis débâcle (indeed his clear implication is that there were not going to be any). But the Flem-Aths picture just such survivors – only from a more Hapgoodian advanced maritime sort of lost civilization – encountering primitive hunter-gatherers in the lands to which they escaped from their destroyed home island. With the stimulus of the arrival of the Atlanteans, these hillbillies at various places around the world promptly go on, according to the Flem-Aths, to take the first steps we know of in the archaeological record towards the farming way of life, in that golden year of 9600 BC. (Plato in the *Laws* never suggests that renewals would come this quickly on the heels of disasters, nor that they would need external stimulation.)

For the Flem-Aths to be so dogmatic about worldwide farming innovation in 9600 BC flies in the face of archaeological knowledge. There is, as we have seen, evidence for a sort of proto-agricultural trend in the low-lying Nile Valley as early as about fifteen thousand years ago, but the Natufian people of Palestine were evolving true cultivation, on the basis of a long period of harvesting but not sowing grasses, at about 9000 BC. In Peru, contrary to the Flem-Aths' claim of 9600 BC yet again, the cultivation of potatoes and other roots starts even later, just possibly going back to about 8500 BC. At Spirit Cave in Thailand (in 9600 BC according to the Flem-Aths, though the sequence actually starts at about 8500 BC), the surviving sample of plant food remains was very small and it is difficult to tell whether wild or domesticated varieties of peas and beans were present, while carbonized rice grains occur only at a later stage in a different Thai cave and there too it is difficult to distinguish between domesticated and wild. Less ambiguous evidence of the farming way of life with pottery only occurs at Spirit Cave at about 6800 BC.

The Flem-Aths are evidently struck by Plato's hypothesis of survival in the world's highlands away from the waters of his cyclical floods and want to tie this in with theories of the origin of plant cultivation in temperate highland zones. They don't pick up on Plato's contention (through the Saite priests) that Egypt was uniquely able to survive both flood and scorching heat – which Atlantologists like Donnelly and Spence thought made it such a good place for their Atlantean survivors to resort to. Earth crust displacement requires Egypt (along with Crete, Sumer, India and China) to have been tropical before the slippage and so not an immediately good place to start farming in: only when it and the other places settled into a temperate regime could the farmers descend from their ancestral highland homes and get civilization going. (I know of no evidence to suggest that Egypt, Crete and the rest were blessed with tropical conditions before 9600 BC.) The Flem-Aths therefore propose an interlude in the Ethiopian Highlands for the ancestors of the Nile Valley civilization; those highlands, they tell us, 'may yet yield surprises for archaeologists'.

With vague claims that earth crust displacement theory can not only explain agricultural origins and the post-Atlantean beginnings of civilization but also the peopling of the Americas and 'puzzling glaciation patterns found in both hemispheres', the Flem-Aths are off on what Atlantologists always do best – making mountains out of myths. And they begin, with a wearying sense of déjà vu for the reader, with that hoary story from a Ute Indian source (via *Popular Science Monthly* in 1880) of the hare-god singed by the sun – already peddled by Donnelly and not heard of here for the last time, either. This tale of the dangerously wandering sun is not treated by the Flem-Aths to a cometary or asteroid explanation: rather, of course, it was crust displacement that produced a sudden apparent shift in the course of the sun, with concomitant scorchings and floodings (the tears of the hare-god, you will recall). It is an interesting case of the way in which myths can be made to help 'prove' several quite different theories of catastrophe. As usual, any tales from anywhere of flooded islands and the like are related to Atlantis by the Flem-Aths, but it has to be said that their myth trawl is mercifully skimpier than is the case with many Atlantological authors and therefore considerably less tedious to plough through, with many fewer of those unpronounceable folkloric names that seem to hold such a fascination for most writers in this vein.

After this first essay in myth-based argument, the Flem-Aths turn to postglacial catastrophism as a mainstay of their evidence for the truth of their Atlantis in Antarctica. They make much of the mass extinctions of animal species at the close of the last ice age, in order to substantiate their notion of cataclysmic mayhem following the latest of Hapgood's earth crust displacements. Since other writers have built on the Flem-Aths' work (ultimately Hapgood's) in respect of this matter of alleged global catastrophe at the end of the last ice age, it is worth looking into their vision of events in some detail, to see how it compares with the findings of geology and palaeontology. Several species including the giant deer, woolly rhino, sabre-toothed tiger, mastodon and some sorts of bear died out in their respective haunts shortly after the final cold phase of the last glaciation. But it is the mammoth that has continued to fascinate ever since the first frozen body of one of these beasts was discovered in the Siberian permafrost in 1692. Another one was better publicized in 1804 and entered into the orbit of the great naturalists of the day like Georges Cuvier, who pointed out the cold-adapted nature of the mammoth in light of the hairy coat and thick layer of fat exhibited by the frozen finds. This observation of Cuvier's is not often reported by the Atlantologists, the Flem-Aths included, since it goes against their theory that vast numbers of these animals were extinguished when an erstwhile temperate habitat suddenly turned very cold. It is true that stomach contents of mammoth carcasses (with mosses, grasses and vegetation from low shrubs) do sometimes indicate slightly warmer conditions than those prevailing today in the regions where they are found, but those slightly warmer conditions were still cold ones suitable for a cold-loving species like the mammoth. The frozen north today has its short springs and summers and even in winter food can be found under the snow: the wear on the mammoths' tusks indicates their use in scraping the snowed-under surface of the ground. The last ice age, moreover, did not end in one go with an unbroken return to warmer conditions: at around 10,500 years ago, after a long period of gradual warming, a cold snap came on over about one hundred years and lasted a further seven hundred, before ending in a few decades.

Even when the ice age was finally over, temperatures never stabilized completely and there have been three periods in the

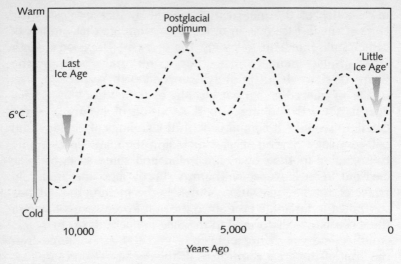

Rising and falling temperatures from the end of the last ice age.

last ten thousand years when average temperatures were higher than they are today, separated by two periods when they were lower. After the initial warming up, there was a slightly cooler spell and then an optimum period when things were warmer than they are today from about 5000 to 4000 BC, followed by another drop until temperatures rose again to peak around 2000 BC, after which a new low (colder than today) followed at about 1000 BC. There was another rise and then came the so-called 'Little Ice Age' of the later Middle Ages. There were similar fluctuations within the hundred thousand years or so of the last ice age itself, with cold stadials and milder interstadials (even if these never reached quite the warmth of interglacial and postglacial times). There is nothing surprising about finding a cold-adapted creature like a mammoth – frozen at some time around the end of one of these fluctuations within or at the end of the last ice age or a bit later – with stomach contents indicating slightly warmer conditions than are met with at the find site today. The circumstances in which the eighty or so mammoth bodies we now have were preserved themselves indicate the basically cold

186

conditions of their time, for they fell into anaerobic mud and silt along river banks or into marshes that later froze over them and became incorporated into the permafrost (even in warmer periods) before serious decay could set in. (Just the same sort of thing happened to an Eskimo family at Barrow in Alaska around AD 1500: they became permanently frozen, till their recent discovery, after summer meltwater got into their home following an accident that killed them all. The well-preserved bodies from the Pazyrik graves of southern Siberia, of about 400 BC, represent a similar case, this time deliberate, of summer burials in soil that subsequently became permanently frozen.) Mammoths, then, were quite simply part of the cold fauna complex, which included woolly-coated rhinos and reindeer, of the cold stadials of the ice age.

Cuvier's sound assessment of the cold-adapted nature of the mammoths is not something the Atlantologists care to highlight. But the Flem-Aths do record Cuvier's remarks, in connection with 'carcasses of some large quadrupeds', about 'calamities which, at their commencement, have perhaps moved and overturned to a great depth the entire outer crust of the globe'. It is worth noting that today's Atlantology pays so much regard to the opinions of a naturalist dead these 168 years, whose extreme catastrophist views were outmoded within a generation of his death. Even so, he wasn't talking about earth crust displacement when he dilated on his 'calamities', though the Flem-Aths would like to have it so: they write of 'Cuvier's theory that mass extinctions were caused by displacements of the earth's crust'. (Hapgood himself comes up with some pretty convoluted arguments about the best known of the mammoth corpses, from Berezovka, to try to accommodate its radiocarbon date of about 45,000 BP which puts it inconveniently into a warming rather than a cooling period for Siberia according to his theory. With some rather give-away remarks like 'can we fit this into our scheme?' and 'of course, there has to be a way out', Hapgood proposes that the Berezovka mammoth fell into a very deep crevasse that was still permanently frozen 'perhaps several hundreds of feet deep': this fissure was then, he suggests, filled in by more of his earth shocks and sealed in the permafrost; after that he has to envisage a long period of heavy river erosion to bring the body back to light, but not before things have turned cold again to keep it preserved as it got back to the surface in our day. In any case, Hapgood seems to have realized that his crust displacements could hardly have been fast enough to flash-freeze whole rafts of species out of existence at a stroke, and he came to emphasize concomitant volcanoes with their dust clouds, poison gas emissions and electric storms as the real killers. His successors have picked up on all that with enthusiasm.)

Palaeontologists agree that there were extinctions of some species at the end of the last ice age – different species in different places and at slightly different times – but they were not caused by any sudden global catastrophe as far as we can see, and it is important to bear in mind that the term 'mass extinction' as used by palaeontology refers not so much to finding hecatombs of animal remains in one spot as to noting that some species that feature in older geological deposits cease to feature in later ones, having somehow or another become extinct. In fact, the most plausible and widely accepted theory of these extinctions is that they were largely caused by hunting overkill on the part of human groups who had become clever enough in the course of the last ice age to spread into new lands like Siberia and North America and develop the hunting skills to carry out the slaughter when the changed environment at the end of the period of glaciation permitted it. Especially in central Europe, the camp sites of the fully modern physical types of the Upper Palaeolithic period are awash with (and sometimes largely built out of) mammoth bones – which occur in these archaeological contexts in far greater numbers than can be accounted for by the frozen bodies found in Siberia. Not all of these bones can have been collected from mammoth graveyards in gullies and along river banks – some of them were hunted and the Palaeolithic cave paintings of western Europe indicate the importance of the mammoth for the Crô-Magnon people. No doubt there were climatic and environmental factors too (it got too cold at times in some places even for the cold-adapted mammoth, drastically reducing their food supply), but the Pleistocene period is not as a whole riddled with mass faunal extinctions at the ends of its ice ages so the human factor is very important at the end of the last one. Talk of 'mass extinctions' is again rather misleading if it suggests massive evidence for such faunal losses, as though Siberia were knee-deep in mammoth carcasses: most of the preserved bodies probably represent herds that had spread to the regions where we find their remains today during milder interstadial phases of the last ice age, or during milder periods than today at the close of the last ice age, and then were caught out when things turned colder again.

The Flem-Aths (and other writers who have come after them, as we shall see) drew on Hapgood for their vision of a cataclysmic end to the ice age with mass extinctions left, right and centre. Hapgood, as is clear from his works, in turn drew on a popular book by Frank C. Hibben called *The Lost Americans*, published as long ago as 1946. It is from Hibben that the oft-quoted notion of worldwide mass extinctions running to forty million animals of one sort or another comes into Atlantological literature. That was entirely an imaginative estimate on Hibben's part and he generally wrote in a colourful vein, though it is interesting to note that his *Prehistoric Man in Europe* of 1959 contains no such extravagances about global mass extinctions. One has a feeling that Hapgood was casting around for anything that might seem to bolster his theory of earth crust displacement and *The Lost Americans* suited his requirements. Hibben's piece of popular science writing was fairly old hat when Hapgood took it up, very old hat by the time the Flem-Aths inherited it, and hopelessly old hat now, although current authors still repeat it, seemingly in entire oblivion of modern detailed work on the stadial/interstadial chronology and the palaeontology of the last ice age and its aftermath.

The other aspect of the catastrophist vision of the end of the ice age, alongside the faunal mass extinctions, is the question of rising sea level and flooding and here too Hapgood and the Flem-Aths did pioneering work that has been drawn on by their successors in the field of Atlantological speculation. The Flem-Aths take up Hapgood's suggestion that it is the weight of ice unevenly distributed about the poles that pulls the earth into the periodic crust slips they all believe in. (Hapgood himself rather abandoned this explanation in his 1970 book *The Path of the Pole*, preferring to concentrate on 'proofs' of displacement rather than theories to explain it.) The Flem-Aths sagaciously add the factor of slight irregularities in the earth's orbit, with consequent gravitational influences of the moon, planets and sun as further complexities contributing to moments of slippage. However such slippages might (or might not, according to orthodox geologists) come about, the Flem-Aths believe they lead to sudden periods of melting for ice-caps previously built up at the poles that now find themselves in warmer latitudes: if these meltings coincide with periods of global warming for other reasons (of the sort the orthodox geologists endorse), then they think the world faces a real problem of rapid and extensive melting with steeply rising sea levels following in short order. (The Flem-Aths reckon that new ice-caps soon form at the new poles – new from a crustal point of view – and the whole thing starts again, to build up to the next slip.) Other Atlantological writers have drawn on the Flem-Aths' vision of catastrophic melting, and built it up even more than they do – so it is important to see what orthodox geology has to say about the process of sea level rise after the last ice age.

Sea level goes down during ice ages chiefly because more precipitation falls in the form of snow in polar and mountainous regions than in warmer times and then fails to melt away to run back into the sea: water evaporated from the oceans becomes locked up in expanding ice sheets. Sea level fell by about 120 metres during the last ice age, which reached its coldest phase at about eighteen thousand years ago. And in fact the ice began to melt by 17,000 BP, with a slow sea level rise in consequence that speeded up after about 14,000 BP to something like 2.4 to 3.7 centimetres per year for a while before about 11,000 BP: hardly the stuff of universal deluge. The cold spell at around 10,500 BP slowed the rate of rise for some seven centuries, but when it accelerated again sea level rose to about 25 metres below its present height by 8,000 BP, since when it has continued to rise more gently (maybe with some fluctuations) till today. The evidence for rates of sea level rise over this period comes in the form of old shorelines, terraces and coral reefs dated for their organic content by means of the radiocarbon and uranium-series methods at various locations in Florida, Barbados, Massachusetts, the Netherlands, Brazil, some

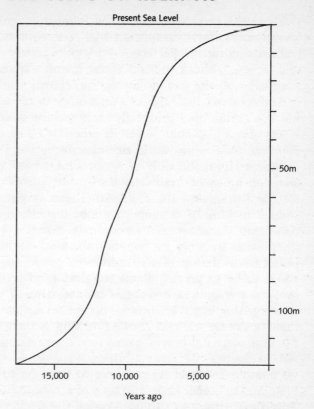

Present Sea Level

50m

100m

15,000   10,000   5,000

Years ago

Rising sea level since the peak of the last ice age.

Pacific islands and New Guinea, with additional information about dated climatic changes from ocean sediment cores, the loess deposits of Eurasia, polar ice probes, Andean lake bottoms and pollen sequences in many sites. But small-scale changes in sea level and short-lived episodes of change are hard to chart in detail and to correlate in different locations. Sediment cores from the sea floors record fluctuations in relative numbers of tiny organisms favouring warmer or colder seas, and fluctuations in the volume of the oceans with implications for temperature change, but the cores are hard to date in fine detail thanks to the inherent probability range of radiocarbon dating and the longish periods covered by samples from the cores, as much as up to a thousand years for any date determination.

There has been speculation that temporary enlargements of the glaciers, for example during that cold snap of a few centuries' duration after about 10,500 BP, could result in extra and especially quick melting when warmer times returned (at not too far off the sort of date we can extract from Plato for the end of Atlantis). But huge amounts of ice would not be involved nor is it certain that unusually rapid melting would ensue, and a rate of sea level rise of even as much as 60 centimetres or so per year for a time would not exactly be world-cataclysmic. Sediments from the Gulf of Mexico have been interpreted to show an influx of freshwater deposits at 11,600 BP (bang on for the *Critias* and the Flem-Aths) that might relate to the sudden melting of a temporary lobe distension of the North American ice sheet, not necessarily caused by temperature fluctuation (or only by temperature fluctuation). But again, radiocarbon dating of the sediments covers too long a time range to be so precise about the date (and on this occasion involves averaging of two dates) and estimates of the size of the ice surge that might be involved do not necessitate spectacularly rapid or drastic sea level rises on melting. Some geologists think the freshwater influx was spread over many thousands of years. Atlantologists, of course, need an episode of rapid and voluminous sea level rise in order to hang on to something of Plato and to bolster their scenarios of a catastrophe sufficient to drive their Atlantean survivors round the world and remove all traces of their former homeland.

After their sortie into the scientific reaches of geology and palaeontology, the Flem-Aths return to myth and even a little dabbling in the discredited business of far-fetched language comparisons, this time between North America and ancient Sumer, on the word of some Soviet linguistic speculators. After that, possibilities are floated for the vast age of the ruins at Tiahuanaco (actually the city thrived from about 500 BC to AD 1000 – we will return to it later), the vast age of the Sphinx (more of that later, too, but there's no reason to shift it from its Egyptian Old Kingdom date of about 2500 BC), and the vast age of the layout of the pyramids at Giza (based on very flawed speculation, as we shall see). The Aztlan name is invoked, without mention of the late date of AD 1168 given by the

Aztecs themselves for their leaving it. There is even recourse to those musings about the Arctic as the original home of the Aryans which the Flem-Aths appear to introduce, without giving it any credence, as a bridge to their own advocacy of Antarctica as the site of Atlantis.

Suggestions that the Arctic may have been warmer in the past than it is now are applied to Antarctica in turn. The whole discussion is conducted in terms of 'before 9600 BC', with no recognition of the complex pattern of cold glacial and warm interglacial periods we know to have obtained during two million years of the Pleistocene era, and seemingly no awareness that the glacial phases are themselves made up of similarly complex patterns of colder stadials and warmer interstadials. Remarks about evidence for warmth-loving faunas in Norway and Siberia are made in complete ignorance of these complexities. There is no mystery about ice-free corridors like the one that permitted the ancestors of the American Indians to pass down North America after crossing the Bering Strait during a time of lowered sea level in the last millennia of the last ice age. The glaciers spread from the north and from mountain ranges like the Rockies and Alps, with ice-free tracts between them.

The Flem-Aths quote bafflingly precise dates for a scheme of earth crust displacements and glaciations/meltings at 91,600, 50,600 and 9600 BC that do not match the known phases of the last ice age as charted by geological science. It is interesting to see that, in a paper of Rand Flem-Ath's of 1981 included as an appendix in *When the Sky Fell*, Hapgood's notion of an earth crust displacement somewhere between 17,000 and 12,000 BP is not refined to the precise date of 9600 BC with which we are so familiar in the main work. Incorporated into the Flem-Aths' scheme of displacement chronology is their suggestion that people were able to travel from Siberia across Beringia, down the Pacific coast of America to California, on to South America and then into the allegedly ice-free region they call Lesser Antarctica – West Antarctica on our maps – any time after 50,600 BC! (After 9600 BC, they think, of course, that another displacement brought this area too into glaciation, causing its inhabitants to flee; they see another influx of people into North

America at this time.) We may wonder where the archaeological evidence is for such a peopling of the Americas (let alone Antarctica) as early as about 50,000 BC, but the Flem-Aths think in any case that it could all have taken place even earlier: 'forty to eighty thousand years would seem to be more than enough time to create an advanced civilization on a temperate island free from external invasion'. Again, they mean West Antarctica, before icing.

When the Sky Fell next treats the reader to a vivid word picture of the cataclysmic end of Atlantis in Antarctica, returning to Solon's account via Plato, but not in Plato's words so that an impression is easily garnered that Solon's Saite informants were talking of worldwide earthquakes and floods and a change in the path of the sun across the sky that are simply not in Plato's account of Atlantis. Then comes the ingenious claim that, shorn of its ice, West Antarctica would not be unlike Plato's Atlantis in size and general topography. Putting Atlantis under today's ice over West Antarctica gives the Flem-Aths a distinct advantage over other Atlantologists who favour non-Antarctic or non-sub-Atlantic locations. They are able to take Plato much more literally about the size, shape and appointments of the island's chief city, for example: after all, there could be golden statuary and racetracks and annular harbours under all that ice, couldn't there? And the Library of Alexandria in Egypt, where Greeks communed in scholarship with Egyptian sages, could have contained wonderful maps from Atlantean times, couldn't it? (Atlantis went under the ice and the Library of Alexandria went up in smoke.) Some of those maps could have been sent to Constantinople and been seen there by Viking Varangians and Muslim seafarers, providing ultimate inspiration for Columbus. So the Flem-Aths conjecture.

They make much of a couple of sixteenth-century maps from the Muslim world that they think, following Hapgood, show evidence of just the sort of old Atlantean sailors' lore that might have come down through the ages. The Hadji Ahmed map of 1559 is said to show more of North America than was known at the time and, moreover, to show it as covered in ice in (about?) 11,600 BC, with Beringia above water. The Flem-Aths illustrate the Hadji Ahmed map with a

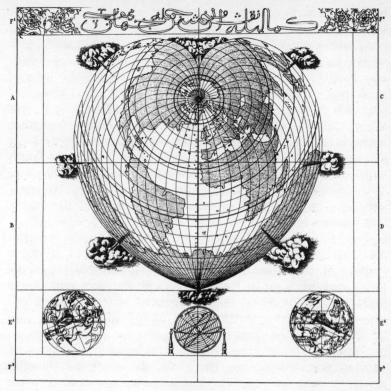

Hadji Ahmed's map.

modern drawing made from it. They do not tell the reader that the map Hapgood illustrates is itself a highly ornate and stylized copy of the original made in France in 1865. Hapgood is very sketchy about the details of the real original. By rendering only the North American part of the French version of the Hadji Ahmed map, the Flem-Aths omit to show us that in the southern hemisphere this map depicts a huge polar continent that reaches up east of Madagascar and west of South America practically to the Tropic of Capricorn! This does tend to detract from any idea that the original makers of the map were guided by sophisticated cartography inherited from an ancient globally seagoing civilization. Hapgood does note, as his borrowers do not, that the suggestion has been made that the layout of the west coast of North America on the map was accidentally arrived at by stitching together the fanciful details shown for the area on the Oronteus Finaeus map of 1532, which splits North America up the middle for the sake of projection of the globe on the flat page. Hapgood disagrees with this suggestion, but he does relate it. Whatever it is, this Hadji Ahmed's map via nineteenth-century France is neither an accurate map of America today nor in the last part of the ice age. (Incidentally, the first map to show North and South America separated from Asia beyond was Waldseemüller's of 1507, probably the oldest map upon which the name 'America' appears. The first chart to show the vast area of the Pacific was Ribero's of 1529.)

More famous than Hadji Ahmed's is the Piri Reis map of 1513, which has loomed large in the arguments of many writers of the Atlantological persuasion since Hapgood's pioneering work on it. Hapgood was much more punctilious about it than most of the subsequent writers have been, drawing attention to the map's many inaccuracies and inadequacies at the same time as arguing for its importance as an indicator of very ancient geographical knowledge and cartographic achievement. The Flem-Aths, while not claiming as others have done that the Piri Reis map is a dead accurate mapping as though from outer space of late Pleistocene geography, do make much of its alleged sophistication of projection and its longitudinal accuracy at twenty-four locations in respect of one another. At the same time, they do not mention its glaring faults at all, which Hapgood wanted to explain as later mistakes and accretions added in stages to a basically accurate prototype of ancient times. The map, of which we appear to have only the left portion, was found in 1929 in the old Sultan's Palace in Istanbul (formerly Constantinople and Byzantium) at the time of its conversion into a museum. It is signed by Piri Ibn Haji Mehmed, known as Piri Reis – Piri the Chief, or Admiral Piri as we might say. It carries the date of 919 in the Muslim calendar, twenty-one years after the discovery of the Americas by Columbus. It was early noted that, unusually for the time, it showed the coast of

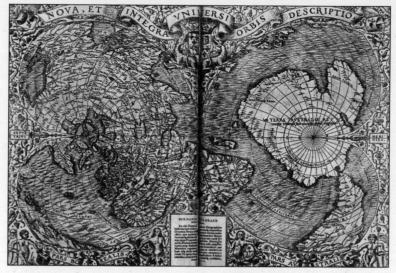

The map of Oronteus Finaeus.

South America in its correct longitudinal position in relation to Africa. Hapgood developed the suggestion that it further showed below that coastline the un-iced coast of part of Antarctica.

But Hapgood was equally aware of the map's manifold inaccuracies, which anyone who glances at it can see for themselves. The Caribbean area is all wrong, with Cuba in the wrong orientation and proportion like fabulous Antilia (and labelled Hispaniola). The Amazon river is on the map twice and some 1,400 kilometres of the coastline of South America cannot be found. Worse still, no sea passage is shown between the tip of South America and the alleged 'Antarctica'. And this 'Antarctic' coast closely resembles neither the present-day ice-bound shoreline nor modern estimates (by echo-sounding) of the underlying land. The map itself attributes its information in this region to Portuguese sailors, and states that the western part is inhabited by white-haired monsters and six-horned oxen. Of the eastern part, which Hapgood and the Flem-Aths would like to see as Antarctica proper, the legend on the Piri Reis map says: 'This country is a waste . . . it is said that large snakes are found here. For this reason the Portuguese infidels

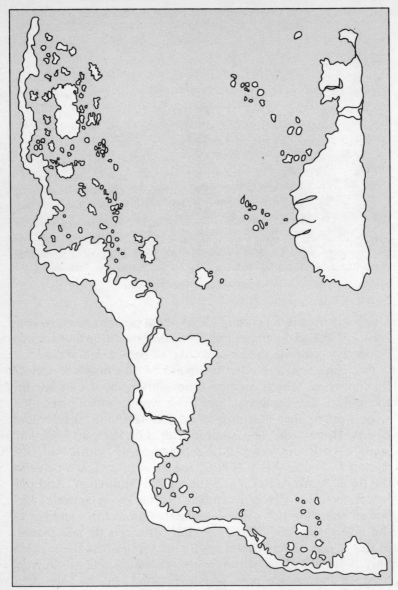

The main outlines of the Piri Reis map.

did not land on these shores and these are also said to be very hot.' Like Hapgood, you have to make unevidenced conjectures about later garblings and corruptions to hold on to any belief that the Piri Reis map could go back to better maps of ancient times. The Reis himself states in a marginal note that his map is a composite of older Greek and Arab charts, of a map by Columbus and of sailors' tales and sketch maps. The Flem-Aths' speculation about transmission of Atlantean maps through Alexandria and Constantinople seems uncalled-for in the light of this map's signal inaccuracy in the key area of 'Antarctica' by which they set such store.

It is even worse with their next exhibit: Athanasius Kircher's map of 1664 from his *Mundus Subterraneus*. He labelled this map as follows: *The Egyptians' and Plato's Account of the Location of the long-since submerged island of Atlantis*. This makes it quite plain that he has simply drawn a map based on what is in Plato as to where Atlantis was situated. Kircher, who published absolutely fanciful 'translations' of Egyptian hieroglyphs (and was, incidentally, the inventor of the magic lantern), was a firm believer in Plato's Atlantis. The most noticeable thing about his map is that it is, to our eyes, upside down, with north at the bottom. There is nothing very unusual in this for his time: maps were often done that way, as can be seen with some of the maps of the fabled islands in the Atlantic, like the Bianco map shown in this book. To say the Egyptians saw their world in the same way as an argument for an Egyptian original of Kircher's map has no force. The Flem-Aths like to see Kircher's map the way he did it so as to invite us to look at a globe of the world from the south polar region and be struck by the similarity of view. Which we hardly shall be, since the Flem-Aths have to disregard Kircher's own labelling of Spain and make it into southern Africa, similarly disregard his labelling of Africa so as to make it Madagascar and overlook the absolute non-resemblance of Kircher's America to the tip of South America they would like it to represent. It is as plain as a pikestaff that Kircher's Spain is in fact Spain, and his Africa is in fact (North) Africa while his America is a general bulge of no particular specificity and certainly not the tip of South America. When the Flem-Aths

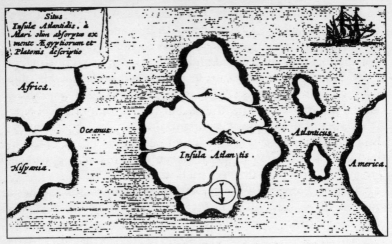

Atlantis according to Athanasius Kircher in 1664.

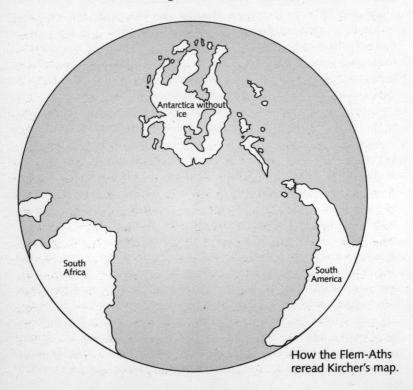

How the Flem-Aths reread Kircher's map.

say (taking it for granted that Kircher's map is based on a much older one) that 'we can immediately see that the Egyptian map of Atlantis represents in size, shape, scale, and position, an ice-free Antarctica', then we can only reply that a map showing Africa like Spain, Madagascar like North Africa and the tip of South America like nothing at all would not be worth tuppence as a map of anything. In any case, Kircher's Atlantis is nothing like the land revealed under the Antarctic ice by seismology, as the maps in the Flem-Aths' book themselves amply demonstrate. Even they more or less acknowledge it but 'nevertheless, the shadow of Atlantis can still be seen in the modern map of Antarctica'. No, not even the shadow, whatever that would mean. All this cartographic juggling only goes to show that, as with amateur linguistics, you can make anything sound a bit like something else if you're not too careful.

The Flem-Aths end their book with a tour of the allegedly mysterious stone-moving capacities, map-making propensities and language-devising aptitudes of the old Atlanteans (the last founded on the flimsiest basis that people around Lake Titicaca still speak a highly regular language). All these hypothetical achievements, together with their supposed inspiration of agriculture all over the world, make the Atlanteans of Antarctica the apples of the Flem-Aths' eye: 'what we are dealing with is not just another lost ancient civilization, it is a lost *advanced* culture, one possessing scientific knowledge that we have yet to comprehend'. In his foreword to their book, the writer Colin Wilson predicts that their work 'will almost certainly earn Rand and Rose Flem-Ath a permanent place in the history of the earth sciences'. The chances of that seem vanishingly small to this writer but they have certainly earned themselves a place in the history of the Atlantis Syndrome by putting Antarctica so prominently on the Atlantological map – as the frequent resort of other authors to their ideas shows. Forget the Mid-Atlantic Ridge, forget the Antilles, forget Bimini or any of the more or less far-fetched locations proposed at one time or another – all of which suffer from the possibility of actually being investigated and found wanting. Antarctica is the place to look for lost

Atlantis. Or rather, not to be able to look for it in the foreseeable future – as with origins for Atlantis in outer space, which we shall come to before we are finished.

Another work by Rand Flem-Ath appeared in late 2000, in co-authorship with Colin Wilson, who has himself written on Atlantis along with so much else in his time, including murder and the occult. (His *From Atlantis to the Sphinx* of 1996 took in such topics as ancient Egypt, Bimini, Hapgood's wandering poles, Antarctica, le Plongeon and Churchward, South America, dowsing, prehistoric art, megalithic alignments, the musings of Jung and the workings of the I Ching.) The chief addition to Flem-Ath's thinking advanced in *The Atlantis Blueprint* is a notion of a network of marker sites around the world established by the Atlanteans before the loss of their homeland, apparently in the first place to monitor tell-tale signs of impending crustal shifts. These were mistaken by subsequent survivors of the disaster for holy places to do with the gods and thus they became the bases for later monuments as diverse as Stonehenge, Lhasa, Troy, Easter Island, Bimini, Canterbury, Carthage, Susa and a host of others. Though this notion of a geometrically arrayed distribution of key sites around the world is by no means a new one, it seems to be in the air again – as we shall see, Graham Hancock and Erich von Däniken are using versions of it in their recent works. Flem-Ath's network shares with von Däniken's a reliance on the classical proportions of the Golden Section but its locations are determined by latitudes and polar alignments that prevailed during Hapgoodian epochs of previous positionings of the poles. The rich possibilitics of this system, with the addition of a special 'X-event' factor when things don't quite fit (a comet, would you believe), are enthusiastically worked out – with a lot of numerological application – by Rand Flem-Ath, who owns to a certain obsessiveness in his pursuit of his material. (He also rather artlessly reveals that his interest in the whole thing was sparked when he was writing a science fiction story about stranded aliens and hearing a pop-song called 'Hail Atlantis'.)

This new work also adds the speculation that it was a long

sojourn in Antarctica after their first appearance in Africa before 100,000 BP that explains the apparent absence of the Crô-Magnons in the archaeological record from that time until their much later appearance in Europe. Flem-Ath has moreover been struck by an article reporting the detection by Landsat satellite surveillance of a circular feature 1,400 metres under the ice of western Antarctica, with a unique magnetic signature. It's enough to remind him of Plato's great circular city of Atlantis with its metal-clad walls. 'Is there a lost city beneath the ice of Antarctica?' he asks, and there's next to no chance of saying a definitive yes or no to that, though one could hardly say it is likely that there is. Flem-Ath would have to get round the conventional geologists' view that the ice of Antarctica is many hundreds of thousands of years old to say 'yes' even to the possibility. (Ice cores have already been drilled that reach through nearly one million years of ice, with some way to go.) He has a go at getting round the geology with old familiar Hapgood material about the mammoths of Siberia, antipodean to Antarctica, as proof that things were warmer near our poles during the last ice age than they should have been according to conventional geology. He still writes without reference to the complexities of glacial/interglacial and stadial/interstadial phases during the Pleistocene, which explain the occurrence of evidence for some warmer conditions during what he seems to assume were unremittingly cold periods.

The Atlantis Blueprint cleaves to Hapgood in all but a few minor points, but it inspires little further confidence in him to learn that in the 1960s he attempted to persuade President Kennedy to support an expedition looking for Atlantis on the Mid-Atlantic Ridge (with the bait of $500,000,000 of gold as divined from Plato), or that at the end of his life he had come to believe in many cycles of lost civilizations in the Americas and the Antarctic going back for a hundred thousand years. It isn't so inspiring, either, in this book to find Finaeus misspelt, Piri mistaken to mean admiral (of a chap named Reis!), the tomb of Ramesses IX relocated to Alexandria and Crô-Magnon man redated back to before 64,800 BP in Europe.

Colin Wilson's contribution to the work appears mainly to consist of a colourful (and simultaneously often quite tedious) trawl through a body of archaeological and historical mysteries of unusually wide range for a book about Atlantis. It's all there, from crystal skulls to the acoustics of the Great Pyramid, from Phoenician exploitation of atomic power (or maybe just powerful sun-focusing lenses) to Colonel Fawcett, from secret chambers at Giza to the Baghdad 'battery', from old balls in Costa Rica to the biggest numbers ever written down in the ancient world (Nineveh did best with 195,955,200,000,000, which is very impressive if you choose to interpret it for no obvious reason as a date given in seconds). We get the Guanches of the Canaries, *Homo erectus* in the Flores Strait, the Templars in Jerusalem and Scotland, the Freemasons, the Book of Enoch, the Dead Sea Scrolls, the Turin Shroud, the goings-on at Rennes-le-Chateau (pages of that) and much, much more. Even the Man in the Iron Mask and Shangri-La get a look-in. There are moments when the reader might be tempted to think that this text contains every major and minor 'mystery' of history except for Joanna Southcott's Box and the Tichborne Claimant. It amounts to a notable example of the genre's ambition to include everything, use everything, explain everything. It is nice, however, to have the minor mystery of the Flem-Aths' name cleared up: Rand Fleming married Rose De'ath.

10

ATLANTIS BY ANY OTHER NAME

Antarctica has figured prominently (if not quite permanently) in the speculations of other Atlantological writers since the Flem-Aths, and the baggage of Hapgood and Hibben transmitted by the Canadian couple looks fair to remain a constant component of the Atlantis Syndrome for ever more.

A writer called Graham Hancock who rarely mentions Atlantis as such has been an enthusiastic propagandist of what I call Atlantological views over the past five years, having cut his teeth in the business of 'alternative' thinking about the past with a book about the Lost Ark of the Covenant in 1992, in which he most ingeniously tracked that fabled relic to a church at Axum in Ethiopia, but did not actually succeed in getting inside to cast an eye over it either on his own behalf or ours. He has also taken time off from terrestrial Atlantological speculation to write a book in 1998 about the so-called Mars Mystery of a giant face with associated structures on the red planet – something that was never a mystery to anyone but fevered 'alternative' thinkers and turned out, absolutely predictably, to have no basis at all once clearer photographs of the Cydonia area of Mars were available. It will be worthwhile to remember that our old friend cometary impact was invoked to explain the extinguishing of the phantom civilization supposed to have built the imagined pyramid and imagined sphinx-like face of Mars.

Hancock's *Fingerprints of the Gods* was his first big sally into Atlantology. He starts this book with that old favourite, the Piri Reis map, which Hapgood and the Flem-Aths made so much of.

(So did Erich von Däniken in his many works advocating a prehistoric interference in human affairs by men from outer space – we shall come to his latest ideas in due course.) All the same objections we recounted to the use of this curious map as proof of a preglacial globe-roaming, cartographically sophisticated, lamentably lost ancient civilization in Antarctica, or anywhere else, still apply. You know: the Caribbean's all wrong, Cuba especially; the Amazon's on twice; a whole piece of South-American coast is missing; there's no sea-passage between South America and 'Antarctica'; the coast of this 'Antarctica' isn't really very like either Antarctica now or as it was in the past, as revealed by seismic soundings through the ice, and may well in fact just be an inaccurate rendering of the further coast of South America below Sao Paulo; the map explicitly attributes its information in this region to Portuguese sailors and throws in white-haired monsters, six-horned cattle, large snakes . . . Hancock tells little of the manifold inaccuracies of the Piri Reis map, though he does mention the Amazon's dual entry and tries to use what errors he notes to suggest the vast age and authenticity of the sources the Reis may have drawn upon. Hancock urges that, despite what Piri says on his own map, he could not have got his information about 'Antarctica' from contemporary sailors of the Atlantic – but then the map is by no means proved to show the real Antarctica at all.

As did Hapgood, Hancock also brings on the Oronteus Finaeus world map of 1532, which does feature – in the right place – something much more suggestive of Antarctica in general shape. Suggestive is the word, since in detail this map of the French geographer Oronce Finé does not accurately represent either Antarctica of the sixteenth century or a putative ice-free Antarctica of the past. The fact that it shows flowing rivers is more likely to be owed to map-drawing conventions of Finé's day than to acquaintance with wonderful maps of yore. Mercator's world map of 1569 merely follows Finé's in its showing of a south polar continent. Philippe Buache's map of 1737 is likewise not remotely an accurate map of land masses beneath the Antarctic ice. Its showing of clear water between the two sections of its south polar continent (and indeed the pole itself at sea) does not reflect the real situation of a West Antarctica as a single land mass and an East Antarctica of many islands (with two large ones) under the ice.

Back with the Reis, Hancock tries to make something of the Turkish map's depiction of a large island in the Atlantic off South America (Piri's map is dotted with islands all over the place). He thinks this large island may suggest knowledge of the Mid-Atlantic Ridge as it might have showed above water here during the low sea level period of the last ice age. But we can't have it all ways with a map that shows the Caribbean in such profuse inaccuracy: what are we to make of that large island to the north, mislabelled Hispaniola, that can only be a grossly distorted representation of Cuba, looking like a pre-Columbian map's Antilia? It can't be Cuba during the ice age, since lowering of sea level could not produce its shape or orientation as shown on the Piri Reis map.

Hancock has so far introduced his old maps in an open-minded style, noting their suggestive possibilities. Then, in a manner all too familiar in this field, we move from possibilities to certainties in one bound. 'We saw that the Mercator World Map of 1569 included an accurate portrayal of the coasts of Antarctica as they would have looked thousands of years ago when they were free of ice,' he writes. It's true that we have had a bit of muted pooh-poohing from him of the academic geologists' belief in the long duration of the Antarctic ice-cap and of the academic archaeologists' denial that there were any civilizations in the world at all before the end of the last ice age – but we thought Hancock was still only pointing to the possibilities of his maps. Now we know he's certain about it. We can only repeat that Piri and Finaeus and Mercator have not provided in their maps any accurate portrayal at all of the preglacial coastlines of the real Antarctica. Hancock, however, drives on and, with an invocation of the Viracochas of old South America, just the sort of chaps who might have preserved the ancient wisdom of Hapgood's map-making seafarers from unfrozen Antarctica, we're off with him to Peru.

Viracocha, before we get any further, was a bearded rain-god of pre-Inca origins taken up by the Inca and believed by them to have created the sun and moon on Lake Titicaca. After going on to create the rest of the world, he travelled around teaching the arts of civilization. This latter trait has caused him to be espoused by assorted Atlantologists as a cover name for a body of antique seers, steeped in the ancient wisdom of long-lost Atlantis (wherever it was), who went round the world enlightening the rest of humanity – who, obviously, could never have bettered themselves without these 'Viracochas'.

In Peru with Hancock, it's rather a case of 'round up the usual suspects'. And we start with the Nazca Lines, that collection of tracks and signs on the ground near the southern coast of Peru that von Däniken famously identified as landing strips and navigational aids for alien flying machines. Hancock plumps for an American astronomer's identification of the figures, like the spider, with constellations in the night sky (Orion in the case of the spider) and of the straight tracks with sightings of star positions through the ages. Lines 'linked to the figure' of the spider, according to Hancock, 'appear' to track the declinations of the belt stars of our constellation of Orion over a long period. Ancient folk tales of the locality apparently link the lines with Viracocha, but how ancient these tales might be is not clear. To judge by the pottery sherds found strewn around the lines, they were made (by removal of surface stones, to reveal the ground beneath) in a period between about 200 BC and AD 600 – the motifs resemble those on the pottery fragments. Hardly the time frame of old Atlantis, on the face of it.

Next stop, Cuzco, the highland capital of the Inca empire from the eleventh century AD. Hancock invites us to marvel at the cyclopean masonry of the Inca buildings of Cuzco and to speculate that the Inca couldn't possibly have built this way but must have inherited it all from bearded Viracochas. Hancock believes that radiocarbon dating is of no use in dating the Inca fortress in Cuzco and 'thermoluminescence, too, was useless'. Well, it certainly would be so in any attempt to date the stones of the Sacsahuaman fortress directly: it's a method of dating previously fired materials like pottery. But associated finds, in a proper archaeological context, like organic remains or bits of pottery can – by means of radiocarbon or thermoluminescence – be used to date stone monuments. And pottery chronology, as we have seen, can be an important means of dating other things with which pottery is found in association. Hancock is satisfied, however, that with regard to Cuzco '"expert" archaeology was still largely the result of guesswork and subjective assumptions'. Guesswork and subjective assumptions are not, it seems to this writer, noticeable for their absence in the work of Hancock himself, however quickly they are sometimes converted into certainties.

The business of the Viracochas gets even better as we go along, when Hancock tells us that 'ancient myths . . . faithfully recorded' by the Spanish conquerors of Peru associate Viracocha with a time of terrible flooding. How he knows that these myths (of whatever vintage in themselves) were faithfully recorded by the Spanish is not clear – and, after all, these Spanish Catholics came with a well-known flood story of their own. All Christian missionaries' accounts from anywhere in the world of alleged flood stories in the native cultures of their subjects are suspect on this count.

Hancock's next port of call is the very spectacular Machu Picchu atop its ridge about 70 kilometres north-west of Cuzco. Here he tells his readers that not everyone accepts the archaeologists' dating of this small town of the Inca empire to the fifteenth century AD: a German professor of astronomy in the 1930s thought it was as old as 4000–2000 BC. The same Potsdam professor and another one from La Paz have worked out by astronomical reasoning that the city of Tiahuanaco on Lake Titicaca might go back no less than seventeen thousand years, pointing to its present location a long way from the lake and on higher ground: apparently they believe it was destroyed by a seismic catastrophe in 11,000 BC, with flooding. However, Hancock does duly report the conventional archaeologists' contention that the principal monuments of Tiahuanaco (like the Gateway of the Sun) date to only some AD 500 at the earliest, with an overall range of radiocarbon dates from about 1600 BC to AD 900 for the whole site. You have to quarrel profoundly with radiocarbon dating to get out of that one. And to no purpose, in any case, since the astronomically achieved datings were arrived at on the basis of 'alignments' subjectively perceived to exist in a jumble of ruined, robbed and patchily restored remains.

Hancock muses on the similarities between stories about

Viracocha (or at least one of his other manifestations) and Egyptian tales about Osiris. He asks if these similarities can just be coincidences: details like these gods' being conspired against, struck down, sealed in a container, cast into the water, drifting out to sea. And the answer is that yes, indeed, these details can very well be coincidences. Everyone who's worked with other people (or lived in a family) knows that conspiracies are always afoot; doing down one's enemies is commonplace; hiding the evidence of crimes is an obvious resort; chucking things into flowing rivers is a good way of getting rid of them; having them get taken out to sea is better still. Human imagination is endlessly creative but there are only a limited number of basic scenarios and plot devices and they are bound to keep cropping up. If a folk-tale resembles another one found among a nearby people at about the same time, there's reason to think about links between the stories: Moses in his basket is a clear case to consider in that light when we recall a similar story about the Mesopotamian ruler Sargon of about 2300 BC. Over enormous distances and separated by vast stretches of time there's scant cause to be impressed by similarities of mythology. Are the similarities between reed boats on Lake Titicaca and Nile boats in Egyptian drawings any more impressive? What do you do when you want to build a small boat for local travel out of locally available materials?

Towards the end of his South American chapter, Hancock ruminates about the present-day inhabitants around Tiahuanaco in a way that reveals a well-established trait of the Atlantis Syndrome. Watching some 'stolid Aymara Indians who walked slowly in the narrow cobbled streets and sat placidly in the little sunlit plazas', he asks himself, 'Were these people the descendants of the builders of Tiahuanaco, as the scholars insisted? Had the ancient city been the work of foreigners with godlike powers who had settled here, long ages ago?' I take Graham Hancock, from his journalistic work in Africa, to be a liberal and progressively minded person and I fear that, with this reliance on the old colonialist strain in Atlantology that Donnelly and Spence so advocated, he may be unconsciously incorporating an unfortunate if not dangerous line of thought into his speculations – certainly it is a naïve one. He appears to incline more to the missionary than the military aspect of colonialist thinking and with that reference to 'godlike powers' we are reminded of Atlantology's essentially religious affiliation. It is really a sort of religion in mufti, posing as history and even as science. God is being let in by the back door in the shape of those Viracocha- refugees from the wise old supercivilization (we may as well call it Atlantis) lost under the ice or wherever. In any case, is it so surprising if civilizations like the Incas' outlive their heyday, go into decline and leave their descendants in altered circumstances? A visitor to medieval Rome, full of cowherds and shepherds, would have wondered whether these people could possibly be the descendants of the supermen who built the Colosseum and the Pantheon.

There follows some rather inconclusive stuff about various items at Tiahuanaco. There are figures holding things that must mean something. Fish-scaled statuary brings to Hancock's mind the story of a fish-like teacher of the Sumerians called Oannes by Berossus. He regales us with the resemblance of some carvings on the Gateway of the Sun to elephants, but even he has to admit that they are what the archaeologists say they are – condor heads throat to throat. But they still look a bit like elephants to him (not to this writer, I may say) and maybe the wily Andeans of old meant elephants as well as condors – and elephants have been extinct in these parts for twelve thousand years! Some other carvings he believes to depict an extinct amphibious mammal called Toxodon that might have persisted in these parts till 12,000 BC, too. 'To my eye,' he says, 'this looked like striking corroboration for the astroarchaeological evidence that dated Tiahuanaco to the end of the Pleistocene.' He thinks this undermines the archaeologists' claim that Tiahuanaco was no older than AD 500, since Toxodon could only have been modelled from life. One can only wonder about Hancock's eye if he seriously thinks the sketch he shows resembles anything modelled from life. He says there are many such depictions at Tiahuanaco but seems unable, like so many of a broadly Atlantological cast of mind, to recognize the powers of the human imagination in creating imaginary beasts. If these pictures have to be of a once-living Toxodon, where did griffins, unicorns and sphinxes

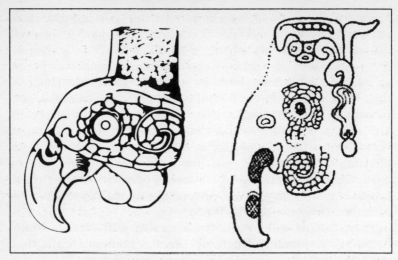

How condors – unstylized left, stylized right – can sometimes be mistaken for elephants.

come from? Do they, too, have to represent once-living realities? But then, Hancock even seems to find it hard to believe that South Americans might have independently hit on the sign (rather a simple one, I should say) of the cross long before the Spanish missionaries arrived: the Inca and Spanish crosses manage to be quite different, however, even given the limitations of this particular bit of graphic design.

Hancock repeats the material already reported by the Flem-Aths about the regularity of the local Indians' language – those poor Aymara that Hancock had wondered about as they sat around in their little sunlit plazas. He wonders now if the alleged superior features of their language could be 'a legacy of the high learning that legend attributed to the Viracochas?', and finishes in Peru with the thought that maybe some of that same high learning could also have inspired the Nazca Lines.

After Peru, Central America. We begin with some alarming but not very obviously relevant remarks about the bloody religion of the Maya and the dire predictions of the so-called 'Mayan Prophecies'. The forecast, extracted by some ingenious writers from various Mayan records, that the world will end in

2012 finds Hancock in a very speculative mood: 'Suppose they knew something we didn't? . . . Suppose, in other words, some truly awful geological catastrophe is already unfolding, deep in the bowels of the earth, as the wise men of the Maya predicted?' 'What wise men?' might be our first retort. (After that, we could perhaps begin to ponder whether it might not be an unconscious part of the strategy of Atlantological writers to unsettle their readers with doom-laden stuff like this, to prepare the psychological ground for their arguments. Ah well, not long to wait now.)

The burden of Hancock's Meso-American enquiries is that essentially the same sort of story emerges here as in Peru of the arrival from elsewhere of teachers oozing ancient wisdom. Here they are called not Viracocha but Kukulkan, Gucumatz, Quetzalcoatl or Votan, but it all comes to the same thing and they are all bearded or white-robed or something of the sort. As Viracocha ended his civilizing career in South America by setting off across the Pacific, so Quetzalcoatl takes off back to the east whence he came in the first place to bring civilization to Mexico and Central America.

At Tula, Hancock spots some more figures mysteriously (for him, at least) holding things: surely not the spears or spear-throwers of the archaeologists. 'I remembered legends which related that the gods of ancient Mexico had armed themselves with xiuhcoatl, fire serpents,' he tells us, and leaves it at that. No quick answers there, then. When he bemoans the Spanish destruction of Mayan records, the 'memory banks of Central America', and grieves over the loss of this 'irreplaceable storehouse of knowledge and history', all fair-minded persons can but agree with him. But his remarks take a turn highly reminiscent of Immanuel Velikovsky at this point. Velikovsky in the 1950s proposed that an astronomical collision (involving a comet that has since become Venus) wrought such incredible havoc on earth that humanity as a whole has wilfully put away all memory of it, except in its multifarious mythologies. Hancock observes, without further justification, that with the loss of the Mayan records 'a chance to shake off at least some of the collective amnesia that clouds our understanding was lost to mankind forever'. He simply cannot know that this bold claim is true: it is more likely that what the Spaniards burned was just a lot more old mythologizing, no doubt interesting but not likely to lift any clouds off our understanding of history. And he really needn't be too downcast about it: after all, if those lost records really did contain much in the way of real history, the scope of Atlantological speculation might have been severely curtailed.

As with Peru, Hancock would like civilization in Meso-America to be as old as possible and he is interested in anything that might cast doubt on the archaeologists' datings and push things further back into the past. Thus he thinks the voluminous pyramid at Cholula may be very old indeed, pointing to a lava flow around its base as a sign of its original great age. Interestingly enough, Hapgood used a similar argument about the round stepped pyramid at Cuicuilco, quoting certain geologists' opinions about the date of its lava flow at as long ago as 7000 BP. Archaeologists put Cuicuilco at after 600 BC and the first settlement at Cholula at about 1000 BC in their chronological scheme of Meso-American cultural developments, with the Olmecs at the beginning of that development in about 1300 BC. That the Mayan calendar can be read back to a start date of 3114 BC is no proof whatever that it was started in 3114 BC (by proto-Olmecs, as Hancock appears to think): only that the system as such can be worked back to that date. In fact the oldest recorded dates of Meso-America, actually put on monuments, only go back to the first century BC. The Olmecs represent the first cultural flowering of this region, but their achievements were not, of course, without an antecedent process, as we saw in our survey of human prehistory in an earlier chapter. However, there were no pyramids of earth let alone stone in 5000 BP or earlier as Hapgood and Hancock would like to think.

Hancock would also like to believe that one of the migrations of peoples into the Americas during the last ice age was of Negroid stock, pointing as many others have done (including Donnelly) to the large Olmec heads of San Lorenzo, La Venta and Tres Zapotes. To say some of these heads are unmistakably African is going much too far: they display traits like wide, flat noses and everted lips that look a bit Negroid but at the same time they show eye shapes and high cheeks that are more Mongoloid. Some 'Negroid' traits, as we might say, were observed by the Spaniards in America from the start and some have been noted among Mongoloid groups in Asia, where the American Indians came from, so we don't need to look to any Negroid immigration into the Americas as such. In any case, these sculptures are works of art and not forensic photographs and we cannot know what artistic motives grew into the expressions we see on them. The same goes for alleged Caucasoid and Semitic features divined in American sculpture and carving. Things become very silly if we try to compare an Olmec head with the Great Sphinx of Giza: the Olmec head has a flat nose and the Sphinx has no nose and there the resemblance ends.

This racial comparing is a preface for Hancock's efforts to link up cultural traits in Egypt and America (in time-honoured fashion since Donnelly and Spence) to indicate the common origin of these cultures in the legacy of an older vanished civilization of the remote past – Atlantis by any other name. After a few cross-cultural examples of no particular force, Hancock moves on to the reassertion, astounding in this day and age, of the Donnellian claim that the ancient Egyptian civilization 'emerged all at once and fully formed'. There was some excuse for Donnelly in the late nineteenth century, none at all for Hancock at the end of the twentieth. The predynastic course of development of Egyptian civilization is now well-known and easily read up in numerous works. I have tried to sketch it in an earlier chapter of this book and in greater detail in my *Riddles of the Sphinx*. Contrary to what Hancock thinks, the hieroglyphs of Egypt – for example – do not first appear in a complete and perfect state and we can – to take another example – track the evolution of tomb building and building in stone from simple beginnings into the early historical dynasties and beyond them to the 300-year development of pyramid building. What we know of Egyptian mathematics, medicine, astronomy and (to a large extent) religion is almost entirely derived from texts that postdate the pyramid age and cannot be used to show that these things sprang into sudden practice at the start of Egyptian civilization as Hancock would like to think. When people like him refer to outdated authorities on Egyptian history (even, as he does, to someone like Wallis Budge who retired from the British Museum in 1924) then their readership needs to know how unreliable their views can be.

With Hancock hypothesis soon turns to certainty: the Olmecs and the Egyptians, and the Sumerians of Mesopotamia too, all got their start from some other civilization, much older. The fact that the Olmecs of Central America are much later than the Old Kingdom of ancient Egypt only means for Hancock that the heads attributed to them must be older and not Olmec products at all, with no need of archaeological evidence to prove it. Or perhaps there was an early input from the Viracochas (Quetzalcoatls if you like) that spluttered nearly out until civilization could be revived with the Olmecs. Hancock produces the familiar list of cultural similarities between Egypt (and Sumer) and the Americas to bolster his notion of a common heritage, including such tidbits as kings after death going to the stars, postmortem journeyings by boat, the destruction of the hearts of the unjust deceased by eating, monsters in the underworld and so on. The equally familiar riposte applies: that there is a limited range of symbolic expressions of ideas about death and the afterlife and inventive human beings are bound to keep hitting on similar ones in similar circumstances. It might be thought something of a disgrace for Hancock to rehash von Däniken's discredited claims about the Palenque tomb lid as showing a man in a machine (actually it's the Mayan Tree of Life) and, what's more, to go on to print a picture of a scene from the Olmec site of La Venta as though it were another depiction of a man in a machine. At Uxmal in Yucatan we are treated to bearded men, serpents and crosses and invited to ask ourselves whether it could be an accident that symbols 'as distinctive as these' should be repeated in widely separated cultures and in different periods. Well, all men grow beards (even Mongoloids), there are snakes everywhere except in Ireland and crosses are just two lines at right angles.

There has been a hint or two already of a novel idea in Hancock's contribution to Atlantology in his *Fingerprints of the Gods*. We recall that the notion was floated of a cultural input into Central America that faltered and almost vanished until the Olmecs got under way. And just now we had Hancock talking of symbols repeated not just in separated places but in different periods. Now comes Hancock's big idea, his first real deviation from an essentially Donnellian version of the Syndrome, owed more perhaps to the Blavatsky tendency than to anything else in Atlantological thinking. 'Not for the first time,' he writes, 'I suspected that I might be looking at signs and icons left behind by some cult or secret society which had sought to keep the light of civilization burning in Central America (and perhaps elsewhere) through long ages of darkness.' Here Atlantology meets theosophy and freemasonry – here we have arrived at The Secret Brotherhood of the Ancient Wisdom, to put it all together and give it a name. (Note how tentatively it is introduced, though, through a string of suspecteds, mights and perhapses.) The idea that a secret society or cult was the means by which the traits of civilization were handed down goes beyond the model of Dark Ages Europe, in which the church may have been a cult but was no secret society, into the realms of Rosicrucianism and theosophy. Secret societies make a convenient addition to Atlantological thinking since their doings would in the nature of things be hard to demonstrate or disprove and their alleged existence helps enormously to cover over the uncertain and elusive aspects of their proponents' theories. There will be plenty of scope for signs and icons to have one's suspicions about, but no hard consistencies or inconsistencies to explain in detail. Any gaps and lacunae in an Atlantological theory, even downright contradictions, can easily be glossed over when one concludes that something secret was always going on, something that might easily come through in an encoded, garbled or debased form in any particular archaeological context.

Once the 'Ancient Wisdom' is out of the bag, the way is open for over-interpretation of such slim pickings as the Popol Vuh (the Mayan chronicle written in the Quiché language using the Spanish alphabet): of the Quiché ancestors it says that 'they were admirable men . . . able to know all . . . they examined the four corners, the four points of the arch of the sky, and the round face of the earth'. Why, then, for Hancock they were consummate astronomers and cartographers: it's as plain as day, just the lads to have drawn the originals of Piri's map. These admirable men were not of course the Maya or the Olmecs before them – they were much greater forerunners and the latter-day peoples only managed to preserve some of their ancient wisdom, which is why the Maya calendar and their maths were really much too sophisticated to run alongside their cruder system of weights and measures. That's the beauty of this theory of a secret brotherhood trying to hang on to the achievements of the past in a changing world: potentially, it explains everything . . . or at least explains it away. Hancock is very impressed with the Mayan 'long count' for its accommodation of vast stretches of time and wonders why the Maya needed it, if not to predict future catastrophes. This, again, is simply to underestimate the drive of the human imagination which is very prone – especially in the religious sphere – to run away with itself into obsessive elaborations of its key ideas, be they notions of long cyclical catastrophe or the need to appease the gods with endless bloody sacrifice.

At Teotihuacan in Mexico Hancock first announces an idea of continuing importance in his thinking, which he shares with several other writers, as he generously acknowledges. The title of his subsequent book, which we shall come to later, vividly encapsulates this idea: *Heaven's Mirror*. The suggestion is that many ancient sites around the world represent in their layouts and principal features the attempt to map on the ground various significant patterns of the night sky on an accurate scale so that the earth becomes a mirror of the heavens. This is not, on the face of it, an over-extravagant, certainly not an impossible, idea. The night skies, especially in climes where the weather made observation both comfortable and productive, were a source of far greater interest to ancient peoples than they are to most of us nowadays. Before Copernicus and Galileo and Newton, the complex movements of the stars and planets were of vast significance – both real and imagined – to people living in pre-scientific cultures. (Needless to say, some of the Greeks did succeed in being more scientific about it all.) From practicalities like calendar-making to flights of mythological and religious fantasy (insofar as any of these things were separated), the mysterious groupings and motions of the heavenly bodies were seen as highly significant. It would not be at all surprising if buildings were often aligned on astronomical sightings and even if, sometimes, whole complexes of buildings mimicked certain constellations. In any given case, it can be quite difficult to demonstrate such alignments since there are so many to choose from for different times of the year in different periods of history. There is, moreover, the frequent difficulty of knowing what particular constellations were in vogue among various ancient cultures. The contention of Hancock and his confrères is that the layout of Teotihuacan reflects the disposition of the solar system and the Milky Way, with an accurate ordering and distance-scaling of the planets out from the sun, including those like Uranus, Neptune and Pluto that were not known to western science until the late eighteenth century and afterwards.

It requires a deal of faith to see in the dozen or so ceremonial buildings of Teotihuacan north and south of the Pyramid of the Sun anything like the far-flung orbits of the sun's planets. Certainly at Giza and its environs in Egypt, a similar proposal that the entire constellation of Orion is terrestrially modelled by pyramids has broken down and been all but abandoned by its proponents, who have included Hancock: too many stars had no terrestrial counterparts, the overall scale and geometry did not turn out to fit at all in reality and all that was left in the end were the three belt stars of Orion with a not very striking similarity to the disposition of the three main pyramids at Giza. Back in 1995 in *Fingerprints of the Gods* Hancock was still reassuring his readers that several other structures on the Giza Plateau, north and south of the three pyramids of Giza, fitted Orion in the sky 'with faultless precision'. This position may indeed have been largely abandoned since but much was built on Orion-by-the-Nile by Hancock *et al*: in particular with regard to their key date of 10,500 BC for the layout of the pyramid plan at Giza. That date makes a rather muted appearance in the 1995 book as 10,450 BC. We can only say that the astronomical significance of Teotihuacan as interpreted by Hancock is not at all demonstrated and the dates he and others would like to assign to the city are at variance with those arrived at by archaeologists on the basis of their overall scheme

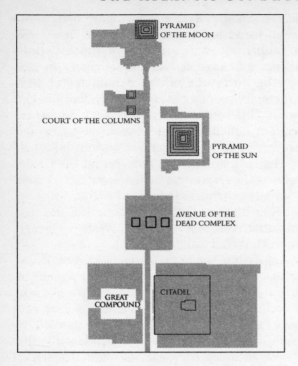

Monuments at Teotihuacan, sometimes interpreted as an image of the solar system.

of cultural development in Meso-America: Teotihuacan was in its heyday between AD 400 and 700. (Quite why it has to be older for Hancock is not really so clear when we recall that the transmission of the ancient wisdom through a secret brotherhood might have gone on at any time – but I suppose on general principles it's nice to make these things as old and venerable as possible and as close to the good old supercivilization as can be.)

Hancock next puts in his plea for the 'message', as he sees it, of all the old mythologies to be heeded, to try to dispel the collective amnesia of the human race about its catastrophic experiences in the past. The displeasure of the gods, a great flood, one man and one woman in a boat, cycles of destruction, the fall of the sun and moon, earthquakes and volcanoes: Hancock asks a series of rhetorical questions about the myths' handling of these themes. 'Isn't it odd that the

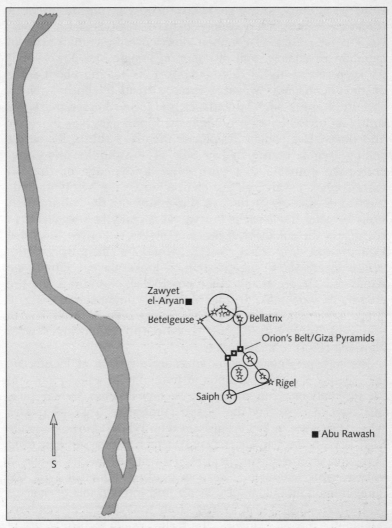

Stars of Orion alongside the Milky Way, and monuments along the Nile fail to match up anywhere except at the three pyramids of Giza.

same symbolic language keeps cropping up in ancient traditions from so many widely scattered regions of the world?' No, for the reasons of common experience on a small scale, of common psychology and of common imaginative powers that we keep reiterating in this book. 'Are we talking about some vast, subconscious wave of intercultural telepathy?' No, I shouldn't think so. 'Or could elements of these remarkable universal myths have been engineered long ages ago, by clever and purposeful people?' Hancock means, I think, his secret society types, trying in the face of mankind's oncoming collective amnesia to record some knowledge of the old catastrophes and the ancient civilization by the highly dubious method of planting mythological narratives in the cultures that grew up after the débâcle. But would it really be very clever to try to use the colourful vagaries of myths to convey historical information, and what exactly would be the purpose? So, again, in answer to his question, it looks like no. Finally, he wonders, 'Or are there other possible explanations for the enigma of the myths?' Insofar as there is any enigma, yes, and those explanations lie in the areas we keep highlighting of common human responses to common experiences with common resort to imagination.

Hancock presents a not-too-inaccurate version of Pleistocene geology and the early evolution of humanity as a background to his speculations about an ancient supercivilization, though he is mistaken in regarding the Neanderthalers as a global species when they were in fact a Eurasian one. Where things get really wild is with the ice age, when Hancock rather outdoes even Hapgood and Hibben in his determination to evoke a catastrophic scenario. There is again no mention of the complicated chronology of glacials and interglacials or stadials and interstadials and no recognition that even ice ages have summers. To go by Hancock, the reader would picture an era of unremitting snow and ice that somehow contrived to end as both a long-drawn-out nightmare of earthquake and flood and an overnight catastrophe of rising waters and mass extinctions, to the accompaniment of electric storms and belching volcanoes right, left and centre. This is catastrophism with a vengeance. He appears to think, moreover, that the evolution of *Homo sapiens*

sapiens occurred in the midst of this glacial environment, whereas both genetic and archaeological evidence points to unglaciated Africa as the home of the fully modern form of humanity. All the objections we saw to the Flem-Aths leaning on Hapgood and Hapgood leaning on Hibben apply to Hancock's version of the end of the last ice age too: if anything, more so. It is an odd thought that a popular work of 1946 could spawn such long-lived and ever-elaborating fantasies as Frank C. Hibben's well-meant *Lost Americans* did.

Hancock's picture of human beings living out their terror-stricken lives during the ice age is quite at variance with what we see in the cultural flowering of Upper Palaeolithic Europe and, for that matter, in the less showy but still resourceful cultures that bridged the end of the ice age in western and northern Europe. As we have seen, the sea level climb after the melting of the glaciers was remorseless but not catastrophically sudden, and quoting a Bible-based geologist of 1895 who suggested that central Europe and England were completely submerged is not sensible let alone persuasive. All this to bolster a notion of universal catastrophe remembered in assorted myths! Hancock, writing in 1995, was even bold enough to dabble with a short-term forecast of similar catastrophe in store – on 5 May 2000 a line-up of Neptune, Uranus, Venus, Mercury and Mars could, he told us, 'be expected to have profound gravitational effects'. Anyone remember anything?

Back with the planets, Hancock offers his readers a very good and clear account of the phenomenon known as 'precession of the equinoxes'. I recommend anyone who would like to understand this aspect of the earth's motion to read Hancock on the subject. Briefly, precession arises because the earth's axis, about which it spins, is not perpendicular to the plane of the solar system in which the earth circles the sun: it is at an angle of about 23½° to that plane, thanks largely to the pull of the moon in its orbit around the earth at an angle to that of the plane of the solar system. Because the earth is spinning, its axis has not become perpendicular over time to the plane of the moon's orbit either but rather it precesses like a wobbling toy top with a line painted round it: its poles very slowly tracing circles and its equator (the top's line) very slowly tipping to and fro. The complete cycle of the wobble takes just over 26,000 years. One of the effects of precession in terms of astronomical observation is that the moment of sunrise at any particular time of the year takes place against a slowly changing background of star patterns.

It was the bold contention of two historians of science in a book called *Hamlet's Mill* of 1969 (though, as is usual in these matters, they were not the first to entertain it) that precession had somehow been understood in the very ancient world, long before its 'official' discovery by Hipparchus in about 120 BC. (He achieved it on the basis of examination of other astronomers' records available to him that revealed the slight observational changes over time.) It is not impossible that older stargazers had hit upon precession before Hipparchus, but de Santillana and von Dechend were inclined to think the discovery to be very ancient indeed and to be reflected in mythologies from all over the world with stories of rotating pillars, props, trees, mills, churns and so on, all seen as images of the wobbled turning of the earth's axis with precession. A host of numerological subtleties to do with years and degrees attaches itself to precession, which enthusiasts like to chase through the arts, mythologies and architectural products of the ancient world, to prove that these things were planned and constructed to incorporate knowledge of precession long before Hipparchus got round to it. Catastrophism meets precession in this idea of ingenious expression through myth and works of art and architecture motivated by myth — especially if something ever went catastrophically wrong with precession in the past, like some big axis slip not a million miles from one of Hapgood's earth crust displacements. As with catastrophe, one may wonder whether myth could ever be a well-chosen vehicle for conveying accurate information about precession. But in *Fingerprints of the Gods* number chasing has a field day with Egyptian and Hindu myths and then with the initiation ceremonies of the Triads (yes, really) and then the quantity of bricks in certain old altars and of stanzas in the Hindu Rig-veda (I am not making this up) – all, apparently, to be seen as memory prompts for ardent students of precession through the ages. The idea seems to be that precession (with or without catastrophic extra wobbles) is an important factor in bringing on ice ages: well, no doubt it is a factor, but it's not the most important, along with variations in the earth's orbital distance from the sun, changes in the output of solar heat, blocking of the sun's heat by interstellar and volcanic dust, and so forth. The further idea that precession mythology might be able to pass on a warning about glaciation to later ages is a house of cards piled up on unsubstantiated claims and flimsy hypothesis after flimsy hypothesis. Better any day to find out about glaciation by the patient methods of geology than to have obscure hints aimed at us via mythology and brick-counting.

And so to Egypt: ever the premier stamping ground of Atlantological thinking. Very sadly, Hancock chooses to start here with the assertion of an old chestnut so thoroughly outmoded that one really does wonder at the reading range of these 'alternative archaeologists'. 'The Great Pyramid', he declares, 'and its neighbours at Giza had emerged out of a black hole in architectural history so deep and so wide that neither its bottom nor its far side had ever been identified.' Not so: the hole and its depth, width and blackness are all in Hancock's head. The architectural evolution of the pyramids – from covered-over holes in the ground before 3500 BC, through flat-topped mud-brick tombs at around 3000 BC, to graves with stone-hewn chambers at about 2800 BC, to stepped pyramids in stone of 2700 BC, to low-sloping true pyramids in 2600 BC, to the Giza pyramids at around 2500 BC – is all very well known and dated. But Hancock rehearses long familiar (and long discredited) doubts about the pyramids' role as tombs and about the attribution of particular pyramids to particular kings. He brings up the never-justified accusation that a Victorian explorer of the Great Pyramid faked the name of Khufu (Cheops) in the roof space above the King's Chamber – this is now wholly exploded by the discovery that the ancient workmen's markings (which include Khufu's name) go round the sides of blocks never exposed till recent years. Curiously enough, first we get the doubts and then the grudging admission that the weight of evidence all the same points to the correctness of the conventional attributions. What was the point, then, of raising the doubts – if not to create a miasma of uncertainty and distrust of Egyptology, so as to let in 'alternative' suggestions in due course?

Like many another exponent of what we shall have to call 'alternative Egyptology', Hancock makes much of the so-called Inventory Stele found near the Great Pyramid for its insinuation that the Sphinx is older than the pyramids at Giza. But even he is obliged to recognize that it is a late work, nearly two thousand years younger than the Great Pyramid. What he doesn't tell us is that it comes from a period of Egyptian revivalism (rather like the Gothic Revival of Victorian England) when the past was being imitated and reinterpreted in an almost romantic fashion. He wants to claim the Inventory Stele as an accurate copy of an original of Khufu's time, when there is absolutely no reason at all to think so and many reasons, including its linguistic anachronisms, to know that it is not.

I have gone into the age of the Sphinx at great length in my *Riddles of the Sphinx*. Suffice it to say here that the 'alternative Egyptologists' have not proved it to be older than the pyramids and their geological evidence, while interesting, is capable of other explanations that do not conflict with academic Egyptological dating to the reign of Khufu's successor Khafre. For Hancock to quote an Egyptologist of over a century ago as an advocate of the Sphinx's great age is like quoting a defunct nineteenth-century medical opinion in a doctor's surgery today. His subjective impression that the Sphinx must be very old is just that: subjective.

Things are often pretty subjective with authors like Hancock. For him, the underground chamber complex of Menkaure's pyramid seems to vibrate 'like the convoluted, multi-valve heart of some slumbering Leviathian'. The entry to Khafre's burial chamber 'seemed to gape like the doorway to another dimension'. At this point, the internal dimensions of the pyramids, in particular the complex arrangements of Khufu's, are discussed in terms of their number significances, in line with the theory that precessional information is incorporated into many of the products, both concrete and mythological, of the ancient world. The dimensions of the Great Pyramid have been used in the past to arrive at theories ranging from Bible prophecy to a universal system of weights and measures. The sceptical response to all such notions is to point out that a sufficiently complex structure with various lengths, angles and volumes built into it is bound to be capable of all sorts of computations with results to suit all tastes. As an American naval officer is said to have retorted to the number-mongers at Giza in the nineteenth century: 'If a suitable unit of measurement is found – say versts, hands or cables – an exact equivalent to the distance of Timbuktu is certain to be found in the roof girder work of the Crystal Palace, or in the number of street lamps in Bond Street, or the Specific Gravity of mud, or the mean weight of an adult goldfish.'

As the pyramids are investigated for their numerological possibilities, so the religious texts of ancient Egypt are vetted for 'encoded' messages about precession. The Pyramid Texts, in particular (since they are the oldest such writings, inscribed in pyramids just a little later than the Giza trio), are rehearsed. These rather barbarous Pyramid Texts, which plainly reflect traditional religious ideas of more primitive times, are frequently obscure but that is no reason whatsoever to speculate with Hancock that they might be translations into Egyptian of Atlantean (or whatever) originals all about precession. In line with his notion of a secret society of seers who passed on their arcane knowledge, Hancock seems to take it for granted that any sophisticated astronomical lore among the Egyptian priesthood would have been encoded in covert and disguised form into Egyptian mythology, but it is not at all obvious why that should be – unless to explain the complete absence of any overt and clear evidence for it. Hancock says that the Egyptians (and Greeks for the most part) are not supposed to have possessed any advanced astronomical knowledge of the kind we have today – I think he means that the Egyptologists and archaeologists are doing this 'supposing'. But, of course, the basis on which the scholars take the line they do is the surely not entirely unreasonable one that the Egyptians' records never evince the slightest acquaintance with modern astronomy (except for some latter-day speculation in Hellenistic Alexandria) – unless you trawl their myths with a vivid and flexible imagination.

Just as he persists in wanting to see Egyptian civilization as springing into existence seemingly out of nowhere (whereas its prehistory before unification under its first king is actually very well-known to Egyptologists), so he would like to see it as relentlessly declining after its initial glories. (This harks back to Plato's degeneration of the Atlanteans as the divine strain became diluted in them over time.) It is a very subjective view, one shared with Donnelly: the pharaohs of the New Kingdom may not have built pyramids like the kings of the Old Kingdom, but they made Abu Simbel and the Colossi of Memnon and their religious writings are a lot less barbarous than the Pyramid Texts. Hancock needs, for related reasons, to try to push back Egyptian civilization if he can to some time nearer the exodus from Atlantis (or whatever) of his supermen with advanced astronomy and so forth. The layout of the Giza complex in about 10,500 BC in the light of the Orion-on-earth hypothesis is one line of argument, and a rather romantic approach to Egypt's oldest records, like the Palermo Stone, offers him another tack. The king listing of the Palermo Stone lacks its opening registers as a result of damage and the Egyptians believed their land had been ruled by gods and demi-gods and 'Followers of Horus' before their first real king of about 3000 BC.

On this slender 'evidence' and in defiance of all archaeology in Egypt, Hancock can speculate about a long line of lost rulers of a lost civilization linking dynastic Egypt back to the lost supercivilization of Atlantis (or wherever). He would like to think certain ruins (like the Osireion at Abydos and the temples by the Sphinx) are older than they are, and that the religious boat burials of the Egyptians can somehow link these strictly riverside people to an ancient seafaring culture. He makes bold claims for agriculture in Egypt as early as 13,000 BC, when the evidence is actually of an early practice of wild plant collecting during hunter-gatherer times in the Nile Valley and not cultivation of domesticated plants. In other parts of the world this collecting of wild grass seeds led on to real agriculture, but it came to nothing in Egypt, where farming arrived late by the standards of the ancient world, in only about 5000 BC. These speculations take Hancock to the Elysian Fields of the ancient Egyptians, Ta-Neteru, the land of the gods: was it from such a land, he wonders, that Osiris and Thoth came at the First Time, in the boats of the seafaring, star-gazing survivors of the lost ancient supercivilization?

Meeting up with his fellow worker and sometime co-writer Robert Bauval, at the mortuary temple of Khafre's pyramid at Giza, Graham Hancock draws near the end of this first long outing of his into Atlantology with a fresh wave of speculation. A picture is conjured up of the Giza site laid out in about 10,500 BC to mimic a particular disposition of the constellation of Orion in the sky of about that time – even if, as we know, the multi-starred constellation by any stretch of the imagination only fits the ruins at Giza and round and about at just three points. There's talk of a continuous cult of Osiris at Giza over eight thousand years – even if there's not a scrap of archaeology to attest to it. Giza is seen as a cunningly contrived provocation to future ages to ferret out its secrets: the Great Pyramid is positively asking for its own violation, so as to yield its store of secret messages to posterity. Both thinkers blithely speculate about zodiac 'houses' at Giza – fish, ram, lion, bull – without questioning whether our zodiacal system goes back beyond the Babylonians of the first millennium BC and without revealing to the reader that it certainly doesn't in Egypt, where a completely different circle of constellations (not on the ecliptic plane like ours) was in vogue for as far back as we have any evidence for Egyptian star maps, about 2000 BC.

Very near the end of *Fingerprints of the Gods*, Atlantis as such is mentioned for the first time, and Hancock faces up to the fact that his Atlantis cannot have been in the Atlantic Ocean where Plato got the whole thing going. Nor can it have been in the Pacific or the Indian Ocean. Hancock in this book plumps for the Flem-Aths' and Hapgood's Antarctica, the victim of 'the dramatic and deadly meltdown of the last Ice Age between about 15,000 and 8000 BC', (flooded, then frozen). Finé's old map is trotted out, for us to admire its ice-free (if not very accurate) rendering of 'Antarctica'. So the remains of the lost civilization 'might today be lying under two miles of ice at the South Pole'. Hancock seems to think that the catastrophic icing of Antarctica reduced its survivors in short order to little more than a Stone Age way of life, albeit they were able to devise those crafty mythological encodements of their advanced astronomical knowledge, and establish the ground plan of the Giza monuments to similarly enshrine their profound understanding of precession and what have you. It's hard to know why they couldn't have kept more of their sophisticated style of life going, these 'master-builders, scientists, engineers, cartographers, mathematicians, medical doctors and the like'. Hancock pictures most of these people going native among the lesser breeds they descended upon after the catastrophe, but with a 'minority of well-organized visionaries' doing their best to salvage something from the disaster. And choosing pyramid fields and the vagaries of mythology to do it! Turning themselves into a secret society to try to transmit their steadily degenerating knowledge through the ages.

At one point, it looks as though all their ingenious efforts have come down for Hancock to little more than a sort of overblown 'Kilroy was here', but he recovers himself to interpret the labours of his visionaries as something more in the way of a warning to future generations of catastrophes yet to come. If such catastrophes are the result of inevitable cycles of precession or crust displacement, we may well wonder why they bothered. What are we going to be able to do about it if and when another one comes along? Mayan Prophecies, the millennial (and failed) predictions of Cayce, even the prognostications of the Watchtower Bible and Tract Society of Pennsylvania are invoked by Hancock in an effort to consolidate the idea of an end-of-the-world threat to our civilization. Rather recklessly we might think, in this book of 1995, Hancock repeats the stuff about a planetary line-up in May 2000, though the voice of caution seems to have come through on that one when he concedes that maybe nothing will come of it (nothing did). For the prodigious efforts of the Atlantean survivors (in planning Giza and giving up their spare time to developing elaborate mythological systems) to have been worthwhile, there have to be catastrophes to come I suppose. Or to put it another way, to make it seem plausible to suggest that there were any Atlantean survivors who went to all this trouble, you need to posit that there are catastrophes to come. Beyond that, the gloomy anxiety of the Atlantological outlook is all too obviously religious in its inheritance. Plato's notion of cyclical catastrophism, not confined to the *Timaeus* and *Critias*, was basically a scientific idea, according to the limitations of scientific knowledge in his day. Maybe he got into difficulties with the *Critias* when a more religious concept of divine retribution interfered with the scientific scheme. There is no religion in Donnelly, just a one-off (non-cyclical) attempt to explain ancient civilizations by reference back to an earlier supercivilization. Spence went in the course of his writings from something like Donnelly's position to a more doom-laden vision. Hapgood was simply trying to bolster his *outré* theory of earth crust displacement with whatever seemed to cast doubt on orthodox geology and archaeology. Hancock, one feels, has emphasized the doom motif as much as anything so as to try and give some plausibility to the theory that ancient monuments and myths were laboriously constructed for some purpose relevant to the world today. Possibly it is unworthy to speculate that scenarios of doom also create an impressionable state of mind in one's readership. For all I know, Hancock is just a gloomy sort of chap.

Hancock's contribution to the development of our Atlantis Syndrome in his *Fingerprints of the Gods* is to emphasize the alarmist tendency in Atlantological thinking, to highlight the idea of encoded messages from the past to the future in mythology and architecture and to make more of the 'secret society' device for the preservation and transmission of the ancient wisdom than any of his predecessors did. His book ends on a note of vague but dismal prophecy, with a bleak visit to the Hopi Indians of Arizona. Is this the sort of thing his readers want, perhaps? To think that it will all soon be over – in 2012 with the Maya, or 2030 with another crust slip?

At all events, by the standards of real archaeology Hancock's dactyloscopy has not begun to demonstrate that a supercivilization ever existed in Antarctica (or anywhere else) or that its ancient lore was transmitted through a line of secret visionaries, by means of an assortment of folk-tales and planning initiatives, into ancient Egypt, Peru and Mexico. The archaeological record of the past is not plastered with the fingerprints of any gods.

11

MIRRORS AND MIRAGES

Graham Hancock returned to the fray in 1998, after his Martian sojourn, with a book called *Heaven's Mirror*, a title that speaks for itself of the theory of celestial patterns copied on the earth. In many ways, it is the same book as *Fingerprints of the Gods*, only with the material in a different order (some of it is new) and excellent photographs. (It's an interesting fact that most books about 'alternative archaeology' have an old-fashioned look to them, with poor photographs of a largely anecdotal character poorly reproduced: *Heaven's Mirror* is an altogether finer product.)

The book begins with the less amiable side of the Aztecs, in a rather sensationally gory account of their bloody sacrifices, a system of priestcraft run mad, or madder than usual. To sustain the idea that a golden thread of the ancient wisdom of Atlantis (or whatever) runs through the later history of mankind – much later with the Aztecs – Hancock wants to believe that a debased misapprehension of an old way of astral initiation into the mysteries of the ancient wisdom came through with the Aztecs in the form of sheer bloody sacrifice. Instead of a pure, spiritual, metaphorical shedding of the body in search of immortality, the Aztecs took it all too literally and actually separated the soul from the body in the most direct fashion: which, incidentally, would highlight the dangers of trying to encode this ancient wisdom in mythological systems! As with many religious practices, it may be doubted that anything really spiritual at all was in the forefront of the Meso-Americans' minds when they tore the hearts out of their victims – religion told them in the crudest terms that this was the way to rejuvenate the sun and postpone the end of the world. From their point of view, we would be well advised to start a massive programme of human sacrifice right now, to try to avert the doom of 2012 according to the Mayan Prophecies!

A less terrifying strain in the American religious outlook was represented by the wise and humane teachings of Quetzalcoatl – so Hancock clings to him as embodying the ancient wisdom of the Atlanteans through the dark ages of human sacrifice. The recent discovery of a speculatively 'Caucasoid' human skeleton (Hancock seems to think fully Caucasian) in the north-western part of the United States at a place called Kennewick, with a radiocarbon date of *c.* 9300 BP, excites him as possible evidence for the presence of those old Atlanteans (or whatever he would like to call them) on American soil before American Indian culture, in some places, took a vicious turn. (I continue to wonder whether Graham Hancock is uneasy about talk of missionary white men among the American Indians.) It is more likely that the Kennewick find simply illustrates the genetic latitude of the peopling of the Americas, with a considerable range of types derived from the Asian populations ancestral to the Amerinds. In any case, Kennewick is just a stray find so far, with its one carbon date – not a context of many related finds with an array of consistent dates. Archaeologists want context and a body of data, not one-offs, however suggestive. (It is interesting that Hancock, no friend of radiocarbon dating as a rule, should cleave to this one.)

There follows the familiar attempt to establish the existence of an advanced geodetic and astronomical science among the American civilizations. Teotihuacan again, with its central avenue now seen as a parallel with the Milky Way, just as the Egyptians sometimes equated the Milky Way with the Nile. Hancock is predictably inclined to be impressed by this common resort to the Milky Way in the two different cultures, but we can only say again that it is in both cases a perfectly natural choice of imagery (from a far from infinite store) and likely to be made by different people in different places and at different times quite independently. And, whatever its achievements (even if they were as spectacular as Hancock claims), star-gazing is not science, however good the observations and records may be. Even if (and when) it might lead to construction of monuments on earth to sight the stars or mimic constellations, it still would not be science.

Hancock is aware in this book that there is a problem with projecting the constellation signs of our current zodiac back into the remote past. The system we employ is not attested before the Babylonians of the first millennium BC, even if some of the signs may go back to the Sumerian forerunners of the Mesopotamian cultures. It isn't much use to point to the Lascaux cave paintings of France with bulls (along with deer and horses and so forth) from about fifteen thousand years ago as suggestive of the possibility of recognition of the Babylonian Taurus. And the fact remains that, until only a few centuries BC, the Egyptians in their rather amateurish and inconsistent star maps used none of the Babylonian signs, giving their attention to a set of constellations that don't even run in the same ecliptic plane as ours and the Babylonians' do but figure higher in the sky. (The zodiac from the Greek-period temple at Dendera is a late hodgepodge of crowded Egyptian plus Babylonian constellations that can't possibly point to the fourth millennium BC as Hancock would like it to.) Similarly, to talk of the very ancient significance of the number 72 as being the years of one degree of change in the sunrise background of our zodiacal system presupposes without justification that the modern zodiac was in use long ages ago and that the division of the circle into 360 degrees (another Babylonian invention) was already in place.

Hancock tries to see evidence for our zodiacal and other constellations in the ground plans of various American edifices, like Uxmal, where the effort seems pretty arbitrary in its plotting: sometimes on, sometimes between and sometimes outside walls. Maybe the identification of Utatlan in Guatemala with Orion is better, but we don't get a plan and it has to be said that Orion is the most striking star configuration in the sky, likely to be isolated in any culture that can see it – just as the Milky Way cannot be missed. Spotting these features of the night sky, even building representations of them on earth (not that such building is anywhere proved) would not be very extraordinary and would not imply a common cultural heritage, let alone the machinations of a secret society of astronomer-priests and builder-scientists.

As with Egypt, Hancock makes much of the allegedly unprecedented nature of cultural developments in the Americas, but again this reflects more his lack of detailed knowledge of archaeology in both places than an absence of evidence in reality. In both regions archaeology has unearthed the evidence for the build-up towards civilization, as we saw in earlier chapters, though in the nature of things that build-up is much less showy than the enduring monuments of the mature civilizations. It is, however, demonstrated by an array of sites with consistent patterns of finds dated by several lines of evidence: it is not a matter of being impressed by things like stray resemblances (imaginary rather than real) between the Sphinx and Olmec heads, as repeated by Hancock in this book, too.

Rather more of the precessional numerology than we enjoyed in *Fingerprints of the Gods* is served up in *Heaven's Mirror*. For example, 72 plus half of 72 and half of the addition of 36 to 72 and 10 times or 1,000 times or 10,000 times the 54 so produced – all these figures are said to feature significantly in ancient structures and myths; along with (for some reason) 600 times 72 to arrive via the height and base circumference of the Great Pyramid at the size of the earth; plus 2160 as the number of years to shift from one of the twelve signs of the zodiac to the next, divided by 10, multiplied by 100, doubled to 4320. On and on it seems to go, all apparently of tremendous significance. Now we're back at the Great Pyramid, Hancock is sure that its precise orientation could only have been achieved by 'master astronomers', but I see no reason to call them anything more than practised star-gazers. Of course, calling them master astronomers lets in the possibility that they not only knew about precession but also understood it. It is, however, one thing (and a pretty speedy thing) to arrive at the points of the compass by star-gazing – quite another, requiring long periods of observation and record-keeping, to identify and quantify the phenomenon of precession – and yet another still to understand why it happens.

The match between the three pyramids of Giza and the belt stars of the Orion constellation is re-emphasized by Hancock in this book of 1998, but the confident assertion of three years earlier about the 'faultless precision' of the correspondences between the rest of Orion and various other constructions close to Giza is not repeated. Indeed nothing whatever is now said about any wider correlation between monuments and stars to reflect a whole Orion on the ground: now it is just the three belt stars and the three pyramids at Giza. If this is an example of the Heaven's Mirror principle, then it's a pretty small mirror in which you can't see much of the heavens. Sadly, too, for Hancock's and Bauval's notion, there remains the oddity that you have to look up to the north in the sky and down to the south on the ground to make even the general correlation. If 'faultless precision' at many points has to give way to mere symbolic resemblance at a few, then all talk of the advanced astronomical knowledge of the ancient priests and the precision of their calculations (and there is much of such talk) comes to naught.

Despite this retrenchment about Orion, much is still made of heaven on earth and the underworld in the sky, and of the amazing significance of a supposed moment of precise matching between the pyramids by the Nile and Orion by the Milky Way at the lowest precessional culmination of 10,500 BC. (The idea is that an observer looking south over the pyramids with the Nile to the left could look up and see Orion – the belt stars at least – in the night sky with the Milky Way to their left in some sort of 'perfect match' at culmination in 10,500 BC.) We may remember it was 10,450 in the previous book: I can never quite see why these seemingly punctilious datings are given to a slow precessional process that looks pretty much the same every year for a great many years. Hancock (and his colleague Bauval) also make much of the rising of the sun behind the Sphinx at the vernal equinox of 10,500 BC, but the same stricture about the slow drift of the zodiac with precession applies – and so does the warning that there is no evidence whatever that the Egyptians knew the signs of the later Babylonian zodiac, Leo included, in 2500 BC when the Sphinx was carved, to say nothing of 10,500 BC when there was no Egyptian civilization at all to carve it. There is also not a shred of evidence to suggest that the Egyptians ever associated sphinxes with Leo even in late times when they became acquainted with the Babylonian zodiac.

Hancock seems inclined to think the Great Sphinx was carved as long ago as 10,500 BC, but he wonders whether only the ground–plan – and not the actual building – of the pyramids was executed as far back as that. Perhaps, he thinks, the secret body of astronomer-priests who continued to beaver away throughout Egyptian history had precessionary theory so completely at their fingertips that they could design the pyramids eight thousand years afterwards to perfectly realize on earth the magic configuration of 10,500 BC. Why? Hancock seems to think it was to advertise their grasp of precession (in other words their high astronomical knowledge) to future generations. Why? Is it going to be the old warning stuff again?

Incidentally, Hancock is constantly chiding Egyptologists with rating the ancient Egyptians and their priests as 'primitive' or 'half-savage'. I know of no Egyptologist who writes or speaks in this vein. On the contrary, no one is in a better position to recognize the subtlety and complexity of Egyptian thought than people who can actually read the ancient Egyptians' works. Egyptologists are well aware that they are dealing with a rounded civilization, whose interest for them arises out of its very complexity. The imaginary Egyptologists that Hancock credits with these imaginary views are straw men set up to be knocked down for their failure to recognize the advanced astronomical prowess (and all the rest of it) revealed by the insights of Hancock and his pals.

In precession Hancock sees a 'great cosmic cycle as a symbol of rebirth and renewal after long periods of apparent extinction'. This is an odd idea, since even prolonged observation of precession over thousands of years (over the full 26,000 for that matter) would see no episodes of catastrophic overthrow as far as we have any reasons to think: the houses of the zodiac don't disappear for ever with the turn of the year, or the drift of precession from one house to the next over some two thousand years. It's all a slow, steady process and all the signs of the zodiac are available for inspection in any given epoch, whichever one the sun is rising from at the vernal equinox at any particular time. If you're looking for a symbol of rebirth and renewal after extinction, then the daily round of the sun and the annual round of the seasons make much more obvious candidates. By invoking the 26,000-year-long cycles of precession, Hancock is certainly making claims of cosmic proportions for the philosophy of eternal renewal that he wishes upon his ancient astronomer-priests. And he is thereby taking the Atlantological vision far beyond Donnelly in the direction of a religion of immortality through everlasting cycles of rebirth (but not exactly rebirth from the extinction of death). On the one hand, a serene process of slow, calm recyclings over tens of thousands of years can be pictured on the basis of the orderly workings of precession, but on the other hand there remains room for catastrophe if the wobbling polar axis of the world should ever slip its bearings and shift the skies about abruptly. (Mind you, if that should happen from time to time, it would make nonsense of attempts to rerun the night skies of yore on our computers or construct precessional chronologies, wouldn't it?)

With the severely diminished example of Giza and Orion's Belt behind us, we journey next halfway round the world with Graham Hancock to Angkor Wat in Cambodia. We get off to a rather dismaying start with his observation that, in ancient Egyptian, Ankh-Hor means 'Horus lives': another of those bits of amateur philologizing with stray words that was already inadmissable in Donnelly's time. You might as well be impressed to notice that the English name for the capital city of modern Egypt makes something like the sound in English of the Greek chi-rho monogram of Christ. (Or that 'Hancock' itself is not a million miles from 'Ankh' – all you need to add is the cock.) And then, because Angkor is apparently about 72° east of Giza (72 is one of those precessional numbers, remember), Hancock finds time to speculate about the vast antiquity of the 360° system.

Hancock's big claim at Angkor is that the monuments on the ground model the serpentine constellation we know as Draco (the snake), rather as the monuments at Giza were supposed (but turned out not) to model the entire constellation

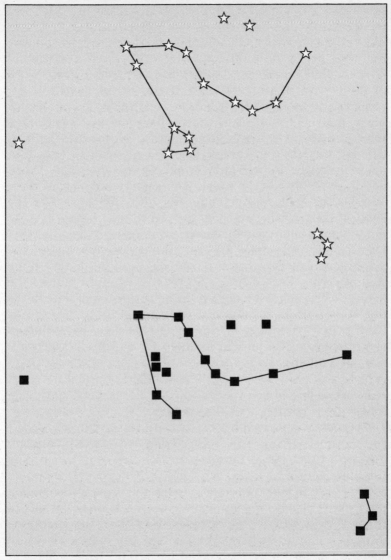

Even the most favourable selection of monuments at Angkor (bottom) makes a poor match for the stars of Draco (top).

of Orion. At least we know that the ancient Egyptians recognized the constellation we call Orion – it is one of only three of our constellations that they did share with us, the rest of theirs being quite different star groupings. There is no evidence that the ancient Cambodians recognized Draco at all in the course of their attested astronomical observations. Moreover, to see anything like Draco at Angkor Wat, Hancock has to make (for no obviously compelling reasons) a particular selection out of a much greater array of temples built at different times and for historically different reasons (which in many instances are well-known and not astronomical). When he has done his best, or worst, with the ground-plan of these temples, he still cannot come up with anything like the faultless precision he was first inclined to see at Giza. It is, to put it bluntly, immediately obvious from his own diagrams that his selection of temples on the ground does not mirror the arrangement of Draco in the heavens. Even he doesn't think the mirroring worked in AD 800–1200 when he knows the temples were built – it will come as no surprise to learn that he thinks the match, such as it was, occurred in 10,500 BC. As there is no archaeology at Angkor of that date, he speculates about rebuilding on ancient locations for which all evidence is lost, or building on the basis of long-preserved star maps (which needless to say we don't have either) or – and the heart sinks – building in accordance with arcane precessionary data somehow encoded in mythological tales.

Hancock is impressed by the serpent iconography of Angkor as a buttress for the idea of identifying the whole monument field with Draco. Snake imagery is first attested in this part of the world in the Rig-veda, the Sanskrit hymns some of which may go back to about 1500 BC, though the serpent-mentioning texts are probably of only about 300 BC. Hancock needs to think they might be much older than that and mentions disputes among Sanskrit scholars and the barmy claims of some enthusiasts that they could be 870,000 years old – in which time-frame only the small-brained, flint-knapping *Homo ergaster/erectus* is ever encountered in the archaeological record, not an obvious candidate for the composition of religious texts in an Indo-European language. While we are with philology, we may pause to be amused by Hancock's speculations about the correspondence between the Sanskrit Bija meaning seed (of the gods) and the ancient Egyptian Bja meaning meteoric iron. 'Perhaps it is a coincidence,' he ventures; and then, enthused by further mythological matchmaking between India and Egypt, he manfully admits that 'it is difficult to resist a comparison'. I think we may take it that, when writers like Hancock find comparisons difficult to resist, something is in the offing that many of us wouldn't find it hard to resist for one moment. He is especially keen to see knowledge of precession in the myths and imagery of cultures widely separated in chronology and location. He talks of a 'hidden link, attenuated across vast gulfs of time and space, adapted to different cultural contexts, but always essentially returning to the same roots': we can only retort that if things are hidden, attenuated and adapted, then how can we know there ever were any common roots? To see in some of the Angkor carvings an image of a mountain 'churned' on its axis with serpentine ropes as a representation of the precession of the equinoxes is far-fetched enough in the first place: to think drawings in certain New Kingdom tombs of Egypt (two thousand years earlier) of what might be a pyramid, with serpents and figures who might have ropes in their hands, amounts to the selfsame thing – that is far-fetched indeed.

To explain how the stellar arrangements of 10,500 BC could have issued in the alleged ground-plan and interior details of the Giza pyramids at about 2500 BC and in the monuments of Cambodia of about AD 1000, Hancock seems from here on in *Heaven's Mirror* to become more and more attracted to the idea of a secret order of astronomer-priests carrying their private knowledge down through the ages and across divergent cultures. He takes Egyptian mythology at face value when it asserts that the first semi-divine rulers of Egypt, before the human kings of their historical records, came to settle in the Nile Valley from somewhere outside Egypt. These were, of course, for Hancock those astronomically adept survivors of a cataclysm that destroyed their original home – Atlantis to you and me. And something like Hapgood's earth crust displacement is evidently thought to have brought that cataclysm about: it never is quite clear how this disaster might be related to the precession of the equinoxes, which as far as we know is a slow, steady process that simply takes our constellations around and up and down in the night sky. You might conceivably take the relentless repetitious shift of precession as an image of eternal recurrence, but it is surely too slow and orderly (without any interruptions, of which we know absolutely nothing) to function well as an image of cyclical catastrophe. At about 10,500 BC Orion was at its precessionary low (and Draco high), and now thirteen thousand years later it is at its high point, poised to sink again with the millennia of precession. So what? Precession is not about to wreak havoc with the world any more than it did thirteen thousand years ago, when Orion started up and Draco started down. It's all a gradual, never-ending, never-starting process. If millenarianism is hope and anxiety over a thousand years, then Hancock's precessional musings constitute a supermillenarianism of truly cosmic foreboding. This is more religion than science.

After visiting an island of Micronesia with impressive megalithic remains whose age he doesn't advertise (they're only about 900 BC), Hancock falls to speculating again on a cataclysmic end to the last ice age, with the novel (for him) addition of a collision with cometary debris at the Flem-Aths' favoured date of 9,600 BC, and further episodes at about 2350 BC and AD 500. All this seems a long way from the majestic round of precession, with these more random bouts of catastrophe apparently invoked to 'explain' cultural decline at the dates in question. Gloomy prognostications of further comet or asteroid collisions help us on our way to Japan's westernmost island of Yonaguni, where we are treated to two different underwater photographs of what is actually the same geological detail, plus several more not so impressive ones of other parts of the Yonaguni formation. This is plainly a natural geological feature. Even Robert Schoch who thought the Sphinx was older than the Egyptologists do, even John Anthony West who thinks it's older than Schoch does, even these two eagerly open-minded investigators evidently think the Yonaguni 'monument' is a natural formation. Its slopes and platforms are not man-made, as is quite apparent through the murky waters of the photographs. Pottery found at the site has yielded dates of about 2000 BC and the Japanese professor who espouses the cause of Yonaguni as a human creation only thinks it's up to three thousand years old. It follows that Hancock's several pages of argument to try to date Yonaguni by working out when it would have been on the Tropic of Cancer (in accordance with changes in the obliquity of the earth's axis – not precession) go for nothing, as a quite pointless exercise. Readers can come to their own conclusions as to how many more pages of Hancock's diverse arguments can be viewed in the same light.

But for Hancock, skating over the extreme dubiety of the evidence at this Japanese island (to put it mildly), Yonaguni is one of many markers set around the globe by the astronomer-priests of that long-lost maritime civilization of his, some thirteen thousand years ago or as near as makes no difference. Hancock is satisfied that all these marker sites are dotted at intervals of numbers of degrees of precessionary significance, testifying to the ancient knowledge of geodesy and scientific astronomy that he attributes to these people.

Where better than Easter Island to look for another such marker? Everyone knows those strange statues of Easter Island, if nothing much else about the place. In fact, the statue building of the Easter Islanders took place (according to radiocarbon dating) at some time after the fifth century AD, up to the seventeenth century. Their own legends tell of their arrival on the island about 1,800 years ago and their nearest cultural affinities are with the Marquesas, about 3,700 kilometres to the north-west. Theirs was a world of war, cannibalism, picture-writing on boards and religion to do with the statues. Hancock sets out to suggest as many parallels – not all of them sound – between the Easter Island of the past several centuries and the Egypt of four or more thousand years ago as he can muster: the original founders of the culture coming from elsewhere allegedly after a flood, the institution of god-like kings, the activities of a bunch of astronomer-priest-architects, the building of sacred mounds. And, well, the Easter islanders' own name for their sacred sanctuaries – the famous Aku – sounds a bit like the Egyptian Akh (one of the components of the soul), doesn't it? He seems ever so impressed to find that Easter Island is on a longitude halfway between Giza and Angkor. Rather revealingly, Hancock even descends to considering 'magic' as a means of moving the statues from their quarries, as per local folklore reported to European visitors after the Dutch got there in 1722 (on Easter Day). Magic of some sort has, of course, been proposed to explain the moving of pyramid blocks in Egypt and the gigantic masonry of Tiahuanaco in Peru. Most writers on these topics mean something more like anti-gravity than Aladdin's genie when they entertain magical explanations for ancient construction works. At Easter Island, as with Egypt and Peru, no magic of any kind is needed to explain the movement of the statuary and modern experiments have succeeded in moving ones left at their quarry sites with methods involving the types of ropes and sledges that were available to their original makers. It is at times like this with Graham Hancock that we see the journalistic flair most clearly showing: the skilful exploitation of whatever is to hand to build up a story, and just about anything will do, even 'magic'. Any amount of scholarly-looking apparatus of notes at the end of such books cannot disguise the essentially journalistic nature of enterprises like *Heaven's Mirror*. Can it be a coincidence, we might ask in Hancockian vein, that several of the chief protagonists of Atlantology in modern times have been, like Donnelly and Spence and Hancock himself, journalists?

We will not tarry over Peru and Bolivia, Nazca Lines and Lake Titicaca, Cuzco and its Sacsahuaman, all over again. Nor over more of the Sphinx and might-be tunnels underneath it, never attested by actual excavation. (As with the Sphinx, there are dark hints of delays and obstructions at Tiahuanaco on the part of hidebound professional archaeologists – to the detriment of potentially wonderful discoveries.) We will not tarry because we have heard it all before and it is all a matter of yet more things that are reminiscent of other things somewhere else and of invitations to be astounded at similar beliefs or imageries shared by different ancient cultures. As always, there is scant recognition that the common experiences of all human life, complex but not limitless, are likely to go on throwing up similar ideas and similar ways of expressing them all over the world. And scant recognition, too, of what the sheer application of manpower can achieve when expense is no object (because the modern idea of commercial expense had not been invented) and time is what rulers and priests want it to be for those labouring under them.

Towards the end of his book, Hancock is plainly wondering what it all might add up to. He has rehearsed catastrophism and diffusionism at length – to what avail? His answer is that his conjectured ancient civilization 'must have possessed knowledge which they believed to be of vital importance to mankind, otherwise they would have had no motive to go to such lengths to disseminate it'. But the lengths to which they allegedly went are really all in Hancock's imagination – the marker sites, the precessional data encoded in structures and pictures and myths, the night skies of yore recorded in ground-plans at Giza and Angkor, the narratives of global catastrophe buried in folk-tales, the cartographic triumphs behind Piri and Columbus. None of these things is an established fact, and all are open to terminally grave doubts. These lengths were not gone to, and there was nothing to go to them for – because no knowledge of vital importance to mankind (precession and cyclical catastrophe, not necessarily related, would seem to be the knowledge in question) has been demonstrated to have actually existed in the remote past to motivate these lengths that were not gone to.

In reality, a tissue of mere speculations, often no better than unoccasioned questions, has been concocted in the interests of a psychological disposition to believe in a unique original inspiration of mankind, a hidden transmission of wisdom and knowledge through a secret priesthood, a system of cosmically ordained catastrophes, a gloomy vision of glacial or cometary or gravitational disaster soon to revisit us (just around the corner in fact), a promise of meaning to life and renewal beyond death. This is indeed a religious concoction: a notable extension of a feature of the Atlantis Syndrome always present but never previously so much to the fore.

Whereas Antarctica had featured boldly in Hancock's *Fingerprints of the Gods*, it – and earth crust displacement with it – is not nearly so prominent in *Heaven's Mirror*. It's as though the mounting religious enthusiasm of the later work makes a mundane location for Atlantis less interesting as time goes by. In unmistakably religious language, Hancock speaks of the ancient world as 'illuminated' by a great theory of 'the meaning and mystery of death and the possibility of eternal life'. He tells of 'a science of immortality' to free the spirit from 'the gross encumbrance of matter'. Anybody who thinks matter is a gross encumbrance is thinking religiously. As befits its cosmic status, Hancock thinks this old spiritual science of his was 'from the beginning . . . as old as the hills . . . with adepts and teachers already present and at work at the dawn of history'. How he could surmise that when the homeland of these adepts and teachers is supposed to be under the ice or the oceans, and consequently not available to have its archaeological evolution assessed, is not at all clear – and only goes to show how mythic all this stuff is.

At least Hancock manages to end *Heaven's Mirror* on a more cheerful note than he did *Fingerprints of the Gods*. Religions may rely to a great extent on doom and gloom and apprehension for their appeal, but a leavening of bright hope is also necessary. Perhaps Hancock is feeling chirpier himself now that he has fully appreciated how the spirituality taught by his ancient seers calls for 'a ruthless stripping away of all attachments to the material world'. He thinks those seers may still be around, after all. If they could keep going from 10,500 BC to plan the pyramids in 2500 BC and have Angkor built till AD 1100, then perhaps their ancient wisdom might also have come through in the creed of the Gnostics of the Hellenistic Levant or, who knows, in the writing of Bacon's *New Atlantis* in the seventeenth century. It may be at work today. The monuments of the world that mimic 'the talismanic sky of 10,500 BC' have not so far been shown to include a terrestrial mirror for Aquarius – Hancock thinks Bimini, no less, might be the place to look for that. But, just possibly mind, it may be that the Aquarius temple is yet to be built, as part of that master plan of the long aeons of precession, just as the cycle shifts sunrise over the Sphinx on the vernal equinox into the constellation of Aquarius, at the opposite end of the thirteen thousand-year semicircle of precessionary change. Think of it –

those secretive heirs of the ancient wisdom working away at this very moment to get their fourth temple built, somewhere on this earth under the twinkling stars! A new religion invented by a journalist? Stranger things have happened in that line.

Graham Hancock in his time has entertained the idea of civilization on other worlds, as his collaboration on *Mars Mystery* in 1998 demonstrates. Interestingly, cometary impact was there proposed as the means by which that (non-existent) ancient extraterrestrial culture was terminated, at some time after about twenty thousand years ago, though it wasn't clear whether the (non-existent) Martian monuments were related to Giza or Angkor and so forth; at any rate, they were surmised to have been created as a warning of the threat of further catastrophes to come. Hancock's universe seems to ooze warnings of disaster. Of course, it predictably turned out that there was no face or pyramid on Mars after all, as many of us could have told the Martian enthusiasts before they ever put pen to paper, as it were.

The chief exponent of the extraterrestrial version of Atlantis, however, was always and still is the Swiss speculative writer Erich von Däniken. He has been at it since the 1960s, often debunked and refuted but seemingly irrepressible: 2000 saw the publication of his *Odyssey of the Gods, an Alien History of Ancient Greece* which, though a slight work in many respects, may be taken to represent the mature expression of his views. With von Däniken we enter an altogether lighter world, with none of the gloom or threat of Hancock's disaster-ridden precessionary round, and very little either of the potentially tedious cargo of mythological, philological and numerological data that can weigh down the offerings of other authors in the field. Von Däniken's many publications have not been notorious for any excessive burden of pedantic scholarship, though they are now graced with the requisite pages of scholarly-looking notes at the back.

In many ways, von Däniken is the *echt* Atlantologist. He has taken the Atlantis theme to its logical conclusion – if logical is the right word in this context. Antarctica was a good try for a place that might conceal innumerable secrets with little or no chance of looking into them, and the oceans hold out the possibility of difficult to explore regions from which murky photographs of ambiguous items can be brought back (Loch Ness does the same job for the Nessie hunters). But there's always the danger that new methods of remote sensing might actually succeed in looking under the ice or making perfect images under water. Of course, the same thing can happen with the nearer reaches of outer space – the good photographs of the Cydonia area of Mars put paid in short order to the pyramid and face on that planet.

But space is practically limitless – sure, you may have to give up on the moon or Mars or anywhere in our solar system in the end, but there's always Sirius or the nebula in Andromeda or some remoter galaxy, full of stars and, presumably, planets, where advanced technologies have perfected faster-than-light or time travel or some such poppycock, to get them here to interfere in human affairs. If patriotism is the last refuge of a scoundrel, then outer space is the last refuge of an Atlantologist. (I wouldn't want it thought that I decry the idea of life on other worlds, including intelligent life with advanced technology: but I think most enthusiasts for the notion of interstellar and intergalactic travel have simply no imaginative grasp of the vastness of the universe in space and time; none of us can have much grasp of it, but it pays to have some.) I suppose in the interests of completeness, we ought to acknowledge that one further refuge beyond even our known universe is theoretically available: Atlantis might exist in another dimension of reality altogether, on the astral plane, say, but somehow able now and then to interact with this world. And, perhaps, if one day a Hancockian religion of Atlantis should ever be established, there will be subtle theologians coming up with an existential sort of Atlantis, spiritually 'real' on account of the allegedly beneficent effect of belief in it.

Back to earth with Erich von Däniken, who is blessedly free of any such mush. In fact, he's notably unsentimental about his alien space 'gods'. He pictures his explorers of the trackless void arriving on earth in the distant past with a more or less well-meaning anthropological interest in our ancestors, dispensing helpful advice in language they taught them. He thinks the aliens would have appeared like gods to our forefathers, adding rather endearingly, 'although we all know that there aren't any gods'.

That they were no angels, in fact, was subsequently demonstrated when they fell out among themselves, went against their orders and even 'had sex with pretty daughters of men'. One wonders at the processes of evolution on other worlds that would have made it possible for them to have sex, let alone want it, with the primitive denizens of our planet: where did they form their idea of prettiness? Does it conform with the tastes of Swiss ex-hoteliers? At all events, interplanetary cross-fertility, with the help of a bit of genetic engineering, brought about a race of mutants, monsters, giants, Titans and the like whose existence is attested in our old friend mythology: 'It must have been a real Frankenstein horror scenario.' It's certainly a farrago of misunderstood biology.

The good aliens eventually took themselves off, back into the depths of the universe, promising to return one day – there's a regrettably religious note. But the bad aliens remained to push our ancestors around with the aid of 'bits and pieces of their original technology'. A picture is painted of solar batteries, hot-air balloons, the odd robot: it all sounds like quite a come-down for people previously able to zoom about the cosmos in spaceships of a technology we cannot even dream about. The offspring of the bad, or baddish, aliens, became the dynasties ruling over the ancient world, both abusing but also teaching their purely earthling subjects a thing or two, intermarrying with humans the while until – like Plato's sons of Atlas – the godlike strain was quite diluted and even the last traces of the old high technology were lost. 'So that is my theory,' says Erich von Däniken.

In *Odyssey of the Gods* von Däniken is concerned to reveal the heritage of the aliens in the approachable mythology and folklore of the Greeks, making much (twenty-four pages' worth at the start of his book) of the story of Jason and the Argonauts. Throughout he errs pretty consistently on the side of a literal reading of all his mythological material: indeed he seems for the most part quite unable to recognize that anything could ever have been made up out of the human imagination, a trait we have seen so often among these highly imaginative writers of 'alternative archaeology'. The animated brazen statue guarding Crete is for him so obviously a robot and not an imaginary development of a piece of statuary that it must have existed. 'But where does the metal monster come from . . . And where did they get the idea of the firespitting dragon? Such creatures never existed in the whole evolution of this planet. No one could have just dreamed it up.' He professes himself very impressed to find that his 1779 German translation of the *Argonautica* of Apollonius of Rhodes of the third century BC uses the word for pilot in connection with the Argo ship; indeed he goes out of his way to assure us that this word is not his own contribution. We could almost be touched by such naivety, as though the word had never been used in connection with any craft before aircraft. But then he thinks the Golden Fleece was some sort of flying machine! (Jonah's whale was a submarine: we aren't confined to the classical world in this odyssey.)

Evidence for his approach to early human history is mostly the routine entries we've had from von Däniken (and others) before. Large bones from China and big hand-axes from Africa are proofs of giants in those days. He says he has 'good reason to believe' that giants built the megalithic temples of Malta, though he doesn't share the reason with us. When he tells us that the great *pithoi* jars of Knossos were storage containers for the fuel (not anything very special, just oil and water) used by the 'rattling, stinking' flying machines of the degenerate sons of the aliens, we might be tempted to conclude that this whole book (perhaps all of von Däniken's output) could be intended as a joke. But he goes on to propose a network of stations around the ancient world, at distances determined by observation of the old golden section rule, where 'these flying tubs' could land. (They seem to have been some sort of hot-air balloon with a steam engine attached.) It's all a bit reminiscent of Hancock's marker sites at locations determined by precessional numerology, only it's more fun since these gods-gone-to-the-bad were evidently touring in search of sex with their priestesses. When their powers had so far declined that they couldn't come any more, the priests just said they were still there in spirit and religion as we know it was born.

When he gets to Delphi (the book is rather disarmingly illustrated with photographs of von Däniken giving a cheery thumbs-up sign at various antique locations), he finds that the mighty slabs of the foundations of the temple of Apollo 'make one think immediately of a helicopter launching platform'. A pity the decrepit aliens' descendants only ran to hot-air balloons with steam engines, then. Von Däniken thinks the original positioning of all these temples and ancient monuments did, however, inspire the later Greeks like Plato and Euclid to their mathematical prowess. He makes the oddly old-fashioned error of confusing the Alexandrian mathematician Euclid of about 300 BC with Euclides of Megara, a contemporary of Plato's, who was not a mathematician. This was a medieval scholars' error and I suggest von Däniken really should invest in a new encyclopaedia: it would pay for itself in no time. (Either that or hire a team of graduate researchers, as some other well-known Atlantological writers do.) Plato and Euclides were fellow pupils of Socrates, but von Däniken has Plato sitting at the feet of this (wrong, non-mathematician) Euclides to learn his mathematics. He also dates the conversations of the *Timaeus* and *Critias* to 401 BC rather than 421, imagining Plato himself to have been there. I suppose it is inconceivable to von Däniken that Plato could have made up any of this dialogue. And it's no surprise to find him taking the whole Atlantis story quite literally from the moment of its appearance in Plato's works. We are treated to all the usual obeisances to Plato's undying devotion to the truth, without any recognition of his philosophical and artistic methods. But von Däniken has added the newish twist of asserting that Plato wouldn't have dared to make up the Atlantis material when the characters of the *Timaeus* were still alive. They may have been alive once (though there are some doubts about Timaeus himself) but they certainly weren't still alive when Plato wrote the *Timaeus* and *Critias*: Socrates dead by judicial suicide, Critias long dead unless he lived to be about 140, Hermocrates killed trying to force his way back into Syracuse in the winter of 408/7 BC, and Timaeus (if he ever existed) necessarily dead some twenty years before the dialogues were composed in about 355 BC.

By taking Plato literally about the great island from which one could go to other islands and a whole continent beyond, Erich von Däniken is satisfied to identify Atlantis, as so many others have done, with America. By taking Plato literally about the gold and silver and orichalcum, he can put his finger like Jim Allen on Peru – after all, might not the ancient Peruvians have made the mysterious alloy out of the rich mineral resources of their land? He is content to attribute the destruction of Plato's Atlantis to the sea level rises of the end of the last ice age (which he announces rather as though none of us had ever heard of this phenomenon before and might be inclined to dispute it). His version of the natural geological formation of Yonaguni has 'broad stairways . . . squares . . . cobbled streets . . . carved monoliths, and even a small tower'. Let's wait for further photographs, Erich. ('Staircases' were claimed at an underwater site west of Gibraltar investigated by Soviet submarine explorers in the 1970s – in fact, they were the results of natural disintegration of basalts.) Von Däniken has no doubts about Bimini either, with 'buildings over which the sea has closed'. The pyramid of Cuicuilco that impressed Hapgood as so provenly old on account of its lava encirclement makes another appearance at a claimed date of seven or eight thousand years ago, though archaeology says it's between twelve and fifteen hundred years old and there was nothing going on there in 7000 BP.

Back with Hapgood, we are also back with Piri Reis and his contentious map. In contrast with his previous treatments of this map, von Däniken does this time admit to a few small discrepancies 'in many cases practically non-existent', which seems a generous way of describing a map with the Amazon on twice and Cuba with the wrong size, shape and orientation, among its many other inaccuracies. He relies on Hapgood's theory that the Reis was trying to marry up an inaccurate Columbian map with a super-accurate Atlantean one, which he thinks must have shown Atlantis itself in the first place. We're told that a German teacher in El Salvador has shown that Mayan texts clearly establish the existence of a city called Aztlan in Guatemala in 12,901 BC and so we're back on von Däniken's old stamping ground: Mayan carvings at Copan in Honduras and Palenque in Mexico with their alleged high-tech indications. He shows a statue from Copan of a figure holding something at his chest which he may be 'operating with his fingers'. We recall the carving of an astronaut at the controls of his spaceship that actually shows the deceased man in association with the Mayan Tree of Life. All in all, von Däniken reckons he has satisfactorily located Atlantis. He says he doesn't want to go searching for

Atlantis but he 'wouldn't mind betting that it lay somewhere in the Caribbean region'.

Von Däniken's contribution to the Atlantis Syndrome is actually to place the essential idea of Atlantis very firmly in outer space. He may put bets on the Caribbean for Plato's particular Atlantis, but the whole concept of a seminal supercivilization behind all merely human endeavours is shifted in von Däniken's approach to somewhere beyond our little planet altogether. I would recommend all Atlantologists to follow him into the outer regions without more ado. Not because he has produced a shred of evidence for his notions, nor even a remotely credible line of argument, but because in the end there's really nowhere else to go.

Sure, there might be a bit more Atlantological mileage, or perhaps we should say fathomage, in submarine speculations about relics of the ancient supercivilization beneath the waves – Hancock continues to harbour them. Published since the first edition of this book, his *Underworld* of 2002 rehearses Bimini and Yonaguni yet again, without enhancing the case for their human creation in postglacial times. His efforts to establish Malta's credentials come to nothing. The underwater features he reports off the south-east coast of India may or may not be artificial productions, but they may also not be as old as he hopes in any case. The patterns detected by sonar off India's north-western coast, deemed by Hancock to indicate submerged cities, cannot be visually identified in their murky waters (too dangerously tidal to dive in) and may, again, be younger than he would like, having quite possibly been subject as much to subsidence as postglacial flooding. The alleged artefacts dredged up from them by grab (not excavated in situ) make a very poor showing as human products of any sort and have no dateable context – even if any of them are old, they do not date the fancied structures suggested by sonar. Schoch has been making similar claims to Hancock's for the region dubbed 'Sundaland' in the south-east Asian archipelago, without producing any 'archaeology' at all. These underwater wonders may linger a while: but really to get into Outer Space with Erich von Däniken right away – and not merely interplanetary either (as the egg-on-the-face on Mars warns) but interstellar or better still intergalactic space, to be on the safe side.

12

MOUNTAINS IN LABOUR

The search for Atlantis will never end. And not all its searchers will wind up in outer space. The attempt will always be made, again and again, to find Atlantis on earth. A book called *Atlantis in America* revived in 1998 the sixteenth-century speculations of men like Fracastoro and Dee, with our old friend the comet as the agent of destruction in 10,513 BC: wonderful the precision these Atlantologists go in for. Another book published in 2000 illustrates very well what a weight of erudition can still be brought to bear in an effort to find some clue to the terrestrial whereabouts of the lost civilization, out of all proportion we might easily think to the results of the enquiry. Andrew Collins' *Gateway to Atlantis* will be the cut-off point of our review of these representative samples of the vast body of Atlantological writings. *Gateway to Atlantis* makes a fitting end since it completely gathers in just about every element of terrestrial Atlantis theory of a remotely plausible character ever proposed and every line of argument ever marshalled. It will very usefully remind us of what we have been about.

Mr Collins (who has previously written about the Garden of Eden and related matters) starts his story in familiar fashion. We find him in a cave on some as yet unnamed tropical island, where he 'almost' feels he is being called to delve into its deposits by 'some unseen *genius loci*'. He soon spots some concentric markings on the rocks which he says resemble lines to be seen in certain megalithic constructions of western Europe. In that characteristic way in which these researchers struggle manfully to retain their objectivity he tells us that it was 'difficult not to see them in terms' of planetary orbits or stellar evolutions. He feels something was being told in these caves of 'archaic events . . . before the dawn of history'. It's hard to say why he felt that way, but evidently he did.

Plato, Theopompus, Pseudo-Aristotle and Strabo are cited by Collins to indicate that the ancient world had knowledge of another continent beyond the ocean; their work can, of course, with at least as much plausibility, be seen simply as evidence that they speculated about other lands overseas very much as we speculate about other worlds in space. For Collins 'it seems certain' that Plato was somehow aware of America and the West Indies: the general lack of references to these lands (and complete lack of details) in classical literature he is inclined to attribute to a situation in which only 'a select few' knew about these things. So the secrecy theme makes an early appearance in Collins: 'information . . . deliberately withheld from the outside world'. Collins thinks Plato might have got knowledge of the transatlantic world through Solon from those priests of Saite Egypt. No sooner is this possibility articulated than it is thereafter taken for granted that he did. But Collins himself is rather stumped by Plato's assertion that the kings of Atlantis (over in the Americas) controlled areas within the Mediterranean, so he does at least entertain the thought that Plato might have made it all up out of family stories of Solon's sojourn in Egypt and various remarks of Herodotus, as we noted earlier on. Collins clings to the possibility that Plato himself may have visited Egypt (though we recall that Plato never says so – only much later anecdotes suggest it): 'It is conceivable that Plato learned of the Atlantis story – or at least found confirmation of it – during his own stay in Egypt.' Many things are conceivable without being demonstrable.

Collins works hard to substantiate the conceivability of Atlantis beyond the Sargasso Sea, despite Plato's claim that its easterly part was next door to Gibraltar. He makes much of Plato's mud shoal in the aftermath of Atlantis, Aristotle's shallows beyond the Pillars of Hercules and the shoals and seaweed mentioned by Pseudo-Scylax (at about the same time as Plato and Aristotle) as blocking navigation beyond a certain Phoenician-occupied island off the African coast. Only in the compilation called Pseudo-Scylax (posing as the work of a much earlier navigator) does seaweed appear in addition to the mud shallows, but it is enough to remind Collins of the floating weeds (actually quite without mud and shallows) of the Sargasso Sea. The Sargasso is, of course, much further to the west than Gibraltar or the coast of Africa, beyond the Mid-Atlantic Ridge. Only by putting together Plato and Aristotle (who was just following his teacher in the matter of mud) with Pseudo-Scylax can Collins come up with what we might call his Pseudo-Sargasso of shallow mud and weeds. (The real Sargasso is between 1,500 and 7,000 metres deep.)

Collins would like to think the Carthaginians had already seen the Sargasso before Plato's time, and it is just possible that they had, though quoting the remarks of a writer of the fourth century AD about a Carthaginian voyage of the fifth century BC is hardly very persuasive. It seems unlikely, moreover, that the square-rigged ships of the Phoenicians and Greeks, with one or two sails and no central rudder, unable to tack against the wind, could ever have reached the Sargasso Sea 'in the teeth of the prevailing westerlies', as L. Sprague de Camp points out. Collins further speculates that the shoals might be a reference to the shallow waters off the Bahamas – Bimini country, in fact. And, 'in accepting the supposition that Plato was alluding . . . to the Sargasso Sea, and perhaps even the Bahamas, we are left with one inescapable conclusion,' he says. It is difficult to see how an inescapable conclusion follows from a supposition about one thing and perhaps another. The conclusion is that 'whether by accident or design, Plato located his sunken island somewhere on the western Atlantic seaboard'. Which plainly, he did not, since it came up practically to Gibraltar in the east.

For Collins the considerable distance between the Sargasso and the Bahamas is accommodated by the suggestion that 'in singling out the Sargasso Sea' (which is a huge assumption on Collins' part since there is nothing at all to suggest Plato was talking about the Sargasso) Plato was just trying to indicate the general location of his sunken island. This cannot be said to be a very rigorous way of arguing. The attempt to add some circumstantial support for associating Atlantis with the Bahamas by means of the coconut is just as weak. A passage in Plato's account of the wonderful fruits of Atlantis, which Collins takes to refer to coconuts, has been interpreted by other translators as a poetic reference to olive trees. Collins is aware that coconuts were not introduced to the West Indies till colonial times – he adopts an unorthodox view of the diffusion of coconut cropping and invokes a Haitian folk-tale about coconuts thrown down to become men and women after a flood to suggest a further antique, Atlantean connection. Ah, there are always the folk-tales! (Collins makes nothing much either way of Plato's assertion of elephants on Atlantis.)

Collins can see as well as most of us that Plato drew on Athens, on Syracuse, on Babylon and Ecbatana and the rest to supply details for his city of Atlantis, but he is determined to believe that none the less some real knowledge of old Atlantis and its topography came through to Plato from maritime sources available at the time – merchants' maps, in fact. Collins wants to strip Plato's Atlantis material of 'its political and fantastic overtones' to show how the story 'preserves knowledge of an island kingdom or empire that thrived in the Atlantic thousands of years before recorded history'. But Plato's political and moral purposes are not overtones, they are his central theme, and the colourful details of his story are the disposable bits, not gems of accurate information brought back across the Atlantic to the ancient world of the Mediterranean by seafarers to the Americas. In the matter of the contentious dimensions of Plato's Atlantis, Collins is content to arrive at a much smaller island than something 'bigger than Libya and Asia together', as Plato puts it. If Plato is not to be taken literally about his lost island's size, why take any of the rest of his details seriously? The attempt to reinterpret Plato as meaning that the sphere of maritime influence of Atlantis was equal in size to that of Libya and Asia is doomed by the simple fact that that is not what Plato says. He says in plain Greek, as we have had occasion to note before, that Atlantis was bigger than Libya and Asia.

Collins concedes that classical stories of wonderful islands in the outer ocean are mostly based on occasional landfalls in the Canaries, Madeiras, even the Azores at a stretch, but he wants to hold on to that mention of an island with navigable rivers dating back to a piece of Pseudo-Aristotle, since only in the West Indies can such a topography be found beyond Gibraltar. It can only be said that the navigable rivers may well be sheer invention or, failing that, derived from reports of navigable rivers on the coast of Africa itself (where there might indeed have been elephants), mixed up with stories of islands. Using a very confusing passage in Pliny and its adaptation by a much later classical author to show that the fabled Hesperides islands were really the West Indies will not work. It relies on taking Pliny's word for it that an earlier geographer said the Hesperides were forty days' sail beyond the Isles of the Gorgons, then identifying the Gorgons' islands with the Cape Verdes, then ignoring Pliny's remark that the sail took you 'past Atlas' (presumably the Atlas range of mountains, which would not be in the direction of the West Indies), then rejoicing that the fourth-century Solinus drops the Atlas detail: after all that, Collins feels 'that we can safely conclude that the Hesperides were indeed the West Indies'.

A similar case of a late authority quoting an earlier one is offered in a further effort to bolster the idea that some people of the classical world knew about the far western reaches of the Atlantic. This time it's thinner than with Pliny and Solinus. Proclus, we may recall, of about AD 450, writes about an obscure Roman historian of perhaps 100 BC who apparently mentioned some islands of the 'external sea', of which three were of immense extent, the middle of these being sacred to Neptune who is our old friend Poseidon in Roman guise. The inhabitants of these islands were said to preserve the memory of a former island 'which was truly prodigiously great', dominating all the islands of the Atlantic. Collins wants to see in all this evidence for knowledge in Roman times of an island group which he readily identifies with the West Indies, where memories of old Atlantis were still being handed down.

We might think it difficult to avoid the conclusion that, like everyone else touching on Atlantis in the classical world, Marcellus was simply building on Plato with no other source material to go on. Or that Proclus was doing that, with or without any Marcellus – for Proclus starts off referring merely to 'certain historians', only bringing in mention of Marcellus and his *Ethiopic History* at the end of his remarks. What the West Indies would be doing in a book about Africa is not obvious. At all events, Collins thinks the three big islands of Proclus-Marcellus were Cuba, Hispaniola and Puerto Rico (the Greater Antilles) and the rest were the Lesser Antilles of the West Indies. Flood stories of the native Caribs of these islands, allegedly related to the Spaniards after the European discovery of the New World, are held by Collins to suggest that postglacial flooding may have broken up a greater landmass into separate islands – and then Phoenician sailors visiting the West Indies before Plato's day may have taken stories of these floods and lost lands back to the Mediterranean world of classical times. This is turning out to be a modification of Lewis Spence's Antillean speculations, with behind him le Plongeon, Brasseur and, it seems, a chap called Hyde Clarke whom Collins has tracked down as the first proponent of Atlantis in the Antilles in 1885. (Let's remember that all flood stories told by natives to Christians are open to suspicion.)

If we are invited to believe that Atlantis was in the West Indies and the later inhabitants of those isles still remembered it, even only folklorically, thousands of years after it was gone, and if their stories are supposed somehow to have been taken across the Atlantic in time for Plato to write them into his *Timaeus* and *Critias*, then we really do need some evidence to show that transatlantic voyages were being made in ancient days. Ideally some sound archaeological evidence of, say, Egyptian or Phoenician materials in the Americas or American materials in North Africa would come to light. And not just stray finds, either, of perhaps coins that could have come from much later collections or the odd Roman lamp or some such one-off item: what we really need is proper archaeological contexts in which whole assemblages of foreign goods are found in properly dated situations in association with native material. It can be confidently said that no such archaeological contexts have ever been demonstrated in the Old World or in the New where dated assemblages of goods from one world have been found in dated situations in the other – not even in one case, let alone the several we should ideally require. This stark fact alone makes the idea of regular intercourse between the western

Atlantic and the Mediterranean before Columbus hardly worth entertaining. In the Delta of the Nile, Minoan materials have been turned up in dynastic Egyptian contexts: all well and good, trade and perhaps even immigration from Crete are indicated. Nothing like this is known in the Americas and no American products have been found in an Old World context.

The best Collins (and all the other fans of ancient transatlantic commerce) can do is to point to certain anomalous or ambiguous circumstances that cannot possibly outweigh the lack of repeated context archaeology. Tobacco and cocaine are, as we've seen, two current favourites in this line, traces of both having been reported in some Egyptian mummies (including that of the great pharaoh Ramesses II), sometimes together and sometimes just the tobacco. Tobacco is attested in Brazil at an early enough date to supply New Kingdom Egypt, but not in Mexico until about 100 BC which is far too late. In any case, tobacco is a plant that may once have been indigenous in Africa, much closer to home for the ancient Egyptians. There is no literary, pictorial or artefactual evidence to suggest the Egyptians were smoking pipes or cigars, so the tobacco was presumably being used in the course of mummification (assuming that its traces are not simply the result of modern contaminations, as they may well be). The cocaine is yet more problematical, being only native to the Americas (though there is another species of the same genus on Mauritius). As far as I know, only one team has so far claimed to have found cocaine traces in an Egyptian mummy and they have not been overly inclined to share their researches with other investigators; indeed, they have gone quiet on the matter. We shall have to await developments on that one, if there ever are any. One might wonder why, if tobacco and cocaine could be traded across the Atlantic from the Americas in Phoenician times, the potato and tomato had to wait until after 1492 to make their way to the Old World. Apart from the exotic substances, it's the usual Olmec 'Negroid' heads and alleged 'Semitic' and 'Caucasoid' features of some New World statuary that have to do duty with Collins by way of further evidence for cross-Atlantic comings and goings in ancient times, along with the shared traits of writing and calendar-making. I cannot help remarking again that the writing and calendar systems of the Old and New Worlds actually have no detailed features in common at all.

An interesting aspect of Collins' methods of argument is illustrated by his handling of the Paraiba inscription. With other writers in this general Atlantological field, we have already seen the tendency on occasions to put in dubious material that they themselves will have to reject almost immediately. It looks like the maximizing of anything and everything that comes their way, even if it has to be dropped almost as soon as it's picked up. It also looks to me like the exploitation of even the dodgiest material to help create a vague miasma of possibilities in the readers' minds, when in fact the material turns out to be quite useless. (It all helps to fill out a big book, too, of course.) The Paraiba inscription from Brazil purports to be a Phoenician record of a voyage from the Red Sea that ended up in South America. Even in the late nineteenth century it was generally recognized as a hoax and is now seen to be 'a fraud perpetrated by Brazilian Freemasons', as Collins himself tells us. Why spend two-and-a-half pages on it, then? In its wake he cites some coin finds, an oil lamp, a sword blade, the odd not-very-well-documented wreck in Brazilian waters, and certain very dubious translations of alleged Punic inscriptions from the Americas (many if not all of which aren't human inscriptions of any sort, let alone Punic ones). Collins admits that all this can't add up to proof of a Phoenician presence in the West Indies. Even if the occasional foundering of a Phoenician (or Roman) ship, blown off course across the Atlantic, could deliver Old World coins or amphorae to the American coast, we would still not be faced with deliberate transatlantic crossings with cultural consequences in the Old World or the New. When it comes to Roman-looking bricks in Mayan structures (with no Latin brick marks, needless to say), I feel we are as it were scraping the bottom of the barrel. And what is the good of Collins' suggestion that it was trade secrecy that kept all reference to Phoenician or Roman transatlantic commerce so successfully out of all classical literature? On that score a complete lack of evidence for something would become the finest available proof of it.

Plato's mention of an Atlantean name in its original, native form impresses Collins. That name is Gadirus, for which Plato offers his Greek-via-Egyptian equivalent of Eumelus. Gadirus is indeed a Phoenician-sounding name, related to the root that today gives us Cadiz out of classical Gades for the Spanish port that faces out into the Atlantic where Atlantis is supposed to have come close to western Europe. But there's really nothing suggestive in Plato's use of this name: Greek Eumelus ('rich in sheep') is not a translation of the Semitic root meaning of Gades (probably 'limit', 'hedge'); it is just a bit of exotic local colour in his tale, taken from the name Gades. It's no proof at all that the Atlanteans spoke Phoenician or that news of Atlantis was brought back to Europe by Phoenician sailors.

There follows in Collins' compendious book a rather unrewarding, as I see it, detour into pre-Columbus legends of Antilia and the Seven Cities, El Dorado and the like. The Phoenician theme is then resumed with the conclusion that the a-t-l element of the name Atlantis is a Phoenician root, out of the Semitic linguistic context of the Phoenician language, meaning 'elevate'. Certainly, this is as good a philological speculation as any other and may well explain the background of the Atlas myth and the naming of the Atlas Mountains. It is not obvious that it would have anything to do with Plato's naming of his lost island. He presumably wanted to give his island a name in the setting of his own culture's mythology and in keeping with the location he chose for it in the already named Atlantic Ocean (so called after the mountains that ran down to it). He may very well, as we have seen, also have had in mind recent memories of the flooding of the little island of Atalante, close to Athens. There is absolutely no reason to connect Atlantis with the fantasy island Antilia (or an earlier version as Atulliae) of fourteenth- and fifteenth-century European maps. This island, as we have seen, was most likely a conjectural reflection of the shape of Portugal projected on to the western Atlantic. The Portuguese 'Ante ilha' is at least as good a philological speculation to explain the name Antilia as anything to do with a-t-l.

Collins' next step is to recall certain American legends of their peoples' coming to their present homes from islands to the east – the Aztecs' Aztlan is, not surprisingly with a name like that, the site we have heard most about. These stories were, of course, recorded very late on by Christian or Christianized writers and local origins for them have been proposed by orthodox historians. When such legends involve emergency crossings of waters in the dark over sands or stepping stones, Collins thinks they might hark back to forced emigrations from some larger landmass in the region of the West Indies that was flooded by the rising sea levels of the end of the ice age. On this interpretation, the peoples of Mexico and Central America (and some of the south-east states of North America) could have come to their historical homelands from somewhere in the Caribbean or the waters of the Bahamas. Collins tells us that seven caves are often mentioned in the folklore as the place of genesis of the people who later left for the mainland: seven caves like the seven bays or seven cities of the fabulous island of the pre-Columbian maps, though the seven in the latter case may be related to a legend of seven bishops who fled to sea from the Moorish conquest of Spain. As a way of putting the ancestors of the Aztecs and so forth on an Atlantis that was more or less the same place as the Antilia of the old maps (until flooding reduced it, that is), all this seems pretty thin, one faint possibility heaped on another, as with Lewis Spence.

By now it is becoming clear that Collins has set his sights on Cuba as the last, best relic of old Atlantis – for him, Cuba is Antilia, as others have suggested despite the different shapes and orientations of the real island and the cartographic fantasy. So Collins wants to cry up the archaeology of Cuba. It is one of the admirable things about his writing that he does often candidly sketch in the objections to his ideas that he clearly recognizes. In this case, he admits that the pre-Columbian inhabitants of Cuba, the Taino, with their New Stone Age style of life weren't really up to much as potential heirs of Atlantean civilization and, worse still, probably only came to Cuba themselves in about AD 500, having originated in the region of the mouth of the Orinoco in Venezuela at the other end of the island chain. In the search for something a little more impressive than the Taino, we get reports of late nineteenth-century claims of mounds, enclosures, a jade axe, a black idol on Cuba: a paltry haul, I should say, and most of it not available for inspection any more. More modern archaeology reveals a picture of mesolithic life on Cuba before the neolithic Taino, with flints, bones and shells, back to perhaps 5000 BC. Some standing stones and earthworks have been compared to the products of farming people in Florida at about 2000 BC and this seems to hearten Collins to go on and write of 'prehistoric culture of immense sophistication', but I should say that would depend on your idea of sophistication. The prospect of cave art is raised before us in this connection, but it doesn't turn out to be anything like Lascaux or Altamira. There are stick men, animals and fish, attributed to the Taino, in certain Cuban caves. Some drawings may be the work of black slaves on the plantations. But there are also, in Cave 1 on the 'Isle of Youth' off the southern coast of Cuba, some geometric and abstract designs that Collins feels are in a different league.

The *pièce de résistance* on this Isle of Youth is a complex of concentric circles, about a metre in diameter, with a 'double arrow' reaching out from its centre; this reminds Collins, as he told us right at the start of his book, of our solar system. He is keen to say how super all this geometric stuff is (no stick men here) but it can't be said that the two small photographs in his book do much to encourage us to share this view. The fact that the caves with geometric designs have what are apparently artificially constructed light holes in their roofs and that the cave with the circles and arrows possesses 'roughly seven bays' encourages Collins to speculate that this was the site of the birthplace of the chiefs of old Antilia (with its seven bays): and further that the circle design with arrow represents the sunbeam penetrating into the womb-cave of their nativity! As to the date of all this, well 'the cave art on Mona [another small island between Puerto Rico and Hispaniola, with art derived from Cuba] probably dates back to somewhere between 5000 BC and AD 250'. In other words, it probably has a vague date of some sort. So all this bric-à-brac of idols and axes and standing stones and might-be-old cave glyphs is being used by Collins to suggest that Cuba could have been the place from which the later Meso-Americans – or at least their chiefs and teachers – originated, to develop their Olmec, Maya, Zapotec, Toltec and Aztec civilizations on the mainland. Cuba and its little island with a cavern of 'roughly' seven bays is Antilia of the Seven Cities, Aztlan, Atlantis!

There follows a straight-faced discussion as to whether Cuba or Hispaniola better fits Plato's description of Atlantis – this despite Collins' earlier recognition that Plato cannot be regarded as wholly reliable in detail and, in any case, neither Caribbean island could conceivably fit Plato's description taken as a whole and at face value. Still, for Collins the mountains of north-west Cuba are Plato's ring of mountains on Atlantis, Cuba's western plain is the great (rectangular?) plain of Atlantis, the Isle of Youth is Atlantis City itself at one end of a now submerged connection to the main island, and the caves of the Isle are the place where Plato's Atlantean dynasty was born. The ever-reliable candour of Collins prompts him to say that 'Sadly, no evidence of a true Atlantean city has been found . . . we have no Atlantean kings, no circular hydraulic systems, no canals and no evidence of maritime activity before the arrival of the earliest Palaeo-Amerindians sometime around 6000 BC.' I like that reference to 'a true Atlantean city' when there's no city there at all, true Atlantean or otherwise, and one wonders at the scale of maritime activity that went on after the arrival of the Palaeo-Amerindians for that matter.

The best Collins can come up with in the way of any more corroboration of Plato on Cuba consists of a couple of pictographs of exceptionally poor quality, apparently representing bulls. One is of unknown provenance somewhere on the island and the other is from the province of Havana. Neither is dated. Associated stick men call the poor old Taino to mind, but perhaps the bulls and men together represent bullfighting and were done by African slaves after Havana built a bullring. Collins would like to think these pictures somehow took us back to Plato's bull sacrifices on Atlantis, but he admits that no bovine bones have ever been found in old archaeological sites in Cuba. It's all a bit thin again.

Not for the first time in our review of the literature of Atlantis, it is myth and folklore that fill the breach when hard archaeological evidence is lacking. Collins talks of Caribbean tales about the Antilles as previously one great island that turned into a string of separate isles in the aftermath of floods; he says there were similar stories in the Bahamas. He rules out a volcanic tsunami (at least in the Bahamas) as the cause of this flooding, which would not of course be permanent if such was the mechanism. He sees that the postglacial rise in sea level was a slow process that submerged, say, the Grand Bahama Bank over many, many centuries between about 8000 and 3000 BC. And then he remembers his cave on the Isle of Youth and has second thoughts about that design of concentric circles and double arrow. Perhaps it doesn't show the sun sending out a beam to fertilize the womb-cave of the old chiefs after all, which may come as a relief to any of us who had difficulty with that interpretation. Recalling, of another cave design, that 'for some reason it bore a resemblance to a comet in the sky', Collins concludes that it must have been a comet that broke up old Antilia and thereby destroyed Plato's Atlantis. The big design with the circles and arrow is an image of comet debris hitting water, like what you see when you kick a pebble into a puddle: a non-seismic, non-volcanic tsunami. 'What if', he asks, 'this cave imagery was recalling some kind of oceanic impact?' He confides in us that 'the feeling that at some time in prehistory the Bahamas and Caribbean had been devastated by a comet impact would not leave me'. Heigh ho! These writers are always seeing 'resemblances', 'for some reason', always asking themselves 'What ifs?' (and building an awful lot on them), speculating about 'some kind' of something or other and 'having feelings' that, no matter how hard they may try, they just can't avoid.

An unusual landscape feature of the region, called the Carolina Bays, is brought on as possible evidence of some antique cometary impact, rather like the Tunguska event of Siberia (which, incidentally, other exponents of 'alternative history' have interpreted as a UFO crash). The Carolina Bays are shallow oval depressions widely scattered over some south-eastern states of the USA, of unknown date and speculative origin. True to the rather scrupulous candour he has earlier shown in his book, Collins tells us that these Bays have never evidenced any traces that might have come from a comet or asteroid and he acknowledges that geologists have not proposed – among their several theories – any extraterrestrial explanation for them. Nevertheless, Collins wants to date them to about 8500 BC and relate them to the fall of a comet, that caused (or at least mightily contributed to) the end of the last ice age. He mentions the notion of an ex-Second World War rocket engineer (no prizes given for guessing which side he was on) that there are two 'deep impact sites' in the ocean east of the Bahamas. He doesn't mention the absence of any sedimentological evidence from seabed cores in the Atlantic of any such disturbance as the deep impact of a comet or asteroid would surely make. Nor has any young lava been identified that would have erupted as a result of the impact, nor is there any extraterrestrial material in ice cores of the required date or any magnetic record of disturbance. As a special explanation for the end of the last ice age, the cometary impact theory leaves much to be desired. For a start, we would have to wonder how all the other ice ages ended – did a comet always come along to finish the job? Needless to say, Collins belongs to the nightmare-scenario persuasion when it comes to the end of the last ice age, and even quotes our old friend Frank C. Hibben at some length from his *Lost Americans* of 1946. (You really would conclude, to go by the Atlantologists, that no up-to-date, let alone scholarly, work had been done on glacial geology for the last half-century.)

So a comet is quite in order in Collins' eyes as an added ingredient to the pictured mayhem of mass extinctions that Hapgood ascribed to earth crust displacement. For Collins, the comet supplies the sudden tsunami to break up Atlantis in the Antilles, and the postglacial rise in sea level renders that flooding permanent. (The comet idea wasn't a new one with the German rocket man: as far back as 1788, Gian Rinaldo Carli suggested that Atlantis may have been sunk by comet strike, Donnelly more than toyed with it, and the idea was renewed with Karl Georg Zschaetzsh in 1922 in his ominously titled *Atlantis: die Urheimat der Arier*, 'the original home of the Aryans'. Alex Braghine used the comet notion in his *Shadow of Atlantis* in 1940 and Comyns Beaumont used it again in 1946 in his *Riddle of Prehistoric Britain*, where the English Channel stood in for the Pillars of Hercules and Athens was in Scotland. Immanuel Velikovsky incorporated cometary vicissitudes into his infamous *Worlds in Collision* of 1950 and Jürgen Spanuth's *Atlantis in Heligoland* went the same way in 1953.)

Collins realizes that all the amateur geologizing and glyph-interpreting rather go for nothing unless it can be shown that there were any people in the region of the Antilles and Bahamas in about 8500 BC to witness his comet, tsunami and flooding. (By this time, he is taking it for granted in *Gateway to Atlantis* that Cuba was the core of Plato's Atlantis and that Plato got it right, even if accidentally, that the catastrophe occurred in 8500 BC – not that that is altogether what Plato says. He is also taking it for granted from hereon that a comet did indeed strike the western Atlantic at that date.) Collins avers that 'outside the constraints of archaeological opinion', a reference I take it to the sober, systematic search for a body of consistent evidence that professional archaeologists demand, outside those constraints 'there is compelling evidence to show that the sunken regions of the Bahamas and Caribbean still hold important clues concerning the historical reality of lost Atlantis'. What we get is some footprints of unknown age in mud-rock, the Bimini Road again and those odd sightings from the air, and reports of underwater caves with bones. It is certainly true that archaeologists are not going to find any or all of that in the least bit compelling as evidence for the previous existence of the 'shining jewel' of Atlantis on Cuba and its empire among the Antillean archipelagos. Collins thinks these areas 'may well' provide us with proof of a settled neolithic culture that was terminated by this cometary impact of about 8500 BC.

'Neolithic' means the New Stone Age way of life of the world's earliest farmers, before the use of metals, usually with pottery but no written records. Even if such a neolithic presence in this region were satisfactorily demonstrated at an early date of 8500 BC (and there is not a scrap of serious evidence for that), we should still be obliged to note that such a way of life was a far cry indeed from Plato's highly sophisticated, indeed luxuriously oversophisticated, kingdom of Atlantis. Collins even seems to think that Plato's ship-filled, canal-ringed city of gold and silver palaces, awash with statuary, may yet be found somewhere near Cuba. Does he seriously think all that could have arisen in a neolithic context evidenced at best by some bones, footprints and dubious marks on the seabed, plus axe, idol, standing stone, earthworks and poor quality pictographs, all undated. A line of Latin poetry comes to mind as one nears the end of Collins' weighty and erudite tome, when a putative bunch of neolithic farmers in Cuba with very little to show for them turn out to be the chief product of all that heavy delving into mythology, geology, philology, cartography, archaeology and cosmology:

Parturiunt montes, nascetur ridiculus mus.
('Mountains are in labour, there'll be born a laughable mouse.')

Horace, *Ars Poetica*, line 139

To pile on top of such a truly laboured construction the idea that, much later, Phoenician merchants (for whom there is likewise not a scrap of serious evidence in the New World) could have taken an accurate memory of this Atlantis back to Plato might strike many as laughable indeed.

Gateway to Atlantis ends in a notable flight of fancy about Cronus, father of the Olympian gods, the Nephilim giants of the Bible, and a voyage from the Levant to Mexico via Britain and Cuba with a black-skinned crew somewhere between 2200 and 1250 BC. Collins opines that 'whether they might have utilized the North-west Passage or the North Equatorial Current via the Canary Isles is open to debate.' He's telling us. There's a strong hint, throughout the closing passages, of that hoary notion of a ruling élite coming in from outside to direct the affairs of the less advanced people they settled among. Something I find difficult to avoid is the feeling that this is the old colonialist attitude resurfacing at the end of the twentieth century, which saw it taken to horrible extremes by the Nazis (no strangers themselves to entertaining every sort of 'alternative archaeology'). There is that familiar and dismaying failure to acknowledge the protean inventiveness of humanity everywhere, in the realm of the imagination as well as of technology.

Collins does not push the notions of a high-tech, scientific ancient civilization or 'ancient wisdom' like some of the Atlantological writers we have reviewed, but his instincts are firmly in line with theirs. And, like the rest of them, he makes much throughout of stray finds and random similarities, yet consistently makes very little of one of the most important aspects of real archaeology: its insistence on full cultural context and repeated association of finds, with corroborated dates. His resort to folklore is positively Donnellian in its recklessness, seizing on anything like tales of fire or stones from the sky as evidence of cometary catastrophe, and quietly downplaying such grotesque and impossible twaddle as serpent-bodied goddesses without navels that inextricably goes with these tales – and reveals their highly imaginative nature.

Lastly, Collins' work evinces that need to subvert the findings, indeed the entire approach, of the academic archaeologists that we almost always find – more or less virulent – in all the writers of 'alternative archaeology'. I suppose that the proponents of theories wildly divergent from the conclusions of the paid, appointed professors are always under pressure to do down the work, the attitudes and even the motives of the professionals. After all, how can it be that the university professors disagree with, worse still ignore, the startling insights achieved by the independent researchers? They must be blind, or hidebound, or jealous, or fearful for their own jobs, surely. The 'alternative archaeologists' seem to find the published work of the professionals unrewarding in its lack of colourful hypotheses, its emphasis on data to do with potsherds and pollen grains, its graphs and sections, its statistics, its satisfaction with modest gains in detailed knowledge and its rigorous testing of all interpretations of its material, old and new. I sympathize with their evident bafflement when faced with the publications of the professionals. But then I would be baffled if I browsed through some article in *Nature* about cell chemistry or stellar physics. (I wouldn't, however, tend to think that the authors of such articles were generally up to no good.) It has to be said that ploughing through books like *Gateway to Atlantis* can itself call for some stern dutifulness on the reader's part, just to keep on with it, not so much to the bitter as the anticlimactic end. Whole tracts of these 'alternative' archaeological writings manage to be both thin and heavy going at the same time, with nothing at all certain to show for it at the end, as I fear more – even among their most well-disposed readers – have found out than would care to admit it.

Collins has not contributed any startling new details to our diagnostic list of features of the Atlantis Syndrome. The literal reliance on Plato, the idea of a vanished primal civilization, the ready resort to folklore, the predisposition to catastrophe, the theme of secret élites, the fixation on transatlantic intercourse before Columbus, the penchant for amateur philologizing and geologizing, the defiance of the academic archaeological establishment – all these are well-worn signs of the Syndrome. To his credit, Collins avoids the seductions of ancient high technology and ancient astronomical science and the whole business of the 'ancient wisdom' in general. What, perhaps, he has highlighted more than most – though he's by no means the only exemplar, far from it – is the potential for hard labour without significant issue that is contained in this whole genre.

13

WHY?

Our review of the Atlantological literature has necessarily been selective: L. Sprague de Camp, writing in the 1950s, reckoned there were already some two thousand books on the Atlantis theme. I have tried to give an account of the development of the main features of the Atlantis argument from Plato through such crucial authors as Donnelly and Spence up to the present time, with an emphasis on recent years when the mass media (and now the Internet) have added new impetus to the whole business. The popularity of science fiction in films and on television has played no small part in readying significant sections of the public for the distinctive Atlantological output of today. Very likely it has directly inspired some of the producers of that output: a melancholy thought.

I wish we had the space to look into the ideas of such luminaries of Atlantology as Otto Muck, Dr Malaise and Commander Nutter. I wish we could examine the very latest offerings on the bookstalls: I see notice of a new book that seeks somehow to link Atlantis with the parting of the Red Sea, the biblical plagues of Egypt and the obscure mummy from Tomb 55, across the way from Tutankhamun's tomb in the Valley of the Kings. Pending further investigation the mind boggles. But books like this and legions more have had to be passed over as we sought to bring together all the truly essential features of that set of associated attitudes to the past, so often running together, that we are calling here the Atlantis Syndrome. Along the way, we have tried always to bring the manifold speculations of Atlantology and 'alternative archaeology' up short, as it were, against the findings and methods of real archaeology, not so much so as to secure a conviction against those speculations with the full weight of scholarly argument as to offer the reader, who may have been impressed by some of the Atlantological literature, another perspective on the notions to be encountered there: the alternative to 'alternative archaeology', you might say. At the same time, we have striven – good-humouredly – to point up some of the inherent shortcomings of the Atlantological outlook.

But our main task now is to make a full characterization of the multi-symptomed syndrome and to ask why its 'victims' (to keep up the medical simile for a moment) are so prone to it – both the writers and the readers of the genre. In what follows, it should not be thought the suggestion is being made that all the proponents of Atlantology have ever presented all the features of the syndrome, or that any particular one of them has shown signs of any particular tendency. We are constructing an overall characterization of a certain sort of approach to the past built up by many authors (and their readers) over a considerable period.

Atlantis started with Plato and in his hands it was never a supercivilization of the sort conjectured by later authors; perhaps in strictly Greek terms it was no civilization at all but rather a fatally luxurious elaboration of an essentially barbarian way of life, for all its inception by a god. At all events, it was no seminal civilization: it wasn't the *fons et origo* of all later civilizations in the world, indeed Athens was its independent contemporary. Both Atlantis and old Athens were, for Plato, but episodes in the ever ongoing cycle of catastrophes and renewals that he saw as the most rational and scientific interpretation to which the world of human experience could be subjected. For him, science and religion were quite bound up together, so that the natural catastrophes were at the same time eras in which the divine light was withdrawn from the world and the equally natural renewals were times when it returned. So rational and obviously true was this scheme of things to Plato that the 'problem' of the real historical location and fate of Atlantis that has exercised so many writers after him would have left him cold, or perhaps amused to think of what he had started. We quoted early in this book several passages of Plato to show how he handled stories in his works.

A few more examples towards the end of our book may help to remind us of Plato's purpose in floating (then sinking) his Atlantis. In the *Republic*, we find Socrates remarking that, 'We first tell stories to children. These are in general untrue, though there is some truth in them.' Again, 'We then make the fiction as like the truth as possible, and so make the lie or untruth useful.' In the *Protagoras* we are asked by Socrates, 'Now shall I, as an old man speaking to his juniors, put my explanation in the form of a story or give it a reasoned argument? . . . I think it will be pleasanter to tell you a story.' In the *Phaedrus*, we recall, Socrates is told to his face that 'It is easy for you, Socrates, to make up tales from Egypt or anywhere else you care to.' Atlantis is just such a tale from Egypt, made up indeed to bring home the truth of Plato's view of history and his warning about the direction that he saw his civilization taking. Aristotle appreciated that, and we would have heard a whole lot less about Atlantis if everyone else had agreed with him.

The literal-minded, not very interested in Plato's science and philosophy, were soon taking him at face value in the classical world. But before the age of European exploration, there was small scope for them to speculate where in detail Atlantis may really have been sited. With the discovery of the New World at the end of the fifteenth century AD, and then the exploration of the Far East and Africa, speculation could run riot and Atlantis was given a new lease of life, or rather a myriad of new leases in places as far apart as Mexico, South Africa, Spitzbergen and Mongolia. But, only justly in view of Plato's Atlantic placing of Atlantis, it was the New World and the western Atlantic that had the biggest pull and the best staying power. In the nineteenth century it was possible for Donnelly to take the idea on in a really significant way by popularizing, if not inventing, the grand theory of a uniquely seminal civilization lurking behind all known ancient civilizations. There was in Donnelly, and in Spence after him, very little of the supercivilization concept. Their versions of Atlantis were Bronze Age or advanced Stone Age entities, full of wonders for their time but not noticeably decked with the sort of achievements in high technology or sophisticated astronomical science or general 'ancient wisdom' that later writers load on to theirs. Still, there was in the very idea of a prior civilization, which influenced and inspired all later ones, the seed of a notion of superiority, of a pristine quality that all the rest only aped and fell away from in their various ways. Donnelly at least did not push this and managed to keep his theories looking as though they belonged in the rational world of nineteenth-century science.

After Donnelly and Spence, there comes a divergence between two different sorts of Atlantological speculation (though Spence's later work foreshadows both developments). This divergence is still with us and nowadays presenting further subdivergences. On the one hand there are the people still looking for a fairly mundane explanation of Atlantis, more or less in terms of conventional archaeology: Thera, Old Anatolia and even antediluvian Cuba are examples of this relatively sober approach. On the other, there are bolder spirits looking to unknown Antarctica or the oceanic deeps for their rather more exotic long-lost civilization. On the whole, the more mundane-minded favour much less in the way of a supercivilization of sophisticated science and ancient wisdom, while the bolder speculators usually add on the hints of anti-gravity, astronomical expertise, spiritual quest and what have you. Atlantologists willing to settle for the Neolithic Antilles or Bronze Age eastern Mediterranean usually employ the catastrophist approach to explain the particular demise of their versions of Atlantis, but tend not to elevate catastrophism into such a cosmic principle as the other group does, with all its apparatus of arcanely encoded warnings and immortal longings. There is within this latter group something of a further division between the high-tech and the Arcadian tendencies: submarines and lasers versus contemplation of stars and navels; anti-gravity makes a good bridge between these two wings, since manoeuvring pyramid blocks or the cyclopean masonry of Tiahuanaco can be attributed either to advanced physics or to superior mentalist powers or a blurry indistinction between the two. Finally, of course, there is the divergence between those who leave their supercivilization rooted on earth and those who project it into outer space.

The possible combinations of traits exhibited in any particular piece of Atlantological writing are large in number, and sometimes quite startling. You may find the supercivilization in question given exalted cosmic origins – and then reduced to clanking around in steam-powered Zeppelins, looking for sex. You may encounter some survivors of another such supercivilization of purely terrestrial origins, lost under the ice or in the deeps, bringing a religion of immortality and anti-materialism to some benighted corner of the world, only to see it collapse for the most part into mass human sacrifice, with just a golden thread of the original ancient wisdom to be detected by the most recherché 'decodings'. You may be invited to see in some vanishingly paltry neolithic or Bronze Age remains the sure sign of the invisible presence of yet another version of the lost supercivilization.

At the core of the Atlantis Syndrome, in both its mundane and exotic manifestations, is a stubborn literal-mindedness that cannot credit the human race with what is actually one of its most obvious traits: its inventiveness. I have wryly commented before on the oddity that these highly inventive and imaginative writers of Atlantology evidently cannot believe that anyone else ever invents anything – whether it is Plato inventing Atlantis, Ute Indians inventing a folk-tale or various human groups around the world inventing civilization. This is where the Atlantologists' powers of imagination fail them: their own imaginations are revealed to be of a strictly trammelled variety after all, rarely if ever breaking out from the prejudices of their own time and place.

I believe it is no undue simplification of the case to say that modern Atlantology is in essence little more than certain vulgar assumptions of western religion and colonialism unthinkingly imposed on to the entire past history of the human race. The conviction that civilization must be a gift from the gods (of one sort or another) and must be introduced around the world by an élite of priests (of one sort or another) is precisely in line with such religious and social prejudices, of a very low order of sophistication it must be said. (There is nothing of this in Plato, who saw civilization as endlessly renewed, reinvented countless times all over the world, in the natural course of events. On the contrary, his Atlanteans are condemned for their imperialism in reaching out for Europe and Egypt.) It is really no wonder that the Nazis showed such an enthusiasm for every sort of Atlantological theory: Nazism was the product of a bunch of romantic autodidacts, stuffed full of the popular prejudices of their time and place (exceptionally spiteful prejudices in their case), bent on expansion – eastward in Europe, rather than in overseas colonies – at the expense of the current inhabitants of the regions they wanted to get their hands on. There is about the Nazis' aspirations and exploits something like a pathological perversion of the romantic adventure stories for boys of the late nineteenth and early twentieth centuries: stories by no means free of inhumane attitudes and assumptions in themselves. Stories of white explorers among, at best, gullible natives, frequently senselessly hostile; and stories of lost tribes and cities and treasures, sometimes presented in a pseudo-Egyptological or pseudo-archaeological context. (It was one of the depressing aspects of the Hollywood revamping of this genre in the 1980s that an apparently liberal sector of an essentially non-colonial country could have carried on so many of the negative traditions of the pre-war empire adventure story ethos.)

The Nazi ideology, horribly romantic, has been the most extreme and pernicious expression of the myth of the divinely sanctioned élite to date, and a far cry you might think from ideas of some secret brotherhood of wise old priests struggling to carry the torch of learning and spirituality down all the dark ages of prehistory and history. But I do believe that some of the proponents of modern Atlantology, especially since the Second World War, might have stopped and thought about the strain of colonialist and missionary condescension – if nothing worse – implied in their ideas. They might yet stop to think that, short of extraterrestrial intervention, every civilization on earth must in any case have been created by ordinary human beings in natural situations, out of their adaptive cleverness of mind – Atlantis in any guise is only a postponement of the recognition of this human potential. If you insist on refusing to acknowledge that any known human civilization created itself in the course of its own experience on earth and likewise insist that each and every civilization got its impetus from an earlier lost civilization, then you only put off consideration of how that earlier civilization came about. Unless you invoke alien invaders or gods like Poseidon you must still seek to enquire (if you really have an enquiring mind) by what natural processes of social evolution civilization can ever come about. And if it can naturally come about once, then like all good things in this world it can come about again and again and the single founding civilization loses even the appeal of primacy since primacy has evaporated as a necessity of explanation. (To say nothing of the fact that not a scrap of reliable evidence for such a primal civilization exists anywhere on Earth.) If you do invoke alien invaders or gods like Poseidon, then you really ought to admit to yourself that you have left the realm of rational enquiry altogether and are merely conjecturing within the imaginative confines established by popular entertainment and religion.

Other psychological forces at work close to the core of the syndrome include anxiety and the lure of the quick fix. The catastrophist outlook that always goes, to varying degrees, with Atlantological speculation is itself of a deeply anxious character. If comets and asteroids can strike out of the blue, if the earth's crust might suddenly pitch us to the poles at any moment, if the precessionary cycle can go haywire, if whole civilizations can disappear without trace, then we are living not just with the threat of car accidents, air crashes, fatal epidemics, political oppression, nuclear war, race hatred, famine and common mortality, as we thought we were, but with something more cosmically unsettling. It may be that those of us with a developed sensitivity to the uncertainty of things are predisposed to Atlantology or, at least, are vulnerable to its appeal. Certainly some of the Atlantological authors appear to think so.

Uncertainty also contributes to the need for a quick fix, either by way of explanation or reassurance or both. If you don't know much about archaeology, haven't given it a lot of thought or ever learned much about it, then a lost ancient supercivilization may look like a readily plausible explanation for the pyramids, or Stonehenge, or Cuzco, or the Nazca Lines (the more so since you are likely to have seen some piece of science fiction that floated the idea or even a 'documentary' programme that espoused it). As we saw earlier, such an explanation will probably chime in with unexamined bits of your mental furniture derived from religion and memories of empire. Not for you the academic papers and excavation reports, full of dry data about pollen grains and potsherds and probability ranges of radiocarbon dates, with distribution maps of unexciting finds and hatched sections through archaeological deposits. You don't need all that – you know how the past works and it's just like recent history. Superior immigrants sort the natives out and missionaries let them in on a few of the profundities, in a simplified form of course. Wouldn't be at all surprising if that was what happened ten thousand years ago, would it? And since we're about to launch ourselves into space (or at least it looked like that a while ago), what more natural than that it was spacemen who brought civilization to Earth? Now anybody can follow an explanation like that, straight off: common sense, really. As L. Sprague de Camp put it in his patrician way when discussing the old diffusionist theories of archaeology to which Atlantology is closely akin: 'Therefore, say the diffusionists, everything must have come from somewhere else – it doesn't matter where. Laymen who read a little anthropology or Atlantism tend to agree with them, perhaps because, never having made an invention themselves, they find it hard to imagine anybody else's having done so.'

The quick fix can be more than a mere explanation: it can be an emotional support, too. Where anxiety is running high, then there is a need for reassurance. This can take the form of something relatively sophisticated like belief in a grand cosmic principle of collapse and renewal that can be spiritually understood in terms of rebirth and immortality. It can take the simpler form of belief in 'space brothers' or at least secret brotherhoods of some sort who helped us out before and might do so again. It may function simply as just some kind of an account of things at any price, that helps to ward off apprehensions about the possible meaninglessness of life. For some writers and readers of Atlantological literature, I think the 'alternative archaeology' idea in general (the specifics hardly matter) serves as an antidote against what they believe to be the bleakness of scientific cosmology and Darwinian evolution. Any alternative scheme of things that went against the tenets of modern science would recommend itself to these people as a potential way round a view of life that they find unpalatable. In specific detail, any new ideas about – say – the age of the Sphinx or the calendrical predictions of Mayan monuments or the real import of ancient carvings from Egypt or the Far East fall like manna from heaven for these unhappy folk. If anything about the current world view of the professional archaeologists could be overthrown, then out could go the whole approach to the past that troubles the 'alternative' enthusiasts so.

Talk of manna is not inappropriate, for we are once more faced with the essentially religious pedigree of much Atlantological thought and wish. This is why the 'ancient wisdom' is never far away in the musings of Atlantology – that not so precious heirloom of the classical world's infatuation with Egypt and Europe's infatuation with Genesis. And if not a religious impetus as such, then at least a romantic one propels a deal of inclination towards 'alternative archaeology'. Some people find modern science, of which modern archaeology hopes to form a part, religiously unsatisfying – many more, in all probability, just don't find it romantic enough, especially in this era of science fiction as popular entertainment. (In today's science fiction there is a lot more fiction than science.) If Atlantology were sold as just another branch of the entertainment industry, we might see little more to cavil at in it, but it is not and so we have more to say.

A further key feature of the Atlantis Syndrome is one often seen among enthusiasts for the unorthodox in all its forms, among sectarians of every sort. It is the sense of belonging, in defiance of conventional authority, to a select coterie of those 'in the know', to a happy band of brothers with privileged knowledge of the real truth of things, versus the vested interests of academic orthodoxy or general public indifference. There can be a whiff of martyrdom, pleasing to some personality types, attached to all this (and followers who might not care for martyrdom themselves often like to lend their devoted support to their martyred gurus). Readership of the works of 'alternative archaeology' and, even more so, participation in the Internet's range of 'alternative archaeology' sites brings together in spirit a wide body of disparate types in a shared enthusiasm, without even the need for the most part to meet one another as real academics might do at conferences or in the pages of peer reviews of published work. The loner personality, which always figures largely among the enthusiasts of this sort of thing, finds a natural home at his keyboard, chasing his interests with a semblance of research (and sometimes even fancied scholarship), without having to face directly the sort of watchful criticism that professional academics are used to dishing out and receiving. In line with this camaraderie of the truly enlightened goes the reliance on unconventional sources of 'evidence' that we have so often highlighted in the course of our review of the literature. This is a truly diagnostic feature of the syndrome: all that number-crunching, amateur philologizing and myth-picking that is supposed to supply, via 'encodings' understood only by the various Atlantological authors and their eager readers, the 'proof' of their theories, along with a host of stray and anomalous finds without proper context. Myth seems peculiarly attractive in this respect. It has it seems lost none of its hoary appeal, which is the appeal of the simple and colourful. But it is not mythology that has had any success in explaining the world, it is science. Myth only explains away.

I have tried to sketch some of the core features of the Atlantological predisposition: the literal-mindedness, the reluctance to credit the common inventiveness of the human race, the underdeveloped capacity to step outside prejudices of time and place, the longing for a quick fix both as explanation and reassurance, and the need to belong to just such a 'secret brotherhood' with esoteric insider information as some writers of Atlantology picture operating in the past. All the readers (the committed ones at least, not just reading for idle entertainment) of the Atlantological genre may be expected to share these traits and the writers of the material often show most of them. But the writers are, in the end, more interesting than their readers and our characterization of the syndrome may be refined by reflecting upon their attitudes in detail. Why, after all, are they writing these strange books of theirs?

Plato was a wealthy man. Whatever the vicissitudes and disappointments of his life, he did not need the money. The worst that any commentator of his own day ever said about him was that he might have plagiarized other writers in the composition of his own works. It is not a charge that was made to stick at the time and there was no suggestion that any plagiarism was, in any case, undertaken for financial gain, nor even for reasons of vanity. It is clear that Plato wrote to propagate his ideas, which were driven by an unusual degree of moral fervour. It seems safe to conclude that no subsequent writer on the Atlantis theme could claim to be so purely motivated by moral considerations, but to what extent any of them is open to the charge of writing just for the money can only be a matter of private opinion. Certainly, money has been made since Donnelly did so well with his books in the late nineteenth century and a glance at the recent bestseller listings is enough to show that money continues to be made out of this genre.

As I remarked earlier, if Atlantology never represented itself as anything more than a branch of the entertainment industry then there would be little to complain about in its money-spinning. In the modern world, in any case, as Dr Johnson observed, no man but a blockhead ever wrote except for money. But not exclusively for the money, I think, in the field of Atlantology. What convinces me of this, in almost all cases, is the sheer devotion to tedium evinced by so many of the writers of this genre. I have had occasion to notice, in reviewing their work, that whole tracts of the output of the Atlantological writers are liable to be extremely tedious to get through, invariably with little reward when at the end the shaky conclusions built up on the feeble foundations of all this labour turn out to be so thin and insubstantial. (I believe a large part of the untutored readership of these volumes can, at best, only mistake such heavy passages for evidence of real scholarship, without necessarily reading them closely.) But whatever the merits of all the labour, labour it is. Many people are well used to working hard at tiresome jobs to make a living and we cannot entirely discount a purely money-making motivation for much of the Atlantological literature, but there is frequently something so dedicated about the pursuit of such dubious material that I think other purposes have to be considered.

We don't find many women writing in this field. Rose has written with Rand Flem-Ath and there is always the Blavatsky phenomenon, though I think we can readily discount her as not really belonging to any of the subdivisions of the Atlantological persuasion that we are interested in here. Among the scholars of orthodox archaeology, there have noticeably always been women – excavating, publishing reports, teaching, writing papers and books. Some of the most distinguished archaeologists and prehistorians have been women. But there are next to no women among the producers of Atlantological material. It may well be that this situation offers us a clue to one of the essential differences between real and 'alternative' archaeology.

There is in fact something rather male about the Atlantological interest in itself, and in the ways its practitioners go about it. With some of the writers of Atlantological literature, though not all of them, there is more than a hint of obsession. (On occasion they will even artlessly admit to it.) It is most obvious in the curious way in which some of them are so determined to make something, anything, of every scrap of data (or pseudo-data) that ever comes their way. It seems akin at times to a collector's mania to possess and show off every beer mat from some brewery or every piece of porcelain from some workshop; akin, too, to the relentless pursuit of some hobby or all-consuming interest in something or other, often with an urge to be seen to command the field. On the whole, men are more prone to these things than women, for whatever reasons. When a treasured theory lies at the centre of such an obsessional interest, then we commonly find that for the proponent of that theory virtually everything is grist to the mill. Professional scholars (on the whole) are more relaxed about their business, perhaps because it is more their business than their personal *raison d'être*. But more than that, the disciplines of scholarship have usually taught them, or their colleagues have brought it home to them, that no theory explains everything and that some data (or apparent data) will always fail to conform to any available theory. They are used to this situation, it goes with the territory. The amateurs, though, rarely have a feel for this.

Often working alone, without the benefit of a professional context in which their efforts will be judged (sometimes quite harshly), the amateurs are all too liable to surrender to the urge to dominate their material with an absolute obsession. Everything must be seen to fit their theory, to play its part in the proof – as they see it – of the correctness of their view. Anything they find in the old literature, anything they stumble across from new research sources, anything they see in the papers or on television, anything anyone tells them: it's all sucked in and more or less hammered into their scheme of things, which must be seen to explain everything, even if it is always the same old sample of everything. In this way it comes about that they often make so much of stray, anomalous, doubtful material that a professional would be content to leave aside as unprofitable without further developments. We have even seen that, on occasions, the Atlantologists may incorporate material that they themselves will have to repudiate within a few pages or less as useless even for their purposes. (And we have also noticed how their enthusiasms are apt to come and go between books.) Everything it seems must be somehow, if only temporarily, bent to their will. (As must, I fear, the judgement of their followers – this is a great field for would-be gurus.) It does look rather obsessive and I think this may explain that capacity of theirs to endure the profitless tedium of some of their material. (Of course, we must be careful not to put it all down to obsession – when the material is as thin and incoherent as the Atlantologists' often is, then you might as well bring in everything you have to hand.) I don't wish to suggest that there have never been any obsessives among the professional scholars of archaeology, but I do hazard that there are more of them among the amateurs of the 'alternative' brand.

To go with the obsessiveness, there is the touchiness. It may be mild and good-natured when someone close to straight archaeology embarks on an unorthodox proposal, or – more usually – it may be virulent like le Plongeon's, a sample of whose invective (against the university teachers of American archaeology of his time) well conveys the flavour of so much Atlantological reaction to real scholarship. 'Not only do they know nothing of ancient American civilization, but judging from letters in my possession, the majority of them refuse to learn anything concerning it . . . The so-called learned men of our own days are the first to oppose new ideas and the bearers of these. This opposition will continue to exist until the arrogance and self-conceit of supposed learning that still hovers within the walls of colleges and universities have completely vanished.' It was the college and university types who laid the basis of our knowledge of American prehistory: le Plongeon was a crackpot so zany that even Atlantologists scarcely lean on him anymore. But they do go on railing at the university teachers in just the same old way. Of course, in many ways this may be natural enough as I've said before, even prudent. If I advance a novel theory, at variance with the ideas of the professionals in a given field like archaeology, and they reject my theory or worse still ignore it, then I am likely to feel touchy about the situation. Perhaps deep down I even wonder whether I may in fact be completely wrong, hopelessly unequipped by my lack of anything but self-education in the field. I feel insecure: and there are so many stratagems available to human beings to compensate for insecurity.

Meanwhile, if I am in the business of selling books about my theory, I may well feel it to be only good business to reassure my readers with a show of pained but plucky defiance against the authorities who deny me. Out of the mix of personal and practical insecurities comes the characteristic range of attitudes to the professionals that so many of the amateurs display. (Incidentally, it is an interesting fact that the only other field in which amateurs show such a driven defiance of the professionals appears to be medicine. On the whole, people leave say physics and structural engineering to their professional practitioners, but large numbers seem to doubt the entire system of orthodox medicine and chase after a whole host of 'alternative' therapies, many of them of a highly dubious nature to say the least. Our health and our past are, it seems clear, our most personal concerns as human beings and we feel freer to go our own way with them than with most other things in life. The proponents of 'alternative medicine' and 'alternative archaeology' would no doubt say 'quite right too'. But I have known people pay a high price for an independent approach to medicine.)

The Atlantologists frequently present themselves as hurt and affronted by the rejection – or worse still the indifference – of the professionals. (Their hurt on occasions can take an oddly childish turn, like a schoolboy sulking over a low mark.) They put the professionals' attitude down to, at best, an unadventurous conformism that blinds them to the insights of the 'alternative' camp. Soon after that relatively mild judgement, they usually go on to accuse the professionals of looking to their own jobs and reputations in wilful disregard of the compelling theories of the 'alternative' thinkers; in the end, dark hints of gigantic conspiracies to do down the noble truths of Atlantology and 'alternative archaeology' in general may be advanced, sometimes with imprecise but unsettling implications about the machinations of national security or religious orthodoxy. Men in Black, you might say. At the least, the Atlantologists usually imply that professional scholars have closed ranks to deny them. Those who know the world of professional scholarship are not likely to recognize it in the caricature frequently put forward by the 'alternative' authors. Archaeology has its rival schools of competing approaches to the study, not noticeably indulgent towards one another and to older generations of scholars. The 'New Archaeologists' of the 1960s, with their emphasis on the methods and outlook of the natural sciences, frequently disdained their predecessors of the old culturally descriptive school; the 'postprocessual' archaeologists of recent years have in turn rather gone back on the science emphasis, in favour at times of something almost subjective enough to embrace a certain degree of 'alternative archaeology'. And I wish I had the space to quote at length from a treasured issue of *Current Anthropology* to show what the academics are capable of saying to one another's faces: it might cheer up some of the martyrs of 'alternative archaeology', at the cost of relieving them of their martyrdom.

No, mutual regard and support have never been noticeably the foremost traits of the academics, however it may look to outsiders. If they appear to tacitly come together to cold-shoulder the Atlantologists, it is more likely to be the result of a shared estimate (needing no consultation) of the negligibility and futility of the 'alternative' workers' efforts, rather than of any fear for their jobs or reputations. It may be a hard thing for the Atlantologists to face up to, but professional archaeologists are as likely as not simply uninterested in their shoddy speculations and dilettante dabblings. What is the use, or even passing interest, of theories that there might just possibly be sort of something to, if – just if – a whole string of feebly based or baseless conjectures turned out perhaps to have something in it? Especially when no means are available for testing the theories generated in this dubious fashion, nor likely to become available, and these theories are at odds with everything we reliably know? You don't need any zealously policed guild of vested interests to steer clear of such unprofitable doings. On the contrary, it is the 'alternative' fraternity who give off an air of solidarity against the professional archaeologists: whatever their own differences, however hopelessly incompatible their own particular versions of the Atlantis theme, they are the ones who come together against the academics in a sort of trade unionism of the Atlantologists. And, as a matter of fact, the record of orthodox science in adopting new theories that are well argued and well supported is rather good: relativity and the carbon-dating revolution in archaeology being cases in point.

It really is shabby to impugn the professionals in the way some Atlantologists do, even if it is understandable. They would be well advised to settle for a role as purveyors of popular entertainment and leave the academic archaeologists alone. As it is, it's as though a skilled and entertaining conjuror were suddenly to claim to possess real psychic powers – whatever they would be – and then question the motives of those who doubted or disdained him. And for all their sniping at the attitude of the academics, the proponents of 'alternative archaeology' are often rather pathetically keen to have on board any sort of academic figure who might be thought to support them. Sometimes it's a case of quoting the work of geologists or archaeologists in a neutral situation where the age of some geological context or some archaeological find might be thought to chime in with an Atlantological proposal, or at least not to directly conflict with it. More usually, it is a matter of making much of the theories of some admittedly academic figure operating right outside his own field. Thus the geological theories of a history teacher or the Egyptological theories of a geologist may figure with honour in the literature of Atlantology. The familiar antagonism to the academic professionals will be set aside in cases like these: such authorities will be gleefully billed as 'respected geologists' though they are pronouncing on Egyptology or 'Harvard professors' though they are purporting to translate alleged graffiti in long dead languages, for which endeavour a lifetime in invertebrate zoology might not be the best preparation. Sadly, even a distinguished career in one branch of learning is no guarantee at all of sound work in another. On the whole, university people know this and respect one another's fields, but laymen often do not and are too impressed by academic qualifications as such even when their possessors have wandered far away from all they really know about.

In this connection, one might ponder the current magic of the mere word 'research'. When I was a boy, research conjured up a picture of men in white coats doing something innovative with test tubes. Later on, I understood it to mean the undertaking of original enquiry – with extremely rigorous standards of scholarship, which would be independently tested – into new fields of learning. Nowadays, for many people research appears to mean no more than doing a lot of reading-up after your own bent of whatever you can lay your hands on in the library and on the Internet, and then speculating about it. This is really playing at research, playing at scholars. So it happens that so much 'old hat' (and the same 'old hat', at that) keeps circulating through all the Atlantological literature, sometimes looking faintly like real fresh research till you chase the notes that appear to support it. The sedulous provision of the apparatus of notes that now seems *de rigueur* in the publications of 'alternative archaeology' is an interesting development: it invokes the aura of scholarship without being scholarly in fact and blurs the distinction between real scholarship and the 'alternative' output in a way that quite possibly takes in a good part of the untutored readership. Some of these Atlantological works carry more notes at the back than a *Flashman* novel, though not above half as entertaining, or in most cases as informative.

On the other hand, the illustrations with which the Atlantological books are furnished, particularly the photographs, are never of a scholarly tinge. Traditionally they have been indifferent photographs, badly reproduced in monochrome, of a random range of ancient monuments more or less related to the text, if possible with one or two studies of the author intrepidly scrutinizing some column of hieroglyphs he can't read in a reasonably exotic tourist location. (This last feature is in line with the personalized 'quest' motif of so much of this school of writing and the sort of blurb its publishers like to put on their dust jackets.) The frequent lack of any close relevance to the text and the anecdotal inclusion of personal appearances marks this mode of illustration off from any scholarly intent. No more scholarly, but certainly much pleasanter to peruse, are the sort of illustrations that have recently been introduced in certain publications: excellent photographs reproduced to a high standard, to the point where one might be tempted to say they are much the best thing in such books. I don't think we can ever expect this standard of illustration as a general rule, however, since the publishers of this literature seem to have concluded – probably rightly – that there is little sales advantage in it: oddly enough, in this visual age, it remains the enchantment of the ideas to be found in these works that sells them. (We have tried with the photographs in this present volume to suggest something of the flavour of both approaches to the matter of illustrating Atlantology.)

And it is the ideas to be found in these works by which they must be judged. I have tried to advertise some of the deficiencies of those ideas and I have had some fun doing it. I hope some, at least, of my readers have shared in the fun. To a large extent, I believe, the Atlantis Syndrome is indeed just fun, and – as I have said more than once – there would not be so very much wrong with it if it truly was presented as just all good fun. (Even if, with some of the more serious practitioners, it can be rather hard going to get to the fun of it at all.) But the Atlantologists will go on putting it out as though it were also the truth, or might be. And so, in the end, I think it is fastidiousness about the truth that requires us to give this genre the thumbs down, for all the fun of it. Not in the end perhaps because it spreads false, or even dangerous, ideas about the past. It isn't alone in doing that and millions upon millions of people across the globe go through their entire lives with their heads full of their local versions of nationalistic and religious untruth, and always will. To some extent, in this area or that, we all do. It may be a regrettable situation, but it is also inevitable.

When it comes to factual claims about the world presented as rational enquiry then I think we should always summon up enough fastidiousness to want to know, as far as we can, what really goes on in the world and what has gone on. It is not possible to know the complete and absolute truth of things but there are sound methods by which some of the truth can be arrived at, more as time goes by, and – perhaps more importantly – by which untruth can be seen for what it is. For all the fun of myth and mystery, the truth as far as we can get to it is more satisfying to a fastidious mind. And the truth has its own charms (while untruth has its own dangers). Fastidiousness of mind calls for scepticism towards all speculative and ill-evidenced modes of enquiry, not cynicism towards the hard-won findings of rigorous scholarship. It could be said of the Atlantologists and their readership that they are too cynical and not sceptical enough. I believe it is the baseless and useless nature of so much 'alternative archaeology' in all its forms that really irritates professional scholars and explains their frequent aversion to ever having anything to do with it at all, let alone combat it. Beyond that, it dismays them to see it propagated among a readership very largely unequipped to judge its worth. It is not as though the professionals were trying to keep their own researches to themselves: there are numerous books and television programmes around that try to put the discoveries of real archaeology before the public, often written by the best scholars in the field. We remarked that it seems as though the findings, the whole outlook, of modern science are neither religious enough nor romantic enough for many people – I aver that there is enchantment in these findings and in this outlook worth more than all the fantasies about the world ever promulgated. (Even if there wasn't, I would still prefer the science to the fantasy.)

But it may be worse than that: for some people, science isn't easy enough either. It takes effort to appreciate its findings and more still to understand its fundamental outlook. Anyone, for example, can see that biological evolution has taken place on this earth, but understanding the workings of mutation, genetic inheritance and natural selection is much more difficult. It is the same with archaeology: the discovery of a flashy tomb like Tutankhamun's is relatively easy to absorb; understanding the religious, cultural and political processes of the Amarna period of Egyptian New Kingdom history to which Tutankhamun belonged requires serious study for which there is no easy substitute. Egyptology is just one specialized discipline within ancient history and archaeology; archaeology embraces both the five thousand years or so of history and the unannalled millennia of prehistory, reaching back millions of years. There is a lot to archaeology, and it's not easily learned and understood. Fantasies about the past, on the other hand, are always essentially simple and easy to assimilate, even when they are decked with astronomical and numerological complexities. Fantasies may be beguiling, but then so is the real story of the human past – and much more intellectually stimulating to try to understand. The underlying attitudes of Atlantology are really too simplistic and crude to offer any intellectual challenge. Trying, on the other hand, to reach any sort of understanding of the processes of primate evolution that could give birth to human consciousness and language, or of the social processes by which civilization could arise in farming-based communities – such effort really is rewarding and fit work for clever and original minds. It promises, moreover, to help humanity towards a better understanding of our place in the giant scheme of biological and cosmic evolution. There's charm enough, and real profundity, in that. Alongside such endeavour, speculation about supermen from outer space or secret brotherhoods of astronomer-priests or lost cities under the ice looks like just what I fear it is: woefully unsophisticated and worse than irrelevant to the real interest of the study of the human past.

FURTHER READING

General Archaeology
Andel, Tjeerd H. van. *New Views on an Old Planet*, Cambridge University Press, 1994
Bahn, Paul G. (ed.). *The Atlas of World Archaeology*, Time-Life Books, 2000
Bell, Martin and Walker, Michael. *Late Quaternary Environmental Change*, London, Longman UK, and New York, John Wiley & Sons, 1992
Cotterell, Arthur (ed.). *Penguin Encyclopedia of Ancient Civilizations*, London, Penguin, 1988
Jordan, Paul. *Early Man*, Stroud, Sutton Publishing, 1999
Mithen, Steven. *The Prehistory of the Mind*, London, Thames & Hudson, 1996
Renfrew, Colin and Bahn, Paul G. *Archaeology, Theories, Methods and Practice*, London, Thames & Hudson, 2000
Scarre, Chris (ed.). *The Times Atlas of Past Worlds*, Times Books Ltd, London, 1988
Sherratt, Andrew (ed.). *The Cambridge Encyclopedia of Archaeology*, Cambridge University Press, 1980
Whitehouse, Ruth and Wilkins, John. *The Making of Civilization*, London, Collins, 1986

Discussions of the Atlantis Question
Babcock, William H. *Legendary Islands of the Atlantic*, American Geographical Society, 1922, reprinted New York, Books for Libraries Press, 1975
Cazeau, Charles J. and Scott, Stuart D. *Exploring the Unknown*, New York, Plenum Press, 1979
de Camp, Lyon Sprague. *Lost Continents: The Atlantis Theme in History and Literature*, New York, Dover, 1970 (originally 1954)
Ellis, Richard. *Imagining Atlantis*, New York, Alfred A. Knopf, 1998

Forsyth, Phyllis. *Atlantis: The Making of Myth*, Montreal, McGill – Queen's University Press, 1980 and London, Croom Helm, 1980

Kukal, Zdeněk. *Atlantis in the Light of Modern Research*, Prague, Academia, 1984

Luce, J.V. *The End of Atlantis*, London, Thames & Hudson, 1969

Ramage, Edwin S. (ed.). *Atlantis – Fact or Fiction?*, Indiana University Press, 1978

Randi, James. *Flim-Flam*, Buffalo, Prometheus Books, 1982

Stiebling, William H. *Ancient Astronauts, Cosmic Collisions*, Buffalo, Prometheus Books, 1984

Story, Ronald. *The Space-gods Revealed*, New York, Harper & Row, 1976, and London, New English Library, 1978

——. *Guardians of the Universe?*, London, New English Library, 1980

Vitaliano, Dorothy B. *Legends of the Earth*, Indiana University Press, 1973

Wauchope, Robert. *Lost Tribes and Sunken Continents*, University of Chicago Press, 1973

Atlantological and Atlantology-related works

Allen, J.M. *Atlantis: The Andes Solution*, Gloucester, Windrush Press, 1998

Ashe, Geoffrey. *Atlantis – Lost Lands, Ancient Wisdom*, London, Thames & Hudson, 1992

Bacon, Francis. *New Atlantis*, Oxford, Clarendon Press, 1974

Berlitz, Charles. *The Mystery of Atlantis*, New York, Grosset & Dunlop, 1969

Blavatsky, H.P. 'Madame'. *The Secret Doctrine*, Pasadena, Theosophical University Press, 1970

Braghine, Alex. *The Shadow of Atlantis*, New York, Dutton, 1940

Bramwell, James Guy. *Lost Atlantis*, New York, Harper, 1938

Cayce, Edgar Evans. *Mysteries of Atlantis Revisited*, New York, St Martin's Paperbacks, 1997

Churchward, James. *The Lost Continent of Mu*, New York, W.E. Rudge, 1926

Collins, Andrew. *Gateway to Atlantis: The Search for the Source of a Lost Civilization*, London, Headline Book Publishing, 2000

Comyns Beaumont, W. *The Riddle of Prehistoric Britain*, London, 1946

Däniken, Erich von. *Chariots of the Gods?*, New York, Bantam, 1971

———. *Odyssey of the Gods: An Alien History of Ancient Greece*, Shaftesbury and Boston, Element Books, 2000

Donnelly, Ignatius. *Atlantis: The Antediluvian World*, New York, Harper, 1949 (original 1882)

———. *Ragnarok, The Age of Fire and Gravel*, New York, Appleton, 1883

Flem-Ath, Rand and Rose. *When the Sky Fell: In Search of Atlantis*, London, Weidenfeld & Nicolson, 1995

Flem-Ath, Rand and Wilson, Colin. *The Atlantis Blueprint*, London, Little Brown & Co., 2000

Hancock, Graham. *Fingerprints of the Gods*, London, Heinemann, 1995

———. *Heaven's Mirror: Quest for the Lost Civilization*, London, Michael Joseph, 1998

———, *Underworld: the Mysterious Origins of Civilization*, London, Michael Joseph, 2002

Hapgood, Charles. *Maps of the Ancient Sea Kings*, Philadelphia and New York, Chilton Book Co., 1966

———. *The Path of the Pole*, New York and London, Chilton Book Co., 1970 (revision of *Earth's Shifting Crust*, London, Museum Press, 1958)

James, Peter. *The Sunken Kingdom: The Atlantis Mystery Solved*, London, Jonathan Cape, 1995

Muck, Otto. *The Secrets of Atlantis*, London, Collins, 1978

Plato. *Timaeus* and *Critias*, Cambridge, Massachusetts and London, Harvard University Press, 1999

Santillana, G. de and Dechend, H. von. *Hamlet's Mill*, Boston, Nonpareil Books, 1977 (originally 1969)

Scott-Elliot, William. *The Story of Atlantis and Lost Lemuria*, London, Theosophical Publishing House, 1962

Spanuth, Jürgen. *Atlantis: The Mystery Unravelled*, London, Arco, 1956

Spence, Lewis. *The Problem of Atlantis*, New York, Brentano's, 1924

———. *Atlantis in America*, London, Ernest Benn, 1925

———. *The History of Atlantis*, London, Rider, 1926

Tomas, Andrew. *Atlantis: From Legend to Discovery*, London, Robert Hale & Co., 1972

Velikovsky, Immanuel. *Worlds in Collision*, London, Gollancz, 1950

Wilson, Colin. *From Atlantis to the Sphinx*, London, Virgin Books, 1996

Zangger, Eberhard. *The Flood from Heaven*, London, Sidgwick & Jackson, 1992

INDEX